W9-BXZ-107

PRAISE FOR
Financing the New Venture:

"Gave us a road map . . . one of Business Builders' principals arranged our lead offering investors for $700,000 and we completed the rest of our financing."
—KEN FRISBEE, FLUID INK TECHNOLOGIES

"We raised $1.7 million on our first go 'round through the first boutique broker-dealer the process led us to."
—CHIP ADAMS, LYNX CORP.

"Entrepreneurs who use the techniques and theories of this clinic will be surprised at how close their possibilities are . . . I have trained over 4,000 investment advisors on how to raise capital and I have helped my clients raise over $1 billion from individual investors."
—STEVE MOELLER
AMERICAN BUSINESS VISIONS, SELL TO THE RICH, INC.

"Insightful materials . . . one of Business Builders' principals raised $600,000 on our next round of financing."
—JOSEPH PERRY, UNIPRISE SYSTEMS, INC.

"The IAAVC is showcasing your Visionary Business Builders' model to launch our national "How to Become a Better Angel Investor Program"—brilliant and timely ideas. Our pilot program drew over 550 investors last October in Denver. Your approach is showing all of us another way to access private capital and how to invest in companies—congrats."
—PHIL RAY, PRESIDENT
INTERNATIONAL ASSOCIATION OF ANGEL & VENTURE CLUBS (IAAVC)

"This has powerfully transformed our plans. We have been closing on new investors and, most importantly, building our business on our terms."
—JOANNE BREM, JOURNEY WELL CENTER FOR INTEGRATIVE HEALTH
PAST SENIOR ACCOUNT EXECUTIVE, AMDAHL CORPORATION

"Since the clinic, we have incorporated into our consulting work with emerging companies most of your strategies. Your are definitely setting new best practices standards for raising equity capital for start-ups."
—RICK NEWTON, DIRECTOR
AMERICAN EXPRESS TAX & BUSINESS SERVICES

"Comprehensive. A must for anyone in the tough stages between start-up and regional investment banking financing."
—H.D. THOREAU
CRUTTENDEN ROTH

"Thanks, 75% of our offering has been down now . . . it is so rare to find a seminar like this . . . so many skills required of a CEO were covered. So thanks."
—MARTIN PHILLIPS
WIRELESS COMMUNICATIONS

FINANCING THE NEW VENTURE

ALSO BY MARK LONG

*Corporate Finance: Unlimited Capital for the
New Century Entrepreneur*

Real Estate: Competing for Capital

Big Money Brokerage

Volume I: The Law and Methods of Real Estate Group Investing

Volume II: Partnership Exchanges and Sponsor Tax Techniques

Real Estate Sponsor Due Diligence

Syndication Management

FINANCING THE NEW VENTURE

BY

MARK LONG

Adams Media Corporation

HOLBROOK, MASSACHUSETTS

Copyright ©2000 by Mark Long. All rights reserved.
This book, or parts thereof, may not be reproduced in any form
without permission from the publisher; exceptions are made for
brief excerpts used in published reviews.

Published by
Adams Media Corporation
260 Center Street, Holbrook, MA 02343

ISBN: 1-58062-207-0

Printed in the United States of America.

J I H G F E D C B

Library of Congress Cataloging-in-Publication Data
Long, Mark H.
Financing the new venture : a complete guide to raising capital
from venture capitalists, investment bankers, private investors,
and other sources / by Mark Long.
p.   cm.
Includes index.
ISBN 1-58062-207-0
1. Capital investments. 2. Venture capital.
3. Long-term business financing. 4. Capital market. I. Title.
HG4028.C4 L587 2000
658.15'224—dc21
99-053196

This publication is designed to provide accurate and authoritative information with regard to the
subject matter covered. It is sold with the understanding that the publisher is not engaged in
rendering legal, accounting, or other professional advice. If legal advice or other expert
assistance is required, the services of a competent professional person should be sought.
— From a *Declaration of Principles* jointly adopted by a Committee of the American Bar
Association and a Committee of Publishers and Associations

Cover and text illustration by Dave Cutler.

This book is available at quantity discounts for bulk purchases.
For information, call 1-800-872-5627.

Visit our home page at www.businesstown.com

TO JOHN

CONTENTS

STEP 1: DESIGNING THE PHENOMENAL MESSAGE / 27

STEP 2: SURVEYING INVESTOR FINANCING™ SOURCES AND APPROACHES / 105

STEP 3: DEVELOPING THE BUSINESS PLAN / 175

STEP 4: IDENTIFYING STRATEGIC ASSOCIATIONS / 185

STEP 5: STRUCTURING THE FINANCING / 203

STEP 6: CREATING THE CAPITAL RELATIONS™ PLAN / 233

STEP 7: DEVELOPING THE
DISCUSSION DOCUMENTS / 281

STEP 8: TESTING THE MARKET
AND LIST ASSEMBLAGE / 291

STEP 9: FINALIZING
THE DOCUMENTS / 301

STEP 10: EXECUTING THE OFFERING CAMPAIGN / 307

IF YOU, OR A CLIENT OF YOURS, ARE TRYING TO PREPARE YOURSELF TO RAISE investor capital to start, grow, or reorganize an emerging business, this book was written for you. This book is the culmination of twenty-five years of research and actual money raising experience.

This book is not about how to "get ready" to access all forms of capital, it is, instead, about how to "get ready" to access investor capital. More specifically, it is about "getting ready" to raise investor capital without the need for credit or collateral. It's a book about how to successfully raise equity money in a tough environment—the world of high-risk capital—from demanding investors and their demanding advisors.

This book has one central theme: There is an unlimited amount of investor capital available for entrepreneurs who are willing to play by the new rules in today's new economy.

This book focuses on three key ideas to "get you ready" to raise investor capital:

Idea #1: Less than one half of one percent of the one million start-up businesses each year in this country qualify for venture capital. The remaining 99.5% of the start-up businesses in America simply do not meet the venture capital industry's investment model of blockbuster first product and "fast track" initial public offering (IPO). (I call this model the Great American Product/Exit Game—GAPE.) With a few very notorious and impressive exceptions, the venture capital industry's track record of investment returns is not spectacular, yet the American entrepreneurial sector, including academia and the press, seem to be locked into the venture capital GAPE paradigm of how businesses are supposed to launch, finance, and grow themselves.

Idea #2: There is a new economy pulling us all into the 21st century. This is an economy of knowledge/creativity, and it requires entrepreneurs to equally value business building principles and practices with product building if they want to meet the agendas of the new economy.

Idea #3: The new economy will have two kinds of business models that successfully attract investor capital:

One will be the ever-present GAPE model of hot product/fast-growth/fast investor-liquidity which only a very small number of companies will be fortunate enough to have.

The other super model that will attract investor capital will be the Visionary Business Builder model detailed in this book. This new model provides entrepreneurs with the theory and strategies that will permit outstanding business growth and investor returns. Eventually even the venture capital investing will embrace this disruptive new start-up model.

The roots of the Visionary Business Builder model are based on the research and findings of Jim Collins and Jerry Porras, authors of *Built to Last*. I have spent the last five years developing this book based largely on their findings. Imagine my excitement, when, just as I was putting the finishing touches on this book, *Inc.* magazine put a picture of Jim Collins on its cover with a caption that read: "21st Century Start-Ups: The Next Generation of Successful New Businesses Won't Look Anything Like Today's." Validation is so sweet after so much sweat.

THE BACKGROUND OF THIS BOOK

When I began this book in 1993, my plan was to build upon my twenty years of experience as a real estate syndicator, lawyer, and seminar educator, to offer a book of strategies and tactics for finding investors and obtaining funding from them. I've been part of this Investor Financing™ game since 1970. I've been at bat over 800 times as a lawyer, corporate finance advisor, or small business entrepreneur for projects or companies trying to access investor capital. I've seen and tried a lot of strategies and tactics. This book is the cumulative learning experiences from all these transactions. Half of the fifty-two syndication projects I promoted as a general partner involved real estate projects in Tulsa, Dallas, and Phoenix. When these markets collapsed in the early 1980s, I had to stare down the gun barrel of many disappointed investors and money raisers. In the early 1990s, when the Southern California real estate market collapsed, I was on the "learning team" again. I learned, among other things, that being a soulmate with your investors and money raisers is a wrenching experience when things aren't going well.

I've had my hand in big business as well. In 1985 I served the Kemper Insurance Company as National Marketing Director for their real estate securities direct investment division. I was brought in midstream to rescue the investor fund raising for a public offering that was poorly positioned from the start. I don't know for sure, but I believe the positioning of this fund was done in lawyers' offices high above the street, instead of in the street where the investors are. Lawyers, CPAs, and executives need to ride the elevator down to the street and walk around more often, and then finalize their documentation only after they have asked investors what they think and feel. I saw seventy-three stock brokerage firms, and thousands of stockbrokers an financial consultants, who couldn't raise investor capital (and more importantly, didn't want to) when the company and its product was not positioned right. Further complicating things for Kemper, they introduced the product at a time when the demand for this product was going from low to nonexistent nationwide. Timing is important. This public offering did reach minimum capitalization, but Kemper wisely realized real estate syndication was not a business close to its core competency—insurance—so they got out.

Some of the richest insight I've had into Investor Financing™ technology has come from my experience as an educator teaching the principles and practices of Investor Financing™. From 1978 to 1998 over 17,000 entrepreneurs and professional advisors have attended my one- to four-day clinics, seminars, and workshops held coast to coast. I'm grateful for the experiences my students have shared during my courses.

So for twenty years I had honed the craft of investor solicitation strategies and tactics: over the course of my own fifty-two syndications, I never failed to raise the needed money. Those law clients who entrusted me as their quasi-corporate financial advisor were pleased with my money raising insights and skills. I always got the money and it was always the hard kind to get—equity capital. So when I branched out from real estate into the world of corporate finance in 1992, it seemed to me to be a small step.

In 1993 I began designing and producing the "Money for Business Builders" clinics. With each clinic I began to realize more and more that teaching entrepreneurs money raising strategies and tactics alone was not going to produce the outcome I wanted. I became convinced that "push" strategies were not the answer. But what was? I struggled with this for a year and a half. I revisited again and again the source material I had discovered. I reviewed both the information I had obtained through my clinics and the data from other sources that I had collected. I was looking for strategies and tactics that would allow CEOs to raise investor capital faster and easier. I wanted CEOs to have a quantum-leap improvement in raising investor capital. I discovered that more strategies and tactics were not the answer.

As my writing, teaching, and researching went on, I came to realize that the quantum leap for entrepreneurs was going to first come from new theory and models of "how to be in business." My basket of strategies and tactics were going to be useful to entrepreneurs, but only after fundamental business models and theories were first attended to.

AN AWAKENING

What I've discovered over the last five years has had a profound effect on my models of "how to raise investor capital." Thanks to many gifted business authorities, consummate deal makers, and visionary entrepreneurs, I have been able to share my thoughts through these books and my clinics as a "guide on the side," not as a "sage on the stage." The data and trends were on my side. All I needed to do was tell it like I had discovered and experienced it. But this took more courage than one might think.

First, it meant I really had to do my homework.

Second, I had to find the confidence to speak up to the entrepreneurial and venture capital industries, as well as academia, and tell them what I had discovered. I was not a scholar and I was not widely known in the industry. I knew that I would have to challenge the sacred cows of many bright and rich people. I would have to be a maverick, and I would have to get my readers and students to suspend judgment until I had presented my entire case. I took confidence from the fact that research has shown that major advances in an industry often are brought about by outsiders who have a fresh viewpoint.

Third, it meant I had to tell my inside support group that I was not ready to raise money for Business Builders, LLC, the company I had founded in 1993. I had to do this in spite of the fact that there was a wide open window of opportunity for the company. My inside support group couldn't believe that I wasn't going to raise the financing needed for the company right away. But I wasn't ready until I had the quantum-leap model in place, and models are not developed overnight.

Finally, in January of 1997, I was ready to begin raising the financing for Business Builders, LLC, which to that point still had no profits—only losses. We had no credit and no collateral. But I practiced the principles of this book and followed the 10 Steps of Investor Financing™ covered in this book, and with the efforts of two boutique broker/dealers, my launch team of advisors, and my Board of Directors, we raised $350,000 of seed capital from forty-five investors. Even more important, as a result of my nine-month march for capital, Business Builders, LLC now has a team of strategically linked principals who have collectively raised and placed over $150 million of equity capital in emerging businesses. This team rallied around me as a result of the inspiration of the Visionary Business model and its promise of extraordinary investor returns. What I did for Business Builders, LLC, I can help you do for your company.

WHO THIS BOOK IS FOR

Anyone interested in entrepreneurism will find this book a good addition to their library. Entrepreneurs on the firing line of launching a business should keep this book on their desks and refer to it often. If you're a member of the launch team of an emerging enterprise, make sure that the CEO of your company has a copy of this book and uses it. One of the key lessons this book teaches is that the CEO must be the person who takes the responsibility for obtaining Investor Financing™. As Peter Drucker says in his book *Managing in Turbulent Times*, accessing capital is one of the CEO's top priorities. Many botched Investor Financings™ occur because the CEO does not take charge of this process.

If you're a product or marketing person who hopes that your business will launch, finance itself, and grow on the strength of your product or marketing savvy, you're playing an outdated and risky game (unless of course you're a .com company in 1999). Most likely most of what you've learned about launching and financing a business hinges totally on product, market positioning or .com strategies. Unfortunately, this is an outdated belief system (paradigm). It's not that it's a completely wrong paradigm, it's just not complete enough to meet the demands of the new century. The extended paradigm for the turbulent times of the new century has to include business building to complement product, market building internet strategies.

As we head into the 21st Century, raising capital is a priority agenda item for entrepreneurs. Business Builders, LLC, has found that 47% of the CEOs in charge of young companies (1–5 years old) are looking for investors. (Our data is the result of hundreds of telephone surveys of CEOs of growth companies in each of the geographical areas where we conduct our "Money for Business Builders" clinics.) Regular subscribers to leading business magazines can attest to the frequency of articles on raising capital. And there is not an entrepreneurial training center in this country that does not include raising capital as part of its curriculum.

A BRIDGE TO THE FUTURE

As a result of the five years I've spent on this project, I'm convinced that a new source of capital for early-stage companies is needed *now* for the next millennium. This new source will itself be bold and in step with the demands the new economic paradigm is forcing on entrepreneurs. Like much of the education community, the capital infrastructure in this country seems to lag way behind the needs of those it attempts to serve. For example, banks could accept as security for loans intellectual assets, yet they don't. Likewise, most equity investors in early-stage private companies are still stuck in old paradigms. For example, the venture capital community believes that entrepreneurs with blockbuster first products and fast-track initial public offering plans are the only ones worth betting on. I'll admit that the Wall Street of the 1990s is telling us a lot about the value component of intellectual capital in the new economy. However, for investors to infer that "only" companies with blockbuster first products and fast-track initial public offering plans or .com behind their name are tomorrow's winners is to misread the scorecard. After all, whatever is on the front page of our tabloids is in reality old news.

In this book I show how a new source of capital is emerging. I call this new source Visionary Capital. Visionary Capitalists are emerging to do business with Visionary Business Builders. Together they will add a new model for launching and financing the business builders of the 21st Century. The theories, tools, and processes of Visionary Capitalists and Visionary Business Builders will become so commonplace in the years ahead that people will wonder in the year 2020 how anybody ever got a business financed with only a strong financial statement, strong product or .com behind their name.

This book will serve as a practical bridge between the realities of raising money today and the financing frontiers ahead of us.

—Mark Long
Del Mar, California

ACKNOWLEDGMENTS

I'M LUCKY TO HAVE SOME SUPERSTAR FRIENDS. THEY WERE MY STRATEGIC alliances that made this book possible. John Halverson, President of Baja Communities, Inc. in San Diego, California, the big brother I never had, challenged and changed my ideas so much that he should have been listed as co-author. His passing on Christmas Eve, 1995 leaves a big hole in many lives. Robert Miles Runyan, retired Chairman of Runyan/Hinche Design Group in Marina del Rey, California, has inspired me through the years on the value and power of corporate creativity.

My former associates at the Ventana Companies in Irvine, California, in true venture capital no-nonsense spirit, kept the pressure on to finish the first edition of this book so I could get back to some real work. Tom Gephart, President of Ventana, showed me daily how Investor Financing™ technology is practiced on a global basis. My associates in Business Builders, LLC, namely, Bill Zures, Jerry Dalton, Chip Adams, Dr. Roger Holland, Dr. Tim Wilson, Terry Ahearn, Walt Miller, Bill Treitler, Dwight O'Neill, Mike Hutchison, Randy Moore, and Jim Neal each made invaluable contributions. Robert Svoboda of Santa Barbara, California, retired Chairman of California Thrift and Loan, helped guide the direction of this project from the start. Cliff Krueger, President of Kerr-Krueger Realty of Escondido, California was always there to give me a boost when my batteries ran low.

I want to thank my former law partner Marshall Thurber of the MetaQuality Institute for all his time and inspiration. He made sure the philosophy of his mentor Dr. W. Edwards Deming was introduced and properly incorporated into this book.

I found the following authorities, and their books, indispensable: James Collins and Jerry Porras for *Built to Last*; Clayton Christiansen's *The Innovator's Dilemma*; Guy Kawasaki's *Rules for Revolutionaries*; Geoffrey Moore's *Crossing the Chasm* and *Inside the Tornado*; Peter Drucker for his *Innovation and Entrepreneurship, Post-Capitalist Society, The New Realities*, and half a dozen others; Joel Barker's *Future Edge*; Regis McKenna's *The Regis Touch* and *Relationship Marketing*; Gary Hamel and C.K. Prahalad's *Competing for the Future*; Michael Ray and Rochelle Myer's *Creativity in Business*; Stanley Davis's *Future Perfect*; William Davidow and Michael Malone's *The Virtual Corporation*; and Kenneth Delavigne and J. Daniel Robertson's *Profound Changes*. All of these books were keystone references. There are many other authorities that I'm indebted to as well, and they are acknowledged in the footnote references.

Several close friends read the manuscript and made invaluable contributions, namely Dick Smithee, Bill Patton, Tim Larrick, Ray Calhoun, Phil Currie, Dan Gara, Jim McMichael, Bill Lofft, Jim Wendling, and Gene Konstant. I want to thank Alex DeNoble, Sanford Ehrlich, and Richard Brooks, professors at San

Diego State College of Business Administration, for their instrumental efforts in helping me launch Investor Financing™ in the academic community.

I want to thank the following for sharing with me the vision that Investor Financing™ should be part of the entrepreneur's continuing education agenda: Hal Hurwitz of Coopers & Lybrand; John Denniston and Richard Kintz of Brobeck, Phleger and Harrison; Mike Collins of Rice, Hall & James and the San Diego Corporate Finance Council; Barbara Bry of the University of California, San Diego *Connect*; Tim Considine of Considine and Considine; Brian Butler of Conlee and Butler; Lisa Hasler of the San Diego Chamber of Commerce; Tiffany Haugen of the University of California, Irvine *Accelerate*; James Kelly; John Ecklein of Ecklein Communications, Inc.; and Greg Beck and Wally Eater of the Orange County Venture Forum.

I'm indebted to Steve Curtis of Newport Beach, California, a superstar entrepreneur and professor of Creativity In Business at the University of California at Irvine. His quiet confidence in this project and steadfast support came at the right time. I remember well Marsh Fisher of Irvine, California, founder of Century 21 Real Estate, encouraging from the "get-go" this project and its direction. He helped me press on.

My hundreds of clients and investment partners, and my thousands of seminar students have each, in some way, made the material in this book possible. As of Fall, 1999, over fifty significant financial institutions and professional advisory firms have stepped to the plate and sponsored our "Money for Business Builders" clinics. I'm especially indebted to Venture Law Group, Tech Coast Alliance, Coopers & Lybrand; Fulbright & Jaworski; Ernst & Young; Arthur Andersen; Jones, Day, Reavis & Pogue; Cruttenden Roth; Silicon Valley Bank; and The Thompson Group. They have made it possible to spread the tidings of this book. Each in their own way are paradigm pioneers.

John King, a Macintosh master, digitized this manuscript and brought a level of organization and formatting that exceeded my expectations. Thomas Johns, Jr., was equally valuable in his proofreading and recommendations—his work gave this project much momentum. I wish them well in their marketing efforts. Catherine Worix and Susan Crouch, my assistants, were there, as always, putting out fires and making possible the quiet time I had to have the past five years in order to develop this book.

I want to acknowledge my daughter, Kristi Long, a grade school teacher in Southern California. She reminds me that the teaching profession is noble, and needed now more than ever before. I trust her example will influence me to keep teaching between deals, clients, and projects. Lastly, I want to thank my youngest daughter Katy Long for sharing with me the hundreds of hours we spent together at various libraries these past few years. She's working hard to prepare herself for the 21st Century, and so am I.

Arthur Rock is an investor who gained fame and fortune by the investments he made in such highly successful start-ups as Apple Computer, Fairchild Semiconductor, Teledyne, and Intel. He has been credited for parlaying $275,000 into $100 million. He has offered entrepreneurs the following challenge:

> *You can walk up to people on the street and ask them if they want to be rich and 99% will tell you, "Sure, I want to be rich." But are they willing to do what's necessary to be successful? Not many are.*

If you are willing to do whatever is necessary to be successful in building your business and raising money for it, then studying this book will be easy. You'll devour it and increase your chances of raising money for your business.

Your timing is perfect to start an enterprise or grow an existing business. The global and national economic and political changes are producing unheard of opportunities. Ignore the doomsayers—they never created anything useful. They only react, second-guess, and exploit people's fears. Remember that the *real* economy is not what economists measure, but what entrepreneurs create and lead. Just as the Berlin Wall was dismantled in 1989, so is big business dismantling itself into little pieces. America's entrepreneurial economy is getting bigger all the time. Dun and Bradstreet reports that 75% of all U.S. businesses have fewer than twenty-five employees. As of November 1997, 19% of all U.S. companies are less than five years old. People, ideas, and money are loose and on the run. How many of these are you going to catch?

Things are going to be different in the new millennium—they have to be. No longer can slow growth, falling margins, and falling market share be blamed on the employees, the government, or foreign trade policies. Entrepreneurs, who are going to lead in the new economy, have to realize they're in a new world, see different paths, and see themselves and their stake in the game differently. They must view their position in the new economy as a position of responsibility, not as a position of privilege. They cannot serve themselves and Wall Street anymore. The entrepreneurs of the new economy have to be prepared like never before. The title of the lead article in *Inc.* magazine's 1997 "State of Small Business" issue drives this point home: "Creators of the New Economy: Amateur Entrepreneurship Is Over. The Professionals Have Arrived."[1]

This book proposes an overall system for understanding Investor Financing™ that is designed to overcome the limitations of previous works on this topic. It is important to understand every component of this system. All of the pieces are necessary to make the whole. None of these pieces used alone will be able to guarantee your success in accessing capital. Raising capital is fundamentally a learning process. It's a tough business, this business of raising investor capital, so permit yourself to use this whole recipe—not just the part that tastes the best. Remember, it is the insignificant events and facts that usually make the greatest impact, because they surprise and make people who are not prepared for them usually stumble. Looking smart is important to investors. This system of Investor Financing™ is based on a lot of small, interacting components. These components are all important and add up.

I am not offering a case-specific, canonical business plan of how every kind of Investor Financing™ campaign ought to be done. However, building on my twenty-five years of experience in raising money and on the work and insights of leading academicians, psychologists, philosophers, scientists, venture capitalists, statisticians, private investors, and investment bankers, I have developed a systematic set of principles and disciplines that integrates a diverse set of business disciplines emerging in the new economy.

A lot of capital is invested every year in emerging businesses. However, there are many companies seeking capital each year who are not part of the chosen few. They do not succeed, because they are not doing the right things. They are not being realistic, are not thinking correctly, and are not approaching Investor Financing™ as a learning and relationship building process. The yellow pages of the phone book and the Internet may have some investor listings. However, finding them is not enough, you must know what to do with these contacts.

Raising money without credit or collateral can be a scary proposition. However, most entrepreneurs only have to do it once or twice in their life. Take comfort in the fact that each year over one million new businesses are launched in the United States. Los Angeles alone reports over 60,000 new business licenses issued each year, and it is common knowledge that not every new business applies for a business license. Investors are just as apprehensive as you are. They sense (and some even know) that a new type of economy is rushing at us. A good portion of the "persuasion process" you will use with investors will consist of concise and incisive revelations about your ideas and enterprise in the context of the new economy. Remember, most of your investors may be ten to twenty years older than you, and their frames of reference are based on old paradigms. It's a time for everyone to be enlightened. Make your investors feel good about all the changes around them. Be a point of light, not a blur of confusion. You want their money don't you?

A $100 BILLION PER YEAR U.S. CAPITAL MARKET

Over $100 billion of investor capital is invested in emerging businesses each year in America. Emerging businesses can access cash through *sources* other than asset-based lenders. This kind of capital is commonly known as investor capital, and it embraces three types: venture capital, investment capital, and an emerging new source—Visionary Capital. These three types of investor capital are supplied by five general *sources*: venture capitalists, visionary capitalists, strategic corporate investors, business angels, and adventure stockholders. The system or discipline for acquiring investor capital is known as Investor Financing™. Illustration I-1 depicts an overall look at the sources of Investor Financing™ for business builders. Where does your enterprise belong in this profile, and what sources appear to be your targets?

INVESTORS WANT SAFE BRIDGES INTO THE NEW ECONOMY

Investors rarely invest in "covered wagon" companies that plan on taking their trip without maps across uncharted territory and terrain without safe bridges. Savvy investors hitch rides with pioneers who have routes and maps, and are guided by scouts who have discovered how to navigate safely in the new territory. The new century entrepreneur must know how to build safe bridges into the new economy. Here are the signs to which entrepreneurs must pay attention.

SIGNS IN THE SKY

The Sputnik space launch in 1957 announced to everyone that the technology that had been evolving during the Industrial Economy had evolved so high that a new era based on yet higher forms of technology had arrived. We called it, fifteen years later, the Information Economy. Information capitalism was credited as the engine of global economic changes.

From 1983 to 1991, the technology of the Information Economy was itself in the middle of a watershed period. In 1991, while the world watched the Gulf War on television, America's guided missiles thought for themselves, and more people than ever realized how powerful information technology had become. America's guided missiles did more than gather and compile data—they made *predictive decisions* based on the data. They were smart missiles with actual knowledge. To put it another way, they were embedded with so many information-rich components that they focused, by themselves, on results that they had to figure out and create. Missiles became the experts. The Information Economy of Alvin Toffler's *Third Wave* was blown away before our eyes on TV. We are now on the watch, alert for an approaching new wave that's right off the beach. It's the Fourth Wave, the Knowledge/Creation Wave.

Information Age economics is the platform of this new Knowledge/Creation Economy. Knowledge and creativity will be the genome of new enterprises.

ILLUSTRATION I-1:
SOURCES OF INVESTOR CAPITAL FOR BUSINESS BUILDERS

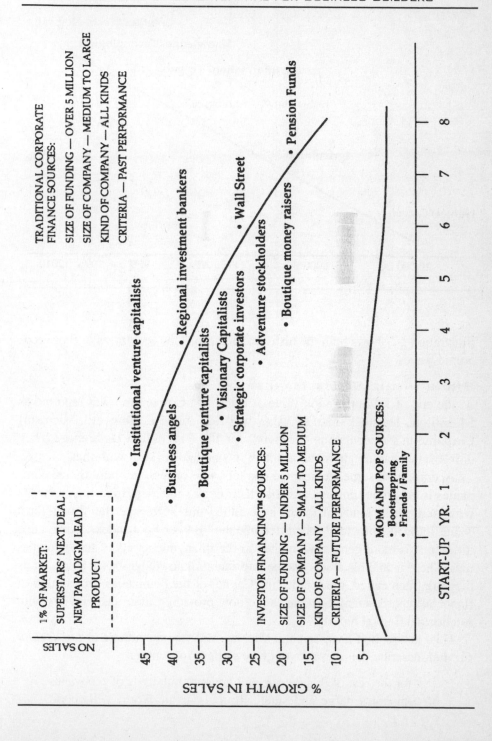

1% OF MARKET:
SUPERSTARS' NEXT DEAL
NEW PARADIGM LEAD
PRODUCT

TRADITIONAL CORPORATE
FINANCE SOURCES:

SIZE OF FUNDING — OVER 5 MILLION

SIZE OF COMPANY — MEDIUM TO LARGE

KIND OF COMPANY — ALL KINDS

CRITERIA — PAST PERFORMANCE

INVESTOR FINANCING™ SOURCES:

SIZE OF FUNDING — UNDER 5 MILLION

SIZE OF COMPANY — SMALL TO MEDIUM

KIND OF COMPANY — ALL KINDS

CRITERIA — FUTURE PERFORMANCE

MOM AND POP SOURCES:
• Bootstrapping
• Friends / Family

• Institutional venture capitalists

• Business angels   • Regional investment bankers

• Boutique venture capitalists

• Visionary Capitalists

• Strategic corporate investors   • Wall Street

• Adventure stockholders

• Boutique money raisers

• Pension Funds

% GROWTH IN SALES

NO SALES

45 40 35 30 25 20 15 10 5

START-UP   YR.   1   2   3   4   5   6   7   8

ILLUSTRATION I-2:
ECONOMIC WAVES

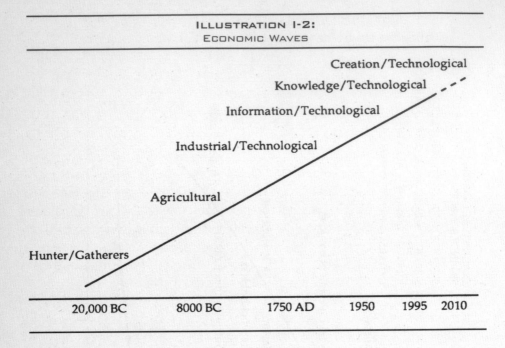

Hunter/Gatherers   20,000 BC   8000 BC   1750 AD   1950   1995   2010

Agricultural

Industrial/Technological

Information/Technological

Knowledge/Technological

Creation/Technological

Illustration I-2 shows both the historical and projected timeliness of these economic waves.

SIGNS IN THE STOCK MARKET

At the end of 1993, the book value of Microsoft Corporation was reported as $4 billion. Its stock market value was $23 billion. How did Microsoft Corporation's Accountants "account" for the $19 billion difference? They didn't. They had no approved accounting standards to deal with that.

According to some studies, the market value of U.S. publicly traded companies is now nine times greater than their book value. Until recently, analysts who study these kinds of things have called this difference the "Long-Term Value Index."[2] Some call this difference the "Bigger Fool Index." Today, this difference is more generally credited to the intangible assets of these companies. These intangible assets are the information/knowledge-based assets, or as they are often called, the Intellectual Capital of the companies. In addition to financial reports, many companies are now providing their shareholders with Intellectual Capital reports.

Here is how Leif Evinssen and Michael Malone, the authors of *Intellectual Capital*, describe the relevance of "Knowledge Accounting":

> . . . for the rest of this decade and beyond, hundreds of thousands
> of companies, large and small, throughout the world will report

Intellectual Capital as a way of measuring, visualizing, and presenting the true value of their businesses.[3]

This new component of the value of a company—its Intellectual Capital, or
embedded knowledge—is becoming the most important asset of the new
economy, even more so than financial capital. Peter Drucker has asserted that,
"Knowledge now has become the real capital of a developed economy."[4]

SIGNS ON THE HIGHWAY

Business opportunities have always been spotted, and even plotted, along new
roads and highways. Nothing has changed today, except the meaning of
"highway." The bricks, steel, and mortar of industrial age highways and
railways gave us plenty of business opportunities. The land, labor, capital, and
infrastructure needs of that era dictated a lot about the business models of the
day. Next, the electrons, switches, and chips of the Information Age opened
up the micro highway of the last fifty years with its crown highway—the
Internet. Now, the optic highways threaten the reign of the electronic network
age. The chieftains of the computer world are closely watching the optical
fiber paradigm and its pioneers. New roads of opportunity are being
trailblazed. These new optical network roads may cause structural changes to
the computer economy to which entrepreneurs and investors have to respond.

SIGNS IN SCIENCE

Entrepreneurs of the new economy have to leave behind deterministic
thinkers like Isaac Newton and Frederick Taylor. Twentieth Century thinkers,
such as Albert Einstein (relativity), Joseph Schumpeter (evolutionary
economics), Max Planck (quantum mechanics), Werner Heisenberg
(uncertainty principle), Henri Poincaré (chaotic processes), and Buckminster
Fuller (synergetics), became path breakers for the new theory of a
nonmechanized, unpredictable universe that functions helter skelter. For
economists, these scientific world-view changes have meant including in their
investigation not only the principles and practices based on equilibria but also
the new principles and practices of complexity. The reductionism of
traditional, stable economics has gone far in explaining the parts and sub-
parts of the economy, but never its whole. Newtonian driven economics is not
powerful enough to explain the global economy maze. Peter Drucker points
out that no existing economic theory explains the main economic events of
the fifteen years between 1975 and 1990. Nor could it have predicted them.
Reality has outgrown existing theories.[5]

Investors Need a New Lens. Investors rooted and conditioned in the traditional, linear, mechanized view of economics may have a hard time relating
to a business plan set in the context and containing the language of the

Knowledge/Creation Economy. Staying in step rarely means staying behind. Venture capitalists, and the companies in which they invest, would love to improve their hit rates from two out of ten to even three out of ten. However, to do this they must stop using old theories and methods, if they want different results. It's no surprise that, beginning in the 1990s, the venture capital industry abandoned start-up companies. High change environments can be scary.

The Knowledge/Creation Economy is Chaotic. How the knowledge asset behaves as an economic resource is not yet certain. Drucker says, "We have not had enough experience to formulate a theory and test it . . . .We therefore know that the new economic theory will be quite different from any existing theory."[6] How different? The Santa Fe Institute in New Mexico is helping provide the answer. Founded in the early 1980s, the Santa Fe Institute has brought leading scientists, academicians, and business people from around the world to study the important developments of chaotic theory in the fields of science, economics, and linguistics. W. Mitchell Waldrop, writing about the Santa Fe Institute, said that it was "a catalyst for change that would have taken place in any case—but much more slowly." He quotes Brian Arthur as saying,

> *By about 1985 . . . all sorts of economists were getting antsy, starting to look around and sniff the air. They sensed that the conventional neoclassical framework that had dominated over the past generation had reached a high water mark. It had allowed them to explore very thoroughly the domain of problems that are treatable by static equilibrium analysis. But it had virtually ignored the problems of process, evolution, and pattern formation—problems where things were not at equilibrium, where there's a lot of happenstance, where history matters a great deal, where adaptation and evolution might go on forever. Of course, the field had kind of gotten stymied by that time, because theories were not held to be theories in economics unless they could be fully mathematized, and people only knew how to do that under conditions of equilibrium. And yet some of the very best economists were sensing that there had to be other things going on and other directions in which the subject could go.*
>
> *. . . Yes! We can deal with inductive learning rather than deductive logic, we can cut the Gordian knot equilibrium and deal with open-ended evolution, because many of these problems have been dealt with by other disciplines. Santa Fe provided the jargon, the metaphors, and the expertise that you needed in order to get the techniques started in economics. But more than that, Santa Fe legitimized this different vision of economics.[7]*

Businesses are more than just simply complex. They are complex and adaptive, as the Santa Fe Institute has postulated.[8] As such, they learn and modify behavior. As Terry Jones, a researcher at Santa Fe Institute, states, "You find in complex adaptive systems some sort of high-level phenomenon, in some sort of big behavior." The more learning, the faster the adaptation and survival. It's the overlap from the natural sciences to the human sciences and economics that makes complex adaptive systems intriguing. "Complex adaptive systems are different, they're problems system specific," states Mike Simmons, Vice President, Academic Affairs for Santa Fe Institute. Investors, once they accept the new science of complexity, have a solid starting point or context for reviewing your business plan. Leif Edvissen and Michael Malone, authors of *Intellectual Capital*, have expressed why entrepreneurs and investors of the new economy have to deal with this:

> *Given the frenzied pace of technological change and the almost instantaneous speed of modern telecommunications, we are flying blindly in a hurricane, depending on instruments that measure the wrong things. (Some of the latest theories about Intellectual Capital even suggest that it is related to Chaos Theory or to complex adaptive—that is, living—systems.) Obviously, this imbalance cannot continue. The sheer wastefulness of resources flowing to the wrong places at the wrong time is dangerous enough . . . We are in enormous danger of losing our direction and flying straight into the ground without even knowing we are heading toward disaster. This alone should chill the soul of every investor, manager or politician . . .[9]*

At the core of the theory of complexity is the conviction that complex systems share similar behavior, so what you learn from one system, such as the immune system, you can apply to another, such as the economy—which explains the conglomeration of physicists, economists, psychologists, mathematicians, and computer scientists all synthesizing their efforts.[10] This synthesis came to a crossroad when Dee Hock, Visa International's first CEO, addressed the Santa Fe Institute in 1993. During his address, he coined a term that described Visa International's structure: "chaordic," a blending of "chaos" and "order" that describes the dynamic tension that results when new science and new business merge.[11]

Entrepreneurs and Investors Have to Deal With This. How does all this new science and "chaordic" philosophy impact early-stage businesses? Plenty. Your investors make their decision to invest based on induction and perception. Both of these cognitive processes are highly driven by the use of analogy—metaphors and patterns. The world view is now accepting a new reality—the science of complexity. If you claim that your business is simple and heading into a controlled or controllable environment—well, there's no analogy, no simile. Investors want things to make sense. Investors and money raisers want to find companies heading into the unpredictable waters of new opportunities, with management theory and tools suitable for the challenge. Savvy investors and money raisers know that the fringes—the edge of chaos in industries and markets—is where new ideas and innovative phenotypes are forever nibbling away at the edges of the status quo. This is where even the most entrenched, old guard will eventually be overthrown. Smart investors and money raisers expect leadership teams to have the capacity and understanding (collectively known as competencies) to navigate "chaordic" enterprises through the messy times of growing the business and shaping new industries and products. Investors want companies that see the dawn of a new age, the age of Knowledge/Creation, in which the top priority will be innovation—the creation of high-value, high-change ideas that produce high growth and high return.

Illustration I-3 compares the former Newtonian-driven economics with the complexity-driven Knowledge/Creation economics.

Signs in the Entrepreneurs

One place to focus attention on for signs of change is in the entrepreneurs themselves. Look around. Do you see the incredible changes taking place in the entrepreneurial landscape? Government, academia, and even Hollywood, in such movies as 1996's *Jerry McGuire*, are exploiting the entrepreneurial revolution.

Entrepreneurism is coming out of the garages. It's not a cottage industry anymore. Small business is now big business. *Inc.* magazine's 1997 issue, "State of Small Business," calls attention to this important sign: "Creators of the New Economy: Amateur Entrepreneurship is Over, the Professionals Have Arrived."[12] The professional entrepreneurs of the new economy see themselves and their roles differently than have amateur entrepreneurs. There is a metamorphosis taking place.

Business Owners are Becoming Business Builders. Entrepreneurs seeking capital, who think like most American business owners, have been missing the mark and the money for some time now. In the past, many start-up enterprises—indeed, probably *most* start-up enterprises—were undertaken by entrepreneurial people who hoped that "their" business would make a lot of money, for as long as possible, and that ownership and control of the company would remain "theirs." Business owners identified and defined themselves largely by their product/service. There was nothing wrong with being a business owner.

ILLUSTRATION I-3:
ECONOMIC PARADIGM SHIFTS

Industrial Economy (Second Wave) →	Information Economy (Third Wave) →	Knowledge/Creation Economy (Fourth Wave)
1. Emerged in the 18th Century	Emerged in the late 20th Century	Will emerge in the 21st Century
2. Industrial revolution	Information revolution	Knowledge/Creation revolution
3. Hand extension	Eye, ear, mouth extension	Brain extension
4. Industrial engineers	Electrical engineers	Business "Imagineers"
5. Standardization	Systemization	Networking
6. Calorie measurement	Bit measurement	Knowledge/creation volume measurement
7. Electronic units	Electronic networks	Optical networks
8. Scale is important	Scope is important	Originality is important
9. *Attributes:* Machinery Energy Centralization Simultaneity Messenger Typewriter	*Attributes:* Information Data Decentralization Multi-time Modem Computer	*Attributes:* Creation Ideas Individuality Free time Message (contents) Conceptor
10. Atoms	Electrons	Photons
11. Money capital intensive	Money capital intensive	Human capital intensive — Money capital less intensive
12. Newtonian/Taylor economics	———→ (The Transition)	Einstein/Deming economics
13. Knowledge is useful information	———→	Knowledge is predictive information
14. Land, labor, capital (tangibles)	Capital intensive hardware & infrastructure (tangibles)	Knowledge, talents, relationships (intangibles)
15. Facts are important	———→	Phenomena are important
16. Incremental changes	———→	high changes (discontinuities)
17. 19th Century physics Determinism and stability	———→	Biology-based connectiveness and chaos
18. Time, space, matter are constraints	———→	Time, space, matter are resources
19. Facts dictate reality	———→	Signals dictate reality

ILLUSTRATION I-3: (CONTINUED)
ECONOMIC PARADIGM SHIFTS

Industrial Economy (Second Wave) →	*Information Economy (Third Wave)* →	*Knowledge/Creation Economy (Fourth Wave)*
20. Life and business seen as mechanical and linear	⟶	Life and business seen holistically ("chaordic")
21. Investors see growth track as straight and deterministic	⟶	Investors see growth track as emergent and surprising
22. In statis — measured by statistics	⟶	In chaos — understood by perception
23. Deductive reasoning	⟶	Inductive reasoning
24. The "one best way" system	⟶	"Plan, Do, Study, Act" cycle to constantly improve the system
25. Primary cause of problems: people	⟶	Primary cause of problems: systems
26. Stay away from edge of chaos because things are stable, and if we change, it will be after empirical data convinces us	⟶	Collide with edge of chaos, because we're organized for it and confident we'll emerge before others confront the changes
27. Re-engineering constantly: "eyes on feet"	⟶	Regenerating through emergence: "eyes on horizon"
28. Organizational transformation: "Things were not done right the first time."	⟶	Industry transformation: "Since things are done right, let's race to the future."
29. Dueling for market share	⟶	Outdistancing competition through lowering prices and increasing customer market and share of customer
30. "Ready — Fire — Aim" and repeat for maximizing ratio of new product hits	⟶	"Plan, Do, Study, Act" and repeat for maximizing learning and knowledge in order to predict
31. Insiders influence the direction of new trends	⟶	Outsiders to an industry (out on the edge) often bring more valuable insight and influence new directions
32. Vertical enterprises	⟶	Virtual enterprises
33. High volume	⟶	High value
34. Satisfied customers	⟶	Loyal and "amazed" customers

However, they did have a hard time accessing investor capital, because there was a lot more to accessing investor capital than current products/services that have a current market. Business owners have had a reputation for "looking at their feet," instead of "looking at the horizon." After all, business owners only have to look out for their own skins. Human nature being what it is, business owners tend to rest on their laurels.

Now a new kind of entrepreneur is showing up to play. This entrepreneur is not just a "profiteer." He or she is cut from the same mold that formed the likes of Dave Packard, Bill Hewlett, Bill Gates, and thousands of others whom I call business builders.

Fire in the Belly. Business builders are people who are in the game because their "fire in the belly" is about important things that need to be done for other people. They will go to almost any length to insure that it happens. Their businesses are not just about personal gain, security, retirement, or control. Their businesses are about destiny, purpose, sharing, and trust. Business owners borrow money and give no stake in their game to anyone else. Business builders create stakeholders in as many people and firms as possible who are in alignment with the mission of the business. Business owners are path finders, while business builders are path breakers. John Sculley, the former president of Apple Computer, Inc., viewed himself this way: "I was driven, not by simple power or raw ambition, but by an insatiable curiosity . . . I considered myself a builder . . . I felt as if I was an architect of new ideas and concepts."[13] Business builders are architects then—dreamers of things not yet created, and draftsmen of plans and actions to make the dream a reality."

Investors Are Not Sharks. Business owners tend to view investors as "sharks" who are going to eat up their profits, control, and security—the last resort suppliers of money. Business builders view investors as partners-in-progress—they are the rocket engine fuel that allows them to get on with the real meaning of life—adding value to as many people as possible that can be served by their special enterprise. Business builders take the perspective that their immediate investors will be their partners and friends for life (even though investors usually don't have this view). Business builders are usually very sensitive to God's calling in their life and are very grateful to have the chance to exercise responsibility for this calling.

WHAT KIND OF ENTREPRENEUR HAS THE BEST CHANCE?

Investors in the new economy are not only looking for business builders as opposed to business owners, they are also seeking out certain types of business builders. Since they know their investment success rides ultimately on the shoulders of the leadership team, they want the best kind of team possible. Not all kinds of business builders will adapt well to the environment of the new century.

There are three different types of business builders, namely: Product/Service Specialists, Traditional Business Builders, and Visionary Business Builders. Each have certain characteristics that indicate the kind of management performance and perspective that may be expected of that particular type of business builder. In Step 1, the complete explanation of the Visionary Business Builder model will begin. The description of Visionary Business Builders here provides a contextual introduction.

An enterprise is initially described and understood inductively by the personalities, track records, skills, attitudes, ideologies, and directions of the leadership team. An honest self-appraisal by an entrepreneur is worth its weight in gold. As you read these three profiles, honestly ask yourself where you fit.

PRODUCT/SERVICE SPECIALISTS

Many entrepreneurs are Product/Service Specialists. They are people whose enthusiasm, energy, and devotion is for their product or service. Most other business issues are boring. Their approach to raising capital is to first impress investors with "what they have," then with "what they do," and finally with "who they are." Attorneys, CPAs, engineers, investors, doctors, architects, scientists, and professors are often good examples of Product/Service Specialists. Ninety-five percent of their time and resources are invested into their expert skills. They are product/service centric. They are product visionaries, not organizational visionaries. Product/Service Specialists exist "inside" a business, and rarely does a business exist "inside" a Product/Service Specialist. They are part of a whole, not a whole. These stand-alone specialists live and die for the satisfaction their craft affords. They are artisans.

Feet Watchers. Product/Service Specialists can discover a rare and significant product/service that is at their feet, but they can lack the patience and discipline necessary to meet the challenges of today's tough market development challenges. Product/Service Specialists have a tendency to be more excited about "what they do" than "what it does for someone else." Shaping the exterior of a connector, for example, is more important to them than shaping an industry. They believe that their benefit to society exists very independently of investors. Product/Service Specialists, as a rule, have a hard time becoming great partners with investors. They may even have a hard time being partners among themselves. They need to realize that they belong on a "business building" team that includes organizational visionaries, if they want to access capital. Companies need Product/Service Specialists. They are the "engineers," allowing the rest of the leadership team to be architects, "imagineering" tomorrow's business as it races to get to the future first.

Part of the Story. A business accessing capital should not develop its persona around the Product/Service Specialist, as a rule, because the perception created is that of "culmination" and "dependence." Exciting businesses that money chases are perceived as "launches," and any one part (the specialist) is not the whole story. Product/Service Specialists are more interested in quickly selling what they have to anyone they can. Product/Service Specialists are not prone to manage paradoxes very well, and paradoxes must be managed in the Knowledge/Creation Economy.

Sought After. These professionals are coveted and nurtured by team builders and their investors, but rarely is the feeling reciprocal. The philosophy of business holds little fascination to a Product/Service Specialist. Their business objectives start out as financial objectives. Rarely do they start out with industry, business, and market objectives.

Product/Service Specialists have an orientation that starts with their fascination about technological "imagineering" ➡ new products ➡ new business ➡ new industry. They do not start with new industry ➡ new business ➡ new products ➡ new technologies.

Maybe a Different Recipe. Product/Service Specialists looking for capital need to realize that their product/service centricity and stand-alone genius, although of keen interest to investors, only represent a small part of the investors' due diligence inquiry. Investors and money raisers know that product life cycles are shortening and a business built solely on the vitality of one product/service is usually doomed. Product/Service Specialists may have a difficult time reading this book. After all, Investor Financing™ is a process that takes a commitment to being in business and loving it, lock, stock, and barrel. Product/Service Specialists may want a different recipe than this book offers.

Spinout Candidates. Product/Service Specialists are sometimes best rewarded in life by staying as employees in organizations that foster "intrapreneurism." This path can often lead to a Product/Service Specialist leading a "spinout" activity for a larger company, with start-up financing coming from the "mother" company. If the "mother" company spreads its warm and caring arms of resources and capabilities over the spinout—then chances are great that the Product/Service Specialist will be in a successful and highly rewarding environment, and on the road to "mission accomplished."

Product Licensing. Financing through product licensing and short-term, self-liquidation, noncorporate structures are also viable strategies for Product/Service Specialists. The simplest roadmap for a Product/Service Specialist is to develop a prototype of the product/service, develop a spec sheet, price the product/service at three to four times the cost, and sell a few to see how users respond. If results are good, then this expert should get a business partner who can handle the intricacies of founding a company.

Product/Service Specialists need to be facilitated into someone bigger than they are by real facilitators—Traditional or Visionary Business Builders.

TRADITIONAL BUSINESS BUILDERS

This is a category of people who have represented the mainstream of American entrepreneurism. "Go for it" people who will bet their farms and futures on their beliefs and aspirations. These beautiful folk represent, more than anything else, the rugged individualism and inventiveness that has become identified with American business. This is the rank and file of the small business community that is forever restless and forever stretching. They exhibit strong product/service expertise, and their faith about what they have and what they can do with it often drives them out of corporate jobs and into the entrepreneurial world. They also have had enough experience and training to know the value of sound business building practices. Like Produce/Service Specialists, they recognize the value of launching their entrepreneurial efforts from the womb of an "intrapreneurial" company that finances "spinout" companies and who support them with organizational resources.

Investors Beware. Traditional Business Builders may really be business owners in disguise and investors try to watch out for this ruse. Investors can have a hard time determining the true intentions and character traits of Traditional Business Builders. Many American investors and money raisers seek out Traditional Business Builders, with plans to build and sell businesses quickly. Getting in and out of an investment quickly (exit centricity) is attractive to many investors, even though this can be the seed of failure for many nearsighted, private investors. There is a lot of drama associated with short-term Traditional Business Builders, and high drama and trust do not mix well. Traditional Business Builders equate long-term with a distant return of capital, ambition with high risk-taking, and commitment as heavy cash investment. Their attention is on the core business (usually a lead product/service) and not on core competencies. They easily get led by their customers, instead of staying out in front of their customers, with new ideas for new benefits that have not yet been thought of by the customer (high change).

The story line of most Traditional Business Builders matches perfectly the latent greed of many investors. Venture capitalists who complain about the mistakes they make in picking the right people in whom to invest, have only themselves to blame. Perhaps their short-term "in and out" investment criteria, when matched with a Traditional Business Builder, prevents both sides from being successful. A truly unfortunate mix is the unrealistic and unprepared Traditional Business Builder and the gullible investor. These are strange bedfellows on a trip to never-never land, and they usually get there. Traditional

Business Builders, and coincidentally their investors, are balance sheet and product/exit centricity driven to the exclusion of almost everything else.

Track Record is the Key. Nowhere is the track record of the leadership team more important for investor consideration than in the case of Traditional Business Builders. Traditional business building implies a short-term orientation—a business will start, grow, and be sold within a span of three to seven years. As a result, there is little room for error. A hot product/service does not guarantee a business success story. Traditional Business Builders exhibit tendencies to be overly product oriented, and less core competency oriented. They think pounding out market share is how to grow. They view the success formula of their enterprises more on "what they do," rather than on "who they are," or "who they are becoming" in the future. Traditional Business Builders, who are successful with their game plans, do not view their current business as their last. They are happy with short trips, and long trips bore them. Shaping the immediate landscape and doing whatever financial engineering is necessary to insure they and their investors get their "exit visas" on time is most important. Shaping the landscape of an entire industry, and doing now what is necessary to get to the future first, is not a voluntary agenda item.

Lots of Money Available. Lest we be too critical, the record book is full of success stories for Traditional Business Builders. These are exciting people and their investors are exciting. There will probably always be a large number of companies in the acquisition market for companies built and financed by Traditional Business Builders. "Exit visas" for Traditional Business Builders and their investors will remain strong. However, Traditional Business Builders that look to the public market for their liquidity and exit should take precautions. These investors, although won over by the past performance of the company, are betting on the future prospects. They invest their bucks hoping the "past bang" means there is a "future bang" as well. IPO (Initial Public Offering) investors deserve leadership teams that win in the long-term arena—and this is a different game. In a nutshell, the soul of Traditional Business Builders, although appearing quite similar to the soul of Visionary Business Builders, is significantly different. It's like saying that Japanese and American executives are alike because both acknowledge the importance of quality management. They are not alike—there are some intrinsic, almost genetically coded differences.

Traditional Business Builders will succeed very well in their Investor Financing™, because America has an ample supply of short-term investors. They will succeed in a spectacular way, if they become Visionary Business Builders. There may even be a few Traditional Business Builders transformed into Visionary Business Builders. There will probably be a few Product/Service Specialists and Traditional Business Builders who discover, during their Investor Financing™ steps, that they have to be Visionary Business Builders just to gain the attention and trust of their targeted investors and money raisers, and to have a large enough universe of stakeholders. Our national clinic experiences have proven this time and time again.

VISIONARY BUSINESS BUILDERS

The Future is Ours. The prospects for a quantum leap forward in the American entrepreneurial experience does not rest on the shoulders of Product/Service Specialists or Traditional Business Builders. Frontiers are always in the future. Products come and go, but talents and resources managed and directed at shaping new industries and markets in an evolving future, have a way of insuring that an enterprise stays around awhile, so that it can realize its full potential. Two of America's greatest examples of Visionary Business Builders are the founders of Hewlett-Packard. In 1937, Bill Hewlett and David Packard started their company with no great ideas for their first products. They only wanted to be in business and make a difference in the long run. According to Bill Hewlett, "We did anything to make a nickel . . . here we were, with about $500 in capital, trying whatever someone thought we might be able to do."[14]

Visionary Business Builders have the same basic skills, talents and experiences as Product/Service Specialists and Traditional Business Builders, but they come to play with a different perspective. They try to impress investors first about "who they are," then "what they do," and finally, "what they have." These people are focused as much on long-term direction as they are on short-term effectiveness. Innovation courses through their veins. They know they have to quickly engineer successful core products/services in order to be in business and attract capital, and are—deep in their souls—architects of enterprises that will endure beyond their first products. They know that products come and go, but they want their enterprise built to last. Like Bill Hewlett and Dave Packard, they are organizational visionaries first and product visionaries second. Innovation and destiny are the compelling drivers of these people. Long-term to them means a point of view about industry evolution and who they are becoming. They know that their companies exist in unstable, fluxing markets. They know it's out of their control, but their role is to innovate and lead through successive emergencies (when the chaotic markets and their stable companies collide) and to reinvent their enterprises. Ambition means aggressive steps, but with minimal risk, through maximum resource leverage. Visionary Business Builders face soberly their first products/services, namely whether or not they are really "breakthroughs." This reality, in turn, allows these visionaries to correctly build the appropriate market entry and development plans. They know there is more than one way to enter a market and get profitable. Commitment means an intellectual and emotional commitment that ensures consistency and constancy. They don't mistake momentum for leadership.

Empathetic, but Not Compromising. Visionary Business Builders empathize with investors who want immediate results and dividends. Accountants and stockbrokers are important to Visionary Business Builders, because Visionary Business Builders deal with existing infrastructures and securities' markets. However, they don't compromise corporate capability building and improvement for the sake of meeting short-term goals that are directed by short-term investor appetites and traditional investor philosophies and values.

Perspective Shifts. Visionary Business Builders decide in advance the timeline of corporate growth and investor liquidity. They have a global viewpoint, even if their market is initially local or small. These entrepreneurs have a 20-year point of view of how, by working hard and smart, they can reshape an industry. They have a 10-year point of view of the kind of Intellectual Capital they need to build in order to be in a position to reshape their industry or create a new one altogether. They have a 5-year point of view of their current processes, products/services, and how to win in their existing markets. They know, and find a way of communicating to their investors, that long-term does not mean that investors necessarily have to be patient for their returns and liquidity.

Long-term business building does not mean long-term investor patience. Visionary Business Builders know that when they are navigating through the rough waters of starting a business, they need to be guided by a lighthouse far away. These entrepreneurs do not see future impact as inconsistent with present impacts. In fact, they believe short-term innovation is brought into clearer focus through a long-term lens. They know that profits and gateways for innovation expand when market share mentality is extended to customer share mentality. Visionary Business Builders are not impressed with having satisfied customers, as are most Product/Service Specialists and Traditional Business Builders. Rather, loyal customers are sought, the kind of customers who bring friends to buy.

Good Obsessions. Visionary Business Builders are obsessed with production and marketing processes and systems, and thus, see to it that they and their vendors actually practice Total Quality Management (TQM) and win loyal customers, because they'll make the investment of time and resources in Structural Capital items that are necessary. With TQM in place, Visionary Business Builders insure themselves the opportunity of having the time and resources to invent and reinvent their futures, instead of mobilizing and remobilizing constantly to restructure and reengineer production processes.

Visionary Business Builders don't want to drive while looking in the rear view mirror and they refuse to play catch-up-style business.

To have long-term intentions and current agendas on Intellectual Capital building requires a very clear understanding of "who we are." The creative and innovative "what to do" for customers is always evolutionary and is always discovered out of a deep awareness of self, destiny, commitment, and data.

Financing is Easier. Visionary Business Builders are able to design an Investor Financing™ message that offers the greatest chance of funding. They spend the time to educate their investor sources about the advantage of becoming visionary capitalists. They get to the heart and meaning of their existence because their existence is inexorably tied to the business with a lifetime view. More questions are answered for investors, sharper answers to the questions are given, and all the right questions are asked. Creating an exciting message insures that a landscape rich in stakeholders is discovered, which in turn means that chances increase for finding more advocate messengers for the final Offering Campaign.

Illustration I-4 provides a comparison of the three kinds of business builders. Some of the comparison points have not yet been explained, but they will be later in the book.

THE WINNERS ARE PASSIONATE

In his song, *All About Soul*, Billy Joel sings the following lyric, "Who's standing now, who's standing tomorrow. You got to be hard as a rock in that 'ol rock 'n roll. That's only part, you know in your heart it's all about soul." This lyric sets the proper context for one of the most important keystones for success. Here's why:

Has your banker ever asked you if you're a "business builder"? Has your banker ever asked you what you care about the most in your business? Have you ever seen a loan application with the following questions: "What is the added-value customer-benefiting direction of your business?" "What is your business's 'success formulas'?" "What is the 'future-value impact' of this 'success formula'?" "Why are you excited about your business?" "At what are you best-in-the-world?" "Do you have a paradigm vision?" "What is the value of your intellectual capital?" "Can your business create more 'knowledges'?" Has an accounts receivable lender ever asked you, "What are the core-competencies of your business?" Probably not.

Well, successful investors and money raisers (the kind talked about in this book) do care about what you and the rest of the principals in your company care about. Their application forms do have spaces for such items as corporate direction, "success formulas," core ideology, "future-value impact," finance sequencing, core competencies, knowledge creation, intellectual capital value,

ILLUSTRATION I-4:
BUSINESS BUILDER PROFILES

Product/Service Specialists	Traditional Business Builders (Tweeners)	Visionary Business Builders
1. Technology → Product → Business	Technology → Product → Business	Business → Product → Technology
2. It's mine	It's ours	It's everyone's
3. What we do	What we do	Who we are and what we're becoming
4. Business issues are boring	Business issues are interesting	Business issues are fascinating
5. Ideology: What's that?	Ideology: Some day	Ideology: Our rudder now
6. Product visionaries	Product visionaries	Organizational visionaries
7. Business owner motive	Business owner in disguise	True Business Builder
8. Investors are a nuisance means to end	Investors are passive partners	Investors are stakeholders
9. Persona is embedded in product/service	Persona is hard to tell	Persona is embedded in core competencies
10. "A finality"	"A tweener"	"A beginning"
11. Exit and liquidity visas are not thought of	Exit and liquidity visas are all consuming	Exit and liquidity visas are important but not all consuming
12. Engineers of a one-time dimension	Engineers of a one-time dimension	Engineers of a short-term time frame and architects of a long-term time frame
13. Sell fast to any customer	Sell fast and people will provide quality later	Quality first and continue to improve it
14. Start with financial objectives	Start with financial objectives	Start with market/industry objectives
15. Product plan	Product plan	Business plan for product and paradigm shifting
16. Structural Capital important	Structural Capital important	Human Capital and Structural Capital important

ILLUSTRATION I-4: (CONTINUED)
BUSINESS BUILDER PROFILES

Product/Service Professionals	Traditional Business Builders (Tweeners)	Visionary Business Builders
17. Raise enough to start selling product	Raise enough to hit home run with current product ideas and get an exit	Raise enough to "pay as we go" as we race to the future
18. If this works, we're in business	"Go for broke" attitude	Tough, careful and Deming-ized
19. Debt/equity: Don't care who invests	Debt/equity: Don't care who invests	Debt: Passive investors Equity: Stakeholder investors
20. Market leadership not a concern, only fast sales	Belief that market leadership is a sustaining and holding on process	Belief that there is no such thing as "sustaining," only a constant cycle of reinventing new leadership all over again
21. Momentum through shortcuts	Mistakes momentum as leadership	Momentum is part of emergence, not leadership
22. Not able to meet the demands of managing a business in the Knowledge/Creation Economy	Barely prepared to meet demands of the Information Economy	Preparing for the Knowledge/Creation Economy
23. "Long-term" means distant return on investment	"Long-term" means distant return on investment	"Long-term" means point of view about industry transformation
24. "Ambitious" means high risk	"Ambitious" means risk taking	"Ambitious" means bold plans for future and small, safe systems to emerge there
25. "Commitment" means large investments	"Commitment" means large investments	"Commitment" means high intellectual and emotional investment and low capital investments
26. Seeks venture capital oriented investors	Seeks venture capital oriented investors	Seeks Visionary Capital oriented investors

attitude, paradigm shifting, enthusiasm, and outsourcing. Investors want to know if you view yourself as a "business builder," or merely as a "business owner."

Successful investors and money raisers have learned that *people* start and run businesses. Traditional asset-based business financing is a nonpersonal credit- and collateral-intensive process. Investor Financing™ is a highly personal, creative, and communications-intensive process. Don't ever mistake investors' interest in the technological and financial condition aspects of your company as a sign that they only measure your request for funding on a strictly quantitative basis. They are equally interested in you and your management team. Investors and money raisers want to know what makes your team tick. They've learned the hard way that "growing a business" is a rocky road. Before they embark on your rocky road, they want to know what's deep in your company's heart and mind—in its soul— that qualifies it to receive their money (or their client's money). They want to know about you, your dreams, and your mission. They want to find out what it is about the principals of the company that drives them to work so hard and long. And they look for that fire in your eyes that indicates that you're a "business builder" for the 21st Century Knowledge/Creation Economy. Successful investors and money raisers quickly weed out people who are not keeping up with the new realities that the Knowledge/Creation Economy is thrusting upon us all.

The essence of your passion and the other intangible qualities that indicate you're a "business builder" show up early. They show up in your business plan, in your very first written or spoken words, and as a twinkle in your eye that indicates something special is going on. The essence of an opportunity has a certain instant feel to it. Investors' intuition plays a big role in their success. They look for early clues. That's why it's important to bare your soul early to investors and money raisers. They always move forward on a deal based on their feelings. They are instantly attracted to management teams brimming over with excitement and anticipation. They know that what is in your soul— your sense of destiny, your attitudes, perspectives, passions, habits, personal characteristics, dreams, and needs, are more deterministic of tomorrow's success than reports about yesterday's events.

Later on, investors and money raisers justify their intuition by crunching your numbers. They let their analysts and accountants "get to know the numbers" while they "get to know the people." If you've sent a good set of numbers on your deal to a candidate investor or money raiser (with whom you haven't yet spent much time), and he/she tells you he/she needs to see more numbers, maybe he/she is really telling you that he/she needs to see and know more of you.

Investors and money raisers know that many valuable "knowledges" are usually earned through failures and disappointments. Investors understand the price of tomorrow's success can be yesterday's pain and failures. On the other hand, "being on a recent roll" is a sign to astute investors and money raisers that your turn to have a "bad hand" may be on the next deal. Investors want to be on your team when it's your turn with the ball, and you're ready to score—no matter where you are on the playing field.

Investors are sensitive to the changing tides of fate. They want to beat the odds. To do this, they have to focus their due diligence process, like a laser, at your very soul. What kind of men and women run your show? Like a spouse, they want intimacy, and they want to know where and with whom you've been in the recent past. And they want to get to know you quickly. They expect "soul mate" status right from the get go.

Once these investors and money raisers "*know about you*" and "*know you personally*," things move fast. Business plans can be short and straight to the point. An Investor Financing™ consists of moving the right bunch of investors and money raisers up the relationship road to your front door—then asking them to participate as family members at dinner.

Smart investors judge the way you located them and then moved into a relationship with them as indicative of how your business probably interacts with its customers. The capital players today know that success in the marketplace hinges on your customers doing business with your company for a long time. Intimacy with your customers is important because customized and codesigned customer centered products/services don't happen by accident. Trust between your company and its customers is very similar to the trust between you and your investors and money raisers. Smoke-and-mirror marketing, hype sales events, and glitzy ad campaigns don't win customers—and they certainly don't find investors and money raisers. It's not enough to simply gain the attention of customers, or of investors and money raisers, by making a lot of noise in the markets. You have to win their trust also. It takes courage to bare your soul early in these relationship-building steps.

Investors and money raisers also know that matters of the soul play a big part in developing and delivering winning products and services. "Knowledge," or "Intellectual Capital" as it is sometimes called, is the driver of new product/service innovations. Where credit, collateral, and offsetting balances are resources considered bankable by traditional bankers, "knowledges" and "future-value impacts" are considered bankable by the visionary investors of the 21st Century. Resourcefulness, not resources, generates Knowledge/Creation Economy assets. Resourcefulness and wisdom are the by-products of the mind and heart at work.

Information—raw data—is abundantly available today. It is easily bartered, bought, and transported. However, information that predicts (the real definition of knowledge) is in short supply. Investors are looking for knowledge creators with a global point of view, who want to build businesses that last. Knowledge creation and business building starts from the soul of inspired and determined people.

The early seeds of knowledge are intuition, insight, hunches, and operating system data. These embryos of knowledge have to be harvested from the individuals and the operation systems they use, in order for the company to improve, exploit, and innovate what it does for its customers. Once done, the souls of the individuals are now part of the soul of the company and its products/services. Investors want companies that have the potential to innovate products/services constantly and who can reinvent themselves at the appropriate times. Investors do not want to invest in a company built around one product or service without assurances that there is talent to create newer and better products and services. It takes new knowledges, not necessarily more information, to expand existing products/services. This innovative, knowledge-based process always starts in the soul of an individual—where the muse first does her dance.

DESIGNING THE PHENOMENAL MESSAGE

STEP 1

Step 2

Step 3

Step 4

Step 5

Step 6

Step 7

Step 8

Step 9

Step 10

1 *To be optimally effective, undertake at the outset the most comprehensive task in the most comprehensive and incisively detailed manner.*

— R. BUCKMINSTER FULLER

ARE YOU REALLY READY?

God, through the Divine Plan, has designed each and every one of us as unique and significant individuals. He has given us all the raw stuff for a great headstart at being great business builders. It is your responsibility to build upon what the Master Designer has already begun by completing "Step 1: Designing the Phenomenal Message."

The principals in your company and your closest advisors (the Inner Circle, see Step 4) will need to be architects and engineers. Like architects, you will need to be both draftsmen and dreamers. At the same time, everyone will have to be engineers to make things work now. The Phenomenal Message consists of the plans and ideas that serve as the blueprint for the business plan (Step 3). This blueprint is equally pragmatic and idealistic. It is one part believable and one part almost unbelievable. It involves current plans that express the voice of experience and reasonableness, and ideas about future conditions that no one has experienced yet and that may seem impossible today.

Fire Up. Your creative resources need to be fired up. The Nomura Research Institute of Japan claims that creation is, in the final analysis, a human activity that explains creativity's substance, foundation, energy, and resulting phenomena.[1] Your chances of catching investors' attention rests on your Phenomenal Message—what you're becoming. You may be in the "no-great-idea-for-the-first-product" predicament Bill Hewlett and Dave Packard had when they started the Hewlett-Packard Company. Step 1 will show you what to do about this.

What You Should Feel. Your ambition and your excitement need expressing. You need to design your Phenomenal Message with all the vividness you can, and it needs the leadership team's signature when done. You need to embrace it completely. When completed, you should have the following perspectives or feelings:

- *Pride*. This is it, we have discovered our David in the marble as did Michelangelo.[2]
- *Confidence*. The future is not coming at us, but we are racing to it, and we know it already.[3]
- *Acceptance*. It is our destiny to do this.
- *Balance*. The description in the business plan is itself like a holographic three-dimensional representation of the nature and soul of our personalities and points of view.
- *Patience*. These points of view explain and give credibility to the view that our company is *not*, in desperation, trying to find the elusive holy grail.
- *Joy*. We already have what we want, and it happens that we have the opportunity to live our dream on a daily basis for twenty years or so.

Step 1 is your opportunity to X-ray your business. It will allow you to find out what's real and what's not. After you complete Step 1, you should:

- Feel confident that you have properly focused on Step 1 because it is responsible for 90% of your funding outcome and success.
- Know your potential and what you can do to enhance it and to leverage it.
- Know your weaknesses and what you can do to transform them into strengths in the future.
- Know the Evidence Points to use to substantiate your claim of a phenomenal enterprise.
- Be prepared to develop your business plan when you get to Step 3.

THE FOUR PHENOMENAL MESSAGES

There are basically four different phenomenal messages that business builders use to access capital. Often two or more of these messages will be used together. The messages are:

- Industry Superstar Message
- Profitable Company Message
- Great American Product/Exit Game Message
- Visionary Business Builder Message

As you proceed through the first three message types, be realistic on how you presently measure up. It may be a sobering, even discouraging study, but only then can the wisdom of committing to the fourth message be fully appreciated.

INDUSTRY SUPERSTAR MESSAGE

Do you think Ted Turner of Turner Broadcast fame has any trouble raising capital for new projects or companies? It's not likely. Once the Mouth of the South (as the big networks branded him) was successful with TBS (track record evidence), his perceived value as a "sure bet" rose considerably. Ted Turner is an Industry Superstar.

The venture capital industry finds the Industry Superstar message very persuasive. An example of how superstars influence the money raising process was profiled in a *Business Week* article titled, "Rewriting the Rules of Venture Capital." D. Blech and Co. was profiled for its use of this first message strategy. This venture capital company makes sure that it recruits "big names" to run the fledgling bio-tech start-ups it backs with its money.[4]

Another example from the venture capital industry appeared in an article titled, "Who Will Feed the Start-Ups?" in *Fortune* magazine:

> Start-ups are feeling the neglect, explains Jack Carston, former Intel Senior Vice President and now a Silicon Valley angel investor. A venture capitalist's most important commodity is time. A partner in a big fund who serves on ten company boards, is not going to have the time at the end of the day to sit down with some unknown entrepreneur. If (an early, unknown) Steve Jobs walked into a mega-fund today, he would have no chance of getting financed. What many of the big venture firms do instead, is to bet on big names—retired or otherwise available company founders—who have made money for them in the past . . . Not surprisingly, no-name entrepreneurs are beginning to look elsewhere . . . There's no venture and there's no capital—at least for start-ups.[5]

A true industry superstar is a rare and significant (phenomenal) occurrence. This kind of person carries a phenomenal message. In our national clinics and workshops, various message exercises are undertaken by all the attendees. Less than two percent of any class has ever had classroom feedback indicating that their message was an Industry Superstar Message. Entrepreneurs who are fortunate enough to raise capital off their name alone are few and far between—in other words, phenomenal.

PROFITABLE COMPANY MESSAGE

An enterprise that is already making a profit is an attractive investment, assuming the "deal points" are favorable. However, most profitable companies seeking capital understand their negotiating position and thus their "deal points" are rarely pro-investor. (Almost by definition, a profitable company already has either collateral or credit to secure their financing and so would not need to obtain financing by the methods described in this book.) It is hard to imagine a profitable company offering investors a deal structure that would be offered by an unprofitable or start-up company. That would be a *really* phenomenal occurrence. The type of capital known as investment capital is attracted to already profitable enterprises. This is where investment bankers are at home.

THE GREAT AMERICAN PRODUCT/EXIT GAME MESSAGE

As you'll learn in Step 2, the venture capital industry has had a strong influence on the way the American emerging business market thinks about securing financing and running a business. This influence has been both positive and negative. On the positive side, the venture capitalists have demanded "nothing but the best." On the negative side, they want to see the best "right now." As a general rule, venture capitalists want enterprises with immediate blockbuster products that will take a company very quickly to profitability, and/or a revenue size that positions the company for a quick sale, or better yet, an IPO (initial public offering) within three to seven years. The kinds of products that drive fast corporate growth and investor liquidity are few and far between. These kinds of fast companies are rare and significant, since there are so few of them. This prompted Peter Drucker to make this observation as long ago as 1985:

> This explains, first, why the high-tech industries follow the tradi-
> tional pattern of great excitement, rapid expansion, and then
> sudden shakeout and collapse. Most of Silicon Valley, and most of
> the new biological high-tech companies as well, are still inventors
> rather than innovators, still speculators, rather than entrepreneurs.
> This perhaps explains why high-tech does not generate enough
> jobs to make the whole economy grow.[6]

THE GREAT AMERICAN PRODUCT/EXIT GAME MESSAGE IS ABOUT PARADIGM SHIFTING

The appetite that venture capitalists have for this message derives from their search for companies with products that are soon going to change the way people live, work, and play. These are products and their companies that will cause disruptive or discontinuous innovations that shift the rules and start "waves of change." Such shifts are called paradigm shifts. As an example, the personal computer paradigm wave actually began in 1971, with the Kenbak personal computer and in 1973, with the Alto, developed by Xerox.[7]

Products that catch an early wave of change caused by a paradigm shift (as opposed to starting it) are also high on the venture capitalist's list. Apple Computer (although not the paradigm shifter) was a paradigm pioneer with its powerful and user-friendly Macintosh Computer. Another example was Microsoft, the premier personal computer wave rider with its focus on the software side of the personal computer paradigm. These are examples of what I call "New Paradigm Lead Products" (NPLP). Since money follows excitement, there isn't anything more exciting for investors than to find themselves investing early in a new paradigm wave rider with the anticipation of fast, high change through the NPLP, and fast, high return through an early IPO.

In our clinics and workshops, every company is asked to write out their product/service description. These are then judged by their peers without identifying company names. Less than one percent of those in attendance are given a New Paradigm Lead Product rating by their peers. The Great American Product/Exit Game Message is a rare occurrence and obviously not many companies have it. Witness the small amount of money invested in start-up stage companies by the U.S. venture capital industry. According to Venture Economics, a Boston research firm, in 1993 only $749 million was invested in start-up stage companies by the venture capital industry. This is approximately 25% of all venture capital invested that year, and this same percentage allocation continues today.

Fortunately for the emerging business market, there is a $96 billion emerging business capital market that isn't as obsessive as the venture capital investors for instant gratification through immediate New Paradigm Lead Products and fast investor liquidity through an IPO. Arthur Rock, a lead investor in start-ups such as Apple Computer and Intel, has said, "I automatically turn down any entrepreneur that mentions how soon his company will go public—I'm not in the stock trading business."[8]

WHAT'S THE VENTURE CAPITAL INDUSTRY'S TRACK RECORD?

How well has the venture capital industry performed for their investors while chasing companies with the Great American Product/Exit Game Message? For some investors it has meant spectacular financial returns. The lucky few who have staked the right fast company have set a standard of good fortune that everyone seems to want to emulate. Who can blame them? However, we would be wise to consider how the venture capital industry has done as a whole. Illustration 1-1 compares the 27-year record

ILLUSTRATION 1-1:
VENTURE CAPITAL VS. STANDARD & POOR'S 500 (ANNUAL RATE OF RETURN)

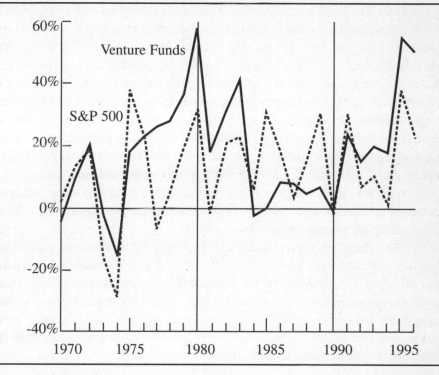

of venture capital performance against the Standard & Poor's 500 Index for the same period.

This information, prepared by Venture Economics[9] conveys several interesting points:

1. The venture capital industry's average annual return over the twenty-seven years was only 14.5%. The safer Standard & Poor's 500 was 13.4%.

2. It shows that the venture capital industry, as a whole, is not generating the kind of returns to justify the risk and lack of liquidity the investor takes when investing in a venture capital fund. For most of this time period, investing in a Standard & Poor's 500 portfolio may have been a better play, considering the liquidity benefits of the Standard & Poor companies.

3. It shows that in the mid- to late-1990s, the hot stock market has had a strong influence on the venture capital industry's returns.

IF YOU'RE IN A DRY HOLE, CHANGING SHOVELS WON'T HELP

I believe the Great American Product/Exit Game model has been responsible for hypnotizing the entrepreneurial and academic leaders of America. Spellbound by the influence of the venture capital industry, America has developed tunnel vision about how to launch and finance an enterprise. Just try to find a textbook, article, or business plan software package that is not developed around the theme of superstars, products, markets, and exits. It's as if entrepreneurs are digging holes, looking for water, but the holes they're digging are dry (that is, finding very little of either corporate performance or investor capital). Then, finding themselves in a dry hole, they change shovels, hoping that if they use better equipment to dig faster the outcome will be different. These dry holes get so deep and dark that it's almost impossible to see anything else. To substantiate my point, let's consider some results from studies done of the entrepreneurial landscape.

In 1989, Bruce Phillips of the Small Business Administration, and Bruce Kirchhoff of the New Jersey Institute of Technology, analyzed business records of the Small Business Database, and discovered that 60% of new companies fail some time during the first six years, and 70% fail some time within eight years.[10]

Michael Gerber, the author of *E-Myth*, presents these findings, citing the Department of Commerce as authority:

> And what we have also discovered is that the people who own small businesses in this country work far more than they should for the return they're getting.

> Indeed, the problem is not that the owners of small businesses in this country don't work; the problem is that they're doing the wrong work.

> As a result, most of their businesses end up in chaos—unmanageable, unpredictable, and unrewarding.

> Just look at the numbers.

> Businesses start and fail in the United States at an increasingly staggering rate. Every year, over a million people in this country start a business of some sort. Statistics tell us that by the end of the first year, at least 40% of them will be out of business.

> Within five years, more than 80% of them—800,000—will have failed.

And the rest of the bad news is, if you own a small business that has managed to survive for five years or more, don't breathe a sigh of relief. Because more than 80% of the small businesses that survive the first five years fail in the second five.

Why is this?

Why do so many people go into business, only to fail?

What lessons aren't they learning?[11]

Let's look for an answer to Michael Gerber's last question, "What lessons aren't they learning?"

One lesson entrepreneurs are not learning is that they have been using the wrong vantage point when looking for solutions to low performance. Too many people take the low road for change and improvement.

Let's look at our dry hole and shovel metaphor. Digging a hole is a strategy to find water, the kind of shovel used is a tactic to achieve that strategy. Changing shovels will not change the status of a dry hole. Entrepreneurs need to more closely analyze their agents for change and improvement. Most start-ups that fail go through many changes, adjustments, and attempts to improve before the plug is finally pulled. Michael Gerber is right when he points out that people are not the problem, rather it's the kind of work they do. Entrepreneurs are not taking the high road to find their way out of difficult business issues.

A HIGH ROAD MODELING LANGUAGE FOR THE 21ST CENTURY

Drawing on the work of Thomas Gilbert in 1978, M.G. Taylor and Associates offer us a look at what they call the Vantage Points Model. This model recognizes that humans form, or hold to solutions and perspectives on, as many as seven distinct levels, as shown in Illustration 1-2. Each level produces a quality or kind of solution for the level immediately below it. Let's look at the levels and see how it works. The entrepreneur who is in a dry hole of the Great American Product/Exit Game philosophy can change tasks (use the right hand with which to shovel), logistics (keep lemonade handy), tactics (use two shovels), strategies (use a different shovel), or policy (we can wait longer). While in the dry hole (that is, the Great American Product/Exit Game), nothing is going to improve, because the culture sees no other way. Now, if the entrepreneur changes his or her basic knowledge and assumptions of business—then there will be a breakthrough. Finding another theory or philosophy of "being in business" is like getting out of the dry hole and

ILLUSTRATION 1-2:
VANTAGE POINTS (FRAMES OF REFERENCE OR MODELS)

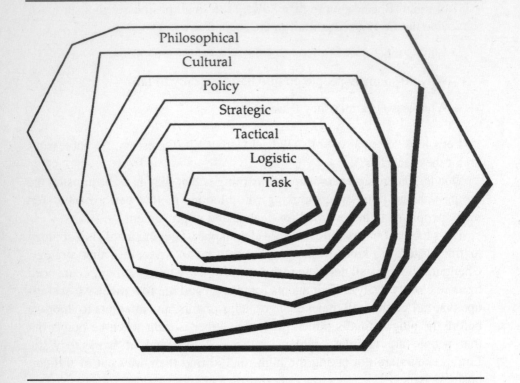

Philosophical

Cultural

Policy

Strategic

Tactical

Logistic

Task

finding another hole on which to work. American entrepreneurs can change their success rate in launching and finding investor capital if they will simply find a philosophy of business that promises a far greater success rate than the Great American Product/Exit Game (GAPE).

The jury is in. The verdict is quite clear. The product/exit centricity game has not produced for the venture capital industry, as a whole, anything close to the returns they expected and deserved for their risk. The American entrepreneurial and academic circles are guilty of emulating the GAPE model and the small business survival record is proof. Truly, we have many GAPEing, dry holes being worked on in this country.

Now some may argue that the business environment is like all other environments in that there is only the survival of the fit few. Thus, no one should be alarmed about the low survival rates in the entrepreneurial sector, or the low investor return rates of the venture capital industry. To entrepreneurs who subscribe to such a philosophy, I say, "Don't ask professional investors to invest in your enterprise." Professional investors are looking for people who believe that God gave us our own minds and spirits to pursue excellence, improvement, and survival. Professional investors don't like the failure rate of American entrepreneurs. Do you? Venture capitalists don't, and that's why they generally stay away from start-ups.

CHANGE YOUR THEORY OR DIE

One of the driving themes of this book, and our work at Business Builders, LLC, is to change the business philosophy, or theory, underpinning the behavior of American entrepreneurs. We know it's a big challenge. Harvard's Chris Argyris, who has worked with mental models and organizational learning for thirty years, puts the challenge this way, "Although people do not (always) behave congruently with their espoused theories, they do behave congruently with their theories-in-use (mental models)."[12] Peter Senge goes on to say, "That is why the discipline of managing mental models—surfacing, testing and improving our internal pictures of how the world works—promises to be a major breakthrough for building [learning] organizations."[13]

We think the numbers speak for themselves. The real question is, what have we learned in the past that can make our future brighter? We are not in the dark. The data is in front of us. My thesis here, is that we have learned the theory or model of business that has driven the entrepreneurial sector of this country in the past, and our models, as Peter Senge says, have determined not only how we make sense of the world, but how we take action.[14] Most entrepreneurs have only seen business start-up challenges through the lens of the GAPE model, and as a result, the American entrepreneur has taken action (culture, policies, strategies, tactics, logistics, and tasks) to support his/her theory. Of all entrepreneurs launching businesses and looking for capital today, 99% are in the dark tunnel, and the light at its end is not the daylight they hope for—it is instead the light of a train, called GAPE, coming right at them.

My hope is that you will be open-minded enough to honestly examine the belief systems that drive your actions and plans. I maintain that the GAPE model of American business design is, at best, a dry hole for the vast majority of start-up enterprises seeking capital and it is, at worst, a business design that will absolutely not support the best corporate and personal success in the new economy.

ONE MORE LESSON—DON'T BLAME THE VENTURE CAPITALISTS

It may appear to some that I'm blaming the venture capital industry for the American entrepreneurs' problems. This would not only be a misinterpretation, but a total misreading of this chapter. Venture capitalism isn't bad, nor is the GAPE model always wrong—it's just a model that supports what venture capitalists have learned is needed to enjoy a high, fast-track investment ride. Obviously, the promise of isolated but huge paydays justifies to the venture capitalist the low rates of return the venture capital industry earns, as a whole, on its portfolio.

The lessons of this chapter are intended to wake up the 99% of the American entrepreneurial sector that doesn't qualify for venture capital. If you think you have a GAPE message, then get your venture capital interviews over as soon as possible. If you're turned down, admit your GAPE model isn't powerful enough. Then sit back and consider that the GAPE model may not be the best business theory or philosophy to use for launching and financing your business. Then remember how powerfully models grip us as we look at things. If you're ready to give up the hold on your outdated business model, you may then be open to another way to launch and finance your business. If so, make a commitment to relax and surrender to the reality that the emerging business capital market is limitless and that this book can show you how to get ready to receive your fair piece of the capital pie.

WHAT CAN WE CONCLUDE SO FAR?

The Industry Superstar Message is a difficult one to achieve. Only a handful of entrepreneurs are lucky enough to raise capital on their name alone. The Profitable Company Message is obviously a valid message that attracts investment capital, but a company with this message will not need this book. The focus of this book is how to raise capital before a company is profitable, or when no credit or collateral is available to raise financing. The third message, the Great American Product/Exit Game Message, is a creation of the venture capital industry, which reflects their preference for fast growing, soon-to-be public companies, driven by New Paradigm Lead Products. Judging by the fact that only a billion dollars a year is placed by venture capitalists in start-up businesses, it is clear that most start-up businesses are unable to develop this message. Finally, it should be noted that not one of these first three messages tells the investor (or the Business Builder) very much about the theory the business will be built upon.

THE VISIONARY BUSINESS BUILDER MESSAGE

Fortunately, there is a fourth Phenomenal Message the Business Builder can use to complete Step 1 of the Investor Financing™ process. It is called the Visionary Business Builder Message. It's both a message strategy for raising capital and a learning organization model for building the knowledge/creation enterprise. All investors, including venture capitalists, will find that the Visionary Business Builder message provides a trustworthy business building theory and due diligence model for the new economy.

All We Had To Do Was Look. This Phenomenal Message has its foundations embedded in the traits and characteristics of the management teams that have led some of the 20th Century's greatest companies. On average, these companies have returned investors 15 times more than either the venture capital industry or the stock market as a whole have returned to their investors. (See Illustrations 1-4 and 1-5.)

THE RESEARCH

The bulk of the research relied on for this Visionary Business Builder Message comes from the work of James C. Collins and Jerry I. Porras, while both were professors at Stanford University Graduate School of Business. Their six-year research effort culminated in their book, *Built to Last: Successful Habits of Visionary Companies*. In their Preface, the authors describe the context of their research:

> We did something in researching and writing this book that, to our knowledge has never been done before. We took a set of truly exceptional companies that have stood the test of the time—the average founding date being 1897—and studied them from their very beginnings, through all phases of their development to the present day; and we studied them in comparison to another set of good companies that had the same shot in life, but didn't attain quite the same stature. We looked at them as start-ups. We looked at them as midsize companies. We looked at them as large companies. We looked at them as they negotiated dramatic changes in the world around them—world wars, depressions, revolutionary technologies, cultural upheavals. And throughout we kept asking, "What makes the truly exceptional companies different from the other companies?"[15]

It should be emphasized that the companies in this research (see Illustration 1-3) have evolved and emerged through the Industrial, the Information, and now the Knowledge/Creation economies.

COLLINS' AND PORRAS' RESEARCH RESULTS

> In a six-year research project, we set out to identify and systematically research the historical development of a set of visionary companies, to examine how they differed from a carefully selected

control set of comparison companies, and to thereby discover the underlying factors that account for their extraordinary long-term position.[16]

. . . [The results are not] about charismatic visionary leaders . . . [nor] about visionary product concepts or visionary market insights. Nor even is it about just having a corporate vision.
. . . [The results are] about something far more important, enduring, and substantial . . . visionary companies.

What is a visionary company? Visionary companies are premier institutions—the crown jewels—in their industries, widely admired by their peers and having a long track record of making a significant impact on the world around them. The key point is that a visionary company is an organization—an institution.[17]

ILLUSTRATION 1-3:
THE COMPANIES RESEARCHED BY COLLINS AND PORRAS

Visionary Company	*Comparison Company*	*Visionary Company*	*Comparison Company*
3 M	Norton	Marriott	Howard Johnson
American Express	Wells Fargo	Merck	Pfizer
Boeing	McDonnell	Motorola	Zenith
Citicorp	Douglas	Nordstrom	Melville
Ford	Chase Manhattan	Philip Morris	RJR Nabisco
General Electric	GM	Procter & Gamble	Colgate
Hewlett-Packard	Westinghouse	Sony	Kenwood
IBM	Texas Instruments	Wal-Mart	Ames
Johnson & Johnson	Burroughs	Walt Disney	Columbia
	Bristol-Myers Squibb		

Why This Is Important—Revisiting Your Message. Remember the first three Phenomenal Messages: Industry Superstar, Profitable Company, and the Great American Product/Exit Game. Does your company fit any of these messages? If so, you can skip the rest of Step 1 and proceed to Step 2. However, if your company doesn't fit any of the first three messages, you can use the fourth Phenomenal Message to raise capital if you follow the rest of Step 1.

Illustration 1-4:
Cumulative Stock Returns of $1 Invested
January 1, 1926–December 31, 1990

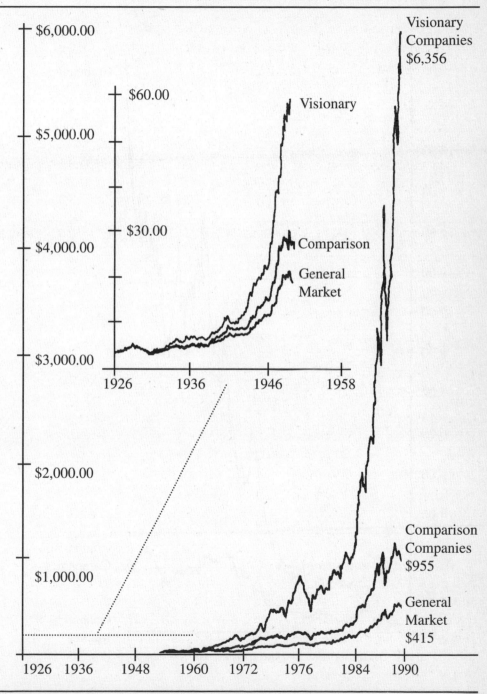

ILLUSTRATION 1-5:
RATIO OF CUMULATIVE STOCK RETURNS TO GENERAL MARKET
1926–1990

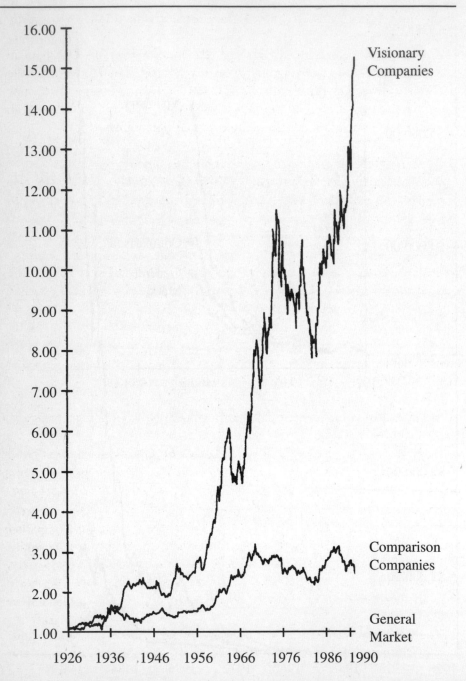

SHATTERING THE MYTHS

Now let's look at the investment performance of the visionary and comparison companies from Collins' and Porras' research as shown in Illustrations 1-4 and 1-5. If you were an investor, which kind of company would you want to invest in?

The book, *Built to Last*, exposes and shatters twelve myths of American business tradition and thinking. All twelve are worth studying. Here are the two most relevant to the Visionary Business Builders message. Note how these two myths represent the heart and soul of the Great American Product/Exit Game message (the venture capital paradigm).

Myth 1: It takes a great idea to start a great company.

Reality: Starting a company with a "great idea" might be a bad idea. Few of the visionary companies began life with a great idea. In fact, some began life without any specific idea and a few even began with outright failures. Furthermore, regardless of the founding concept, the visionary companies were significantly less likely to have early entrepreneurial success than the comparison companies in our study. Like the parable of the tortoise and the hare, visionary companies often get off to a slow start, but win the long race.[20]

This of course was Peter Drucker's observation when he stated, "Successful entrepreneurs do not wait until the muse kisses them and gives them a 'bright idea.'. . . Those entrepreneurs that start out with the idea that they'll make it big—and in a hurry—can be guaranteed failure."[21]

Myth 2: Visionary companies require great and charismatic visionary leaders.

Reality: A charismatic visionary leader is absolutely not required for a visionary company and, in fact, can be detrimental to a company's long-term prospects. Some of the most significant CEOs in the history of visionary companies did not fit the model of the high-profile, charismatic leader—indeed, some explicitly shied away from that model. Like the founders of the United States at the Constitutional Convention, they concentrated more on the architecture of an enduring institution than on being a great individual leader. They sought to be clock builders, not time tellers. And they have been more this way than CEOs at the comparison companies.[22]

The Visionary Business Builder Message is largely derived from the findings of *Built to Last*, using some of the most appropriate principles and recommendations from that book as they relate to designing a powerful message for investor presentations.

Anyone Can Learn How To Do It . . . Collins and Porras point out that " . . . just about anyone can be a protagonist in building an extraordinary business institution. The lessons of these companies can be learned. . . . Gone forever—at least in our eyes—is the debilitation perspective that the trajectory of a company depends on whether it is lead by people ordained with rare and mysterious qualities that cannot be learned by others."[23]

. . . But First, Put On Different Glasses. Collins and Porras are very clear about your first move:

> One of the most important steps you can take in building a visionary company is not an action, but a shift in perspective.[24] . . .
> If you're involved in building and managing a company, we're asking you to think less in terms of being a brilliant product visionary or seeking the personality characteristics of charismatic leadership, and to think more in terms of being an organizational visionary and building the characteristics of a visionary company. . . . We had to shift from seeing the company as a vehicle for the products to seeing the products as a vehicle for the company.[25]

HOW TO PRESENT THE VISIONARY BUSINESS BUILDER MESSAGE

Venture capitalists, strategic corporate investors, adventure stockholders and business angels may still be stuck on the Great American Product/Exit Game model or paradigm. They may not even be aware that there is a better business model in which to invest—The Visionary Business Builder model. They may be looking through the old glasses, unaware that there are better glasses to see the game with today. Your job is to help them put on a new pair of glasses—the Visionary Capitalist glasses. Once on, these investors can see the Visionary Business Builder. It may require all the patience, effort, and help you can muster. Remember, the evidence is on your side that the investors' long-term interest lies in your commitment to launch and build a visionary company and in your short-term money raising interests—as you'll see as you work through Step 1.

Here are three questions most investors want answered when you're presenting your Visionary Business Builder story.

WHO ARE YOU?

The Disciplines. Investors want to know who you are. If they're smart, they will want to know what kind of Business Builder you are (see the discussion in the Introduction) and what your message is. You should tell them and you should walk your talk. You begin to walk the Visionary Business Builder talk by organizing everything from A to Z along the Visionary Business Builder model. The five Disciplines of the Visionary Business Builder are the context of this model. They are the heart and soul of the theories and philosophies of the Visionary Business Builder. As such, these five Disciplines dictate, more than anything else, the direction of your strategies, policies, tactics, and logistics.

The five Disciplines establish the context for everything an investor wants to know about a Visionary Business Builder. They are your most sacred and serious promises to your investors. They are the promises of who you are. These Disciplines are:

1. Intelligently build the organization first, then focus on products/ services.
2. Boldly love your destiny.
3. Fanatically hold two opposed ideas at the same time and remain functional.
4. Passionately preserve the core and drive for progress.
5. Systematically innovate.

In this step our attention is going to be primarily centered on the first Discipline: "Intelligently Build the Organization First, Then Focus on Products/Services." Following the extended section on Discipline 1, there is a summary of the other four Disciplines.

WHAT ARE YOU PLANNING TO DO?

The Strategies. Each of the five Disciplines present various strategies. These strategies are the action steps you promise will be executed by the business now and over time. Naturally, these strategies must be consistent with the five Disciplines. These strategies are the actualization and manifestation of the Discipline with which they relate. So, we call them Discipline Strategies. These strategies will be preliminarily incorporated into the business plan design during Discipline 1's analysis and finally into the business plan during Step 3.

WHAT HAVE YOU DONE?

The Evidence. Each strategy of each Discipline has Evidence Points. These Evidence Points are presented during Discipline 1's discussion on how to design your business plan. That discussion is intended to bring it all together in a cohesive format—the template for your business plan.

Discipline 1 forms the core of Step 1. It's called, "Intelligently Build the Organization First, Then Focus on Products/Services."

DISCIPLINE 1: INTELLIGENTLY BUILD THE ORGANIZATION FIRST, THEN FOCUS ON PRODUCTS/SERVICES

The essence of this discipline, according to Collins and Porras, is to " . . . concentrate primarily on building an organization—building a ticking clock— rather than on hitting a market just right with a visionary product idea and riding the growth curve of an attractive product life cycle."[26] One of the clearest examples of entrepreneurs practicing this discipline was Bill Hewlett and Dave Packard, the founders of Hewlett-Packard. Bill Hewlett told Collins and Porras in an interview, "When I talk to business schools occasionally, the professor of management is devastated when I say that we didn't have any plans when we started . . . Here we were, with about $500 in capital, trying whatever someone thought we might be able to do."[27] Do you think venture capitalists would have found the start-up Hewlett-Packard very exciting? I don't think so.

Discipline 1 separates the wannabes from the real Visionary Business Builders. It requires your leadership team to walk the talk of the first four strategies and requires your team to take a different perspective about launching a business than you were probably taught. Here is how Collins and Porras describe the climate:

> *In courses on strategic management and entrepreneurship, busi-ness schools teach the importance of starting first and foremost with a good idea and well-developed product/market strategy, and then jumping through the "window of opportunity" before it closes. But the people who built the visionary companies often didn't behave or think that way. In case after case, their actions flew in the face of the theories being taught at the business schools.*
>
> *Thus, early in our project, we had to reject the great idea or bril-liant strategy explanation of corporate success and consider a new view. We had to put on a different lens and look at the world back-ward. We had to* shift from seeing the company as a vehicle for the products to seeing the products as a vehicle for the company. *We*

had to embrace the crucial difference between time telling and clock building.[28]

The Visionary Business Builder prescription is the antidote to the high anxiety caused by so many pundits and advisors trying to convince us that their data signifies the entrepreneurial age is destined to be a world of job insecurity. Their assessment begs for attitudes like "protect yourself," live a "portfolio life," and forget "company loyalty"—it's dog eat dog. However, this does not mesh with human motivation at all. What knowledge/creativity workers want are options. The choice to either stay with one company for a long time, (because it affords extrinsic and intrinsic rewards and is built to last), or the choice to disregard security and cast their talents elsewhere.

Many investors are impressed with Silicon Valley's claims that it can take an entrepreneur with a great idea and instantly package up seed capital, management team, distribution channels and IPO. These fast companies are exciting to watch. These same investors also know these fast companies are not the rule, but rather the exception to the rule. A lot of wise investors want an alternative to fast-built companies. They want built-to-last companies. The advent of virtual corporations does not have to mean companies come and go virtually overnight. Investors are nervous with all the drama caused by the quickening pace of product cycles and the implication that companies must therefore be predestined to have short lives as well.

DESIGN IT AND THEY WILL COME

Blueprints precede building. Investors want to see your blueprint. If you're launching a business that's all you can really do anyway. In the popular movie, *Field of Dreams*, the hero was encouraged to build a baseball field and was promised that if he did, they (the customers) would come. The hero persisted because he knew a very phenomenal ball park and ball game was in the works. At the heart of Discipline 1 and its strategies is the promise that if you design the phenomenal message—Visionary Business Builders at work— your investors will be pulled into a relationship with you. "Step 6: Creating the Capital Relations™ Plan" is built on the principle that raising investor capital is a "pull" not a "push" process. You'll always win investors more through attraction (pull) than promotion (push).

Design Is Affected by the Environment. Like the architect designing a building, the Visionary Business Builder has to take into account current and future environmental factors. These environmental factors dictate a lot about what kind of organization to build and how to build it.

An Environmental Design Lesson from the Old Model T. Henry Ford observed long ago a very important principle of finance. He noticed that it was his organizational environment that mattered most. In his day, his perception of his organizational environment was a "closed" environment. Here is how he described it:

> The place to finance a business is in the shop, and not the bank . . . . The money has to come out of the shop, not out of the bank, and I have found that the shop will answer every possible requirement . . . What is needed is a heavier dose of brains and thought and wise courage . . . when that is done, the business will begin to make its own money.[29]

> Entrepreneurs, however, have been caught in the dilemma of not being able to find their "shop" and thus find their financing. Stanley Davis, in *Future Perfect*, observes why:

> The dilemma for managers is that dominant organization models (of the business) are the last link in the progression to develop, and are not likely to occur until the shape of the economy is fairly mature. While the new economy is in the early decades of its unfolding, businesses continue to use organization models that were more appropriate to previous times than to current needs.[30]

In Henry Ford's day, the "shop" was easy to identify. However, the closed organizational models of Ford's day do not work well in the new open environments of the Knowledge/Creation Economy.

We Are All Back To Zero. When a new economy arrives its new rules affect everyone. W. Edwards Deming would refer to this as a structural change. With structural changes everyone is starting over; no one has a head start. Everyone goes back to the baseline to start over. We are in just such a situation today. The new economic paradigms of the Knowledge/Creation age are taking us all back to zero. We are in the midst of redefining the meaning of organizational environment. Thus, it is no longer clear to many where or what their "shop" is and thus, where they can obtain their financing.

So Where Do We Go From Here? In their widely acclaimed book, *2020 Vision*, Bill Davidson and Stanley Davis point out where to start planning your organizational design:

> Since you should organize in relation to the kind of business you will be in, that not yet existing business is the best source of information for what the future organization should look like.[31]

So, we're back again to one of the requirements of Discipline 3, namely, looking into the future. Davis and Davidson suggest that you work backwards from a time in the distant future to determine your organizational design today—your "shop," as Henry Ford put it. And what does your future tell you? The "Imagine a Paradigm Vision Into Your Growth Plan" Strategy of Discipline 3 creates a compelling view of your future world. If your Paradigm Vision work is enthusiastically and exhaustively undertaken, you're literally standing on your road map for organizational design and financing potential.

Your Paradigm Vision should not explain your future business by any of today's industry standards. This kind of result is precisely the outcome predicted by James Moore, author of the best seller, *The Death of Competition*. In his study of the new order, he explains the new organizational design:

> In place of "industry," I suggest an alternative, more appropriate term: business ecosystem. The term circumscribes the micro-economies of intense co-evolution coalescing around innovative ideas. Business ecosystems span a variety of industries. . . . Opportunity environment is the space of business possibility characterized by unmet customer needs, unharnessed technologies, potential regulatory openings, prominent investors, and many other untapped resources . . . thus, shaping cohesive strategy in the new order starts by defining an "opportunity environment." . . . It is more important to see a company within its food "web," than in competition with superficially similar firms bundled together in an industry. . . . The dominant new ecosystems will likely consist of networks (webs) of organizations stretching across several different industries, and they will joust with similar networks (webs), spread across still other industries.[32]

Illustration 1-6 summarizes these shifts, while Illustration 1-7 shows one way of visualizing the web.

Lessons From a Noisy Highway. The influence of the *condition* of an opportunity environment is also important to the Investor Financing™ process. For example, any start-up communications/information company in the early and mid-1990s was able to ride a wave of frenzy caused by everyone honking and speeding on the opportunity environment known as the information highway. Bill Lofft, President of Adcom Information Services, Inc., speaking at one of our clinics, stressed the importance of the press coverage given to the new infobahn environment while his company

Illustration 1-6:
From Entity/Industry to the Web

Yesterday: From Company and Industry	Today: To Ecosystem Web
Corporate positioning	Web positioning
The "closed" company	The virtual company
Innovation done by the company	Innovation done by the web
Competition	Co-opetition
Business boundaries (market/ industry/nation) is a given	Business boundaries *created* out of choice
Economic performance: measured by company performance and industry average	Economic performance: measured by strength of alliances and the web's performance
Growth: measured by company growth	Growth: measured by the web's growth
Business plan is for the company	Business plan is for the web
Capital comes from outside the company	Capital comes from "within" the web
Cooperation: measured by how well a company does with its suppliers and customers	Cooperation: measured among all the players in the web (including the competition)
Competition: measured between product and product, or company and company	Competition: measured between webs
Leadership measured by sales and profits	Leadership measured by *values* and *influence* in the web. Business boundaries created out of choice
Loyalty: employee to company	Loyalty: independent contractor to its web
Paradigm Pioneering on an industry basis by a revolutionary company — so small shifts	Paradigm Pioneering is multi-industry — "new space basis" by many co-evolving companies, usually led by an outsider who also leads the web — so huge shifts

ILLUSTRATION 1-7:
THE WEB: A PLACE TO FINANCE YOUR BUSINESS

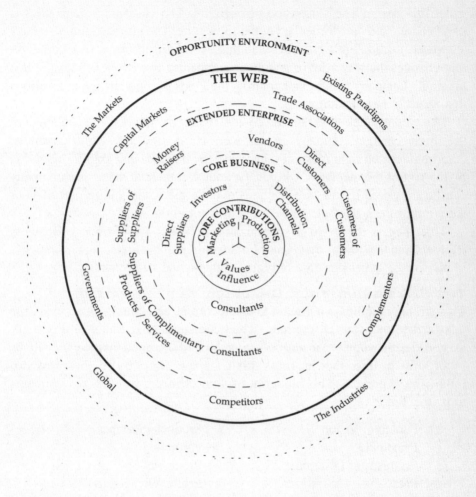

was seeking a secondary round of financing in order to ride on the new infobahn highway. Originally Adcom had attracted $500,000 of seed capital provided by several local business angels found through a boutique broker/dealer firm. This was quickly followed by several million in equity capital from one Wall Street investment banker and three strategic corporate investors. This was followed by another equity placement of several million through a regional stock brokerage house with an investment banking division that arranged some institutional investors again from Wall Street. This whole process spanned three years.

THE CHAORDIC WEB—THE ORGANIZATIONAL BLUEPRINT

Dee Hock, of VISA International fame, told the Santa Fe Institute in 1993 that companies have an organizational design for thriving in a chaotic world. He called his design The Chaordic Organization. The chaordic organization is part "chaos" and part "order" all at the same time. The ultimate aim is to have a "power position" in a chaordic web that evolves itself into a new paradigm that changes the way a lot of people or companies live, work or play. Today, no single company creates and controls the kinds of high change innovations that result in new paradigms.

Many companies co-create and co-evolve new paradigms. The challenge of the high change company in its web is to find the right channels, communicate the right messages, and have the patience and skill for adoption by the rest of the members. Ultimately, your commercial value as a company can be measured by the size of the economic pie when you're part of your web, minus the size of the pie when you're not in the web.

This then is the "virtual" organizational model for Visionary Business Builders and the "shop" that Henry Ford would pull his financings from, with, in his words, "a heavier dose of brains, thought and wise courage."

THE "DESIGNING YOUR CHAORDIC WEB" STRATEGY

This strategy requires your team to use its brains and courageously walk the talk of the other four Disciplines (which are summarized later in this step), as you design your organization—your chaordic web. This design will be incorporated into the business plan during Step 3 of this Investor Financing™ process. This blueprint of your chaordic web has ten elements to it (the Ten P's):

- Paradigm Vision
- Principals
- Promises of Discipline 2
- Path
- Positioning

- Products/Services
- Partners
- Processes
- Profits/Ownership
- Projections/Liquidity

These ten elements need to be addressed within three frameworks: your Identity, your Launch Plan, and your Growth Plan.

Your Identity. The first three chaordic web elements define who you are and what basic principles will guide your company. The discussion of these first three elements usually constitute the opening sections of your executive summary and/or business plan.

The remaining seven elements should be discussed within the context of both the Launch and Growth Plans. These plans can be defined as follows:

ILLUSTRATION 1-8:
THE CHAORDIC WEB ELEMENTS AND THE RELATIONSHIP WHEEL OF THE LAUNCH
PLAN AND GROWTH PLAN

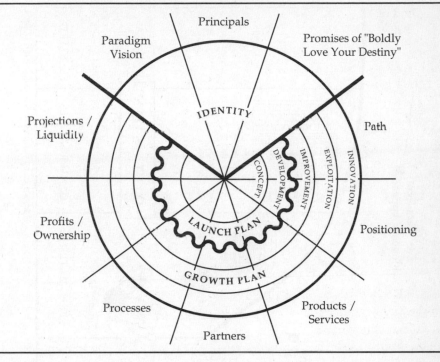

***The Launch Plan* (see page 66).** This is the specific plan that describes everything that the business will do until it reaches a point of profitability, usually a 6–24 month period of time. It is a short-term plan to get the company going and prove to investors the entrepreneurial skill of the management team and its capacity for Discipline 3's requirement to do well in the short run. A well conceived Launch Plan can provide a stable cash flow base, which can be an important antidote to the usually unpredictable market creation challenges for the company's new product initiatives of its Growth Plan.

***The Growth Plan* (see page 83).** Less specific than the Launch Plan, but detailed enough to substantiate that management has done its homework. It can cover any time frame, but should never be less than 3–5 years. This Growth Plan shows investors the path toward the Paradigm Vision. Illustration 1-8 depicts the Ten P's and these three time frames.

Step 3 will discuss more about the "hows" and "whys" of business plan preparation.

ILLUSTRATION 1-9:
PARADIGM ADOPTION LIFE CYLCE

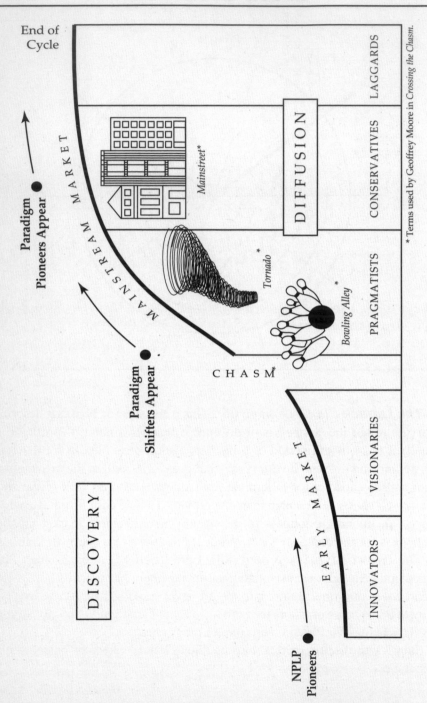

What a Vision Is	What a Vision Is "Not"
■ Highly imaginative	■ A mission statement
■ Idealistic	■ A prophecy
■ Fits core ideology	■ Factual assertions
■ Fits culture	■ Reality
■ Fits destiny promise	■ True or false
■ Sets high standards	■ Static
■ Inspires enthusiasm and courage	■ Constraining
■ Well articulated and easily understood	
■ Fits Core Competency Agenda	
■ Calls for sacrifice and emotional investment[29]	

YOUR IDENTITY
1. THE PARADIGM VISION

"Open with a bold, sweeping, almost controversial opening statement." This quote of Brook Byers, of Kleiner, Perkins, Caufield & Byers, is solid advice. Remember, investors, like most people, are drawn into intimacy by possibilities, rather than realities, by the promise of things to come, rather than proven accomplishments, and perhaps by seduction.[33] Seduce your investors. Spend whatever time is necessary to develop a Paradigm Vision. Remember, like all marketing efforts, you only get one chance to make a good first impression.

The Dream

The Paradigm Vision descriptions in your business plan anticipate what your company is trying to become. They are concept descriptions of ambition without regard to resources. They are the elements of the corporate growth track that relate to the big picture—the race to the future. They convey the leadership team's strategic intent, sense of direction, ambition for discovery, love of destiny, and E=commerce commitments. They describe how the company can capitalize on its years of careful work developing its intellectual capital, Internet based systems, and holding onto core ideologies, to finally bring to market a New Paradigm Lead Product that unlocks a mega-market and supports the company's quest for E=commerce leadership.

Anticipating the future and developing a Paradigm Vision requires your company to understand the art of anticipating new paradigms and what to do about them. A more detailed discussion about the Paradigm Adoption Life Cycle (PALC) is presented in Illustration 1-12A-E and Illustration 1-13A-E. Illustration 1-9 gives an overall look at the PALC.

Once you've developed your Paradigm Vision, a picture of the rare and significant will emerge—a vision of your phenomenal company. The characteristics of a vision, as identified by Burt Nanus, author of *Visionary Leadership*, are listed in the table above.

The Vision Question. The beginning of any Paradigm Vision work can start by answering this crucial question:

> What do our customers and competitors believe to be impossible, but if it were done, would fundamentally change the way everyone (customers and even competitors) would live, work, or play?

ILLUSTRATION 1-10:
TWO PARADIGM VISION STATEMENTS[37]

Total quality	To build a motor car for the great
Market leadership	multitude . . . it will be so low in
Technology driven	price that no man making a good
Global	salary will be unable to own one . . .
Focused growth	everyone will have one. The horse
Diversified	will have disappeared from our
—*Westinghouse, 1989*	highways, the automobile will be
	taken for granted.
	—*Ford Motor Company*

ILLUSTRATION 1-11:
A PARADIGM VISION STATEMENT TEMPLATE

To _____ for _____
    YOUR DESTINY — THE NPLP   YOUR MARKET OR OPPORTUNITY ENVIRONMENT

It will be so _____ that no _____
    MOST ATTRACTIVE PRODUCT FEATURE   CUSTOMER/MARKET

will be unable to _____ one. Everyone in _____
    OWN / HAVE / RESIST   YOUR MARKET

will have one. The _____ will have disappeared,
    CURRENT PARADIGM

the _____ will be taken for granted.
    YOUR DESTINY — THE NPLP

Your answer to this question will inevitably require your company to do "discovery work" about Paradigm Shifters in the Bowling Alley and Mainstreet parts of existing paradigms.

If statistics mean anything, your work in developing the Paradigm Vision may be one of your only opportunities to engage in this important process. Only 3% of America's senior management's time is spent on building a corporate perspective of the future.[35]

As you might expect, developing a Paradigm Vision is often not easy. Some fun examples of people "in the know," who couldn't see beyond existing paradigms have been compiled by Joel Barker, one of the leading researchers in the field of paradigms:

"It is an idle dream to imagine that . . . automobiles will take the place of railways in the long distance movement of . . . passengers."—*American Road Congress, 1913*

"There is no likelihood man can ever tap the power of the atom."—*Robert Millikan, Nobel Prize winner in physics, 1920*

"[Babe] Ruth made a big mistake when he gave up pitching."—*Tris Speaker, 1921*

"Who the hell wants to hear actors talk?"—*Harry Warner, Warner Brothers Pictures, 1927*

"I think there is a world market for about five computers."—*Thomas J. Watson, Chairman of IBM, 1943*

"The odds are now that the United States will not be able to honor the 1970 manned-lunar-landing date set by Mr. Kennedy."—*New Scientist, April 30, 1964*

"There is no reason for any individual to have a computer in their home."—*Ken Olsen, President of Digital Equipment Corporation, 1977* [36]

Where Tomorrow Begins. Take a close look at the two vision statements in Illustration 1-10. Which one would get an investor's juices flowing? Which of the two is set in the context of Paradigm Pioneering? Which one specifically sets a direction?

If you answered Ford Motor Company, you're right. Can you be as bold and visionary? You will find it helpful to use the Ford statement as a template for beginning the work on your own Paradigm Vision (see Illustration 1-11).

2. THE PRINCIPALS

Investors in emerging companies want a team who will make the impossible come true. They begin their early investigation of a business by examining the

CEO and the leadership team. When investors say they "back" a company, they mean they "back the people" in the company. The "people factor" is deterministic. Arthur Rock, speaking at the Harvard Business School, stated how he views the "people factor":

> If you can find good people, they can always change the product. Nearly every mistake I've made has been in picking the wrong people, not the wrong idea . . . Most entrepreneurs have no problem coming up with a good strategy, but they usually need all the help they can get in developing and implementing the tactics that will make them successful in the long run.[38]

Teams Win Games. Investors know that lack of team play can spell disaster. They want a "team," even if it's small or has been assembled through strategic associations (Step 4). It is rare to find investors who are willing to back the efforts of one individual alone. Smart investors want to see your current, and future, leadership team plan. They want to know who is responsible at the top, in production, in marketing, and in other possible departments. If your company is at an early developmental level, and you're the only principal, then investors will want to know when the other key members of the team are scheduled, how much they will be paid, and how much stock they will be entitled to through purchase or performance.

The Dream Team

The 1992 U.S. Olympic Basketball Team was nicknamed the "Dream Team." The new economy's all-star enterprises will also be dream teams. This will be the age where "Imagineers" will be holding the top spots in the new growth businesses. The scientific and electronic engineers that starred in the Information Economy will still be marquee players, but they won't be alone. The "dreamers," the "right brainers," and the conceptualizers will be all-stars as well. What counts in the Knowledge/Creation Economy is rapid problem-spotting, linked to rapid problem-solving.

The Game Plan. The ideal team has three principals that constitute top management—the core team. Their plan is to do big business, but not be a big business. They are chaordic web visionaries guiding, influencing, and connecting ideas and relationships through the web's communication channels. They win web loyalty by being "ring givers," not by dictating rules like emperors. Their power lies in the perception that they alone have the map to the gold. They are the architects of ideas and strategic brokers that are the catalyst for the web to make and move whole products, and the markets that buy them.

The "Big 3" are Imagineers. Two are complementary and the third is the link between them. The two complementors will be the problem-spotter and the problem-solver. The link will be the CEO.[39]

Winning Disciplines and Big Prizes. The Dream Team has the five Disciplines of the Visionary Business Builder model and plays it to win. The ideal Launch Plan provides enough incentive for the three Imagineers of the Dream Team to launch the business. Investors want to know if each of the "Big 3" contributed cash and sweat equity to the business and if they own healthy portions of company stock and options.

The Problem-Spotter

In the Information Age, this was the Director of Marketing. The one in charge of developing the markets for the company's high volume products/services. Companies with high value products/services, since they're customer specific, will require principals who have more specialized knowledge of the customer group. However, savvy marketing knowledge alone will not cut it. The "cult of the customer" is an obsession with the problem-spotter. They don't visit customers, they live with them. The closeness achieved by the part-time "in-house" CFOs and CIOs, or the intimacy of personal coaches, simulates the kind of closeness the new problem-spotters have with their customers. Their personal goal is to find needs their customers are not even aware of yet. They hope along the way to spot problems that, if solved, would amount to paradigm shifts. They are the new paradigm spotters. These problem-spotters of the Visionary Business Builder team know that the company's first products/services must be carefully positioned in existing markets, using existing paradigms.

The Problem-Solver

This used to be the Director of Production, who took what came out of R&D ready for high volume production and made sure the company had capacity. Problem solvers are really R&D specialists operating with an "outside the box" mind set. Problem solvers deserving of the title "Imagineers" are involved in the relentless quest for new applications, combinations, improvements, exploitations, refinements, and product category divisions—in short, innovations for solving an array of emerging problems. They are the rule breakers—the new paradigm shifters.

The Strategic Broker

The person who links the problem-spotter and problem-solver together is the CEO. This Imagineer understands enough about technologies and customers to imagine the potential for innovations. The CEO is more than just the entrepreneur that organizes the Launch Plan and raises the capital. He or she is the "ideapreneur" that facilitates the synergy among the three Imagineers. The CEO manages "idea flow" and is the organizational visionary. He or she is the catalyst for the "Big 3" Imagineers to create the initial Paradigm Vision for the company. The CEO is the one everyone depends on to orchestrate the partnerships and alliances to build a highly successful chaordic web.

The CEO is the one who can mobilize resources to pioneer any of the paradigm shifts the problem-spotter or problem-solver discover. He or she is the paradigm pioneer—the champion of all the company's causes. It's no secret that the CEO is the most vital position in an emerging company, and the investors know this. The CEO is always the point person in charge of leading the Investor Financing™ process. The CEO is the standard setter. He or she personifies the spirit of the company. The stock market reactions to the selection of a company's CEO can be electrifying. When it was announced that John Sculley had found his next job at Spectrum Information Technologies, Inc., the company's stock soared 46% higher that day. Four months later, when John Sculley resigned from Spectrum, its stock fell 66% in value.

Investors in early-stage enterprises need to feel confident that the CEO is going to walk through walls, if need be, to complete the needed Investor Financing™. Champions perform regardless of the odds. Investors want to be with a hard-as-nails CEO. It takes nothing less than champions to launch, relaunch, or grow enterprises today. The CEO is the one responsible for accessing capital—it is not done by committee. It is the job of the CEO, and no one else. Even if money raisers are contracted with (see Step 2), the CEO must be prepared to help the money raisers, and if necessary, take over from the money raisers if they do not perform well.

Something Less Than the Dream Team

Companies that try to launch with less than the "Big 3" present to investors and themselves special considerations. Let examine the possible scenarios:

CEO + 1. A qualified CEO can successfully launch the business with either a problem-spotter or problem-solver. These two founders can usually make a convincing argument in their Launch Plan that the remaining member of the "Big 3" will be found soon, especially if a generous stock acquisition plan is offered.

CEO + None. Lone rangers are not high on any investor wish list. It is possible (though not probable) for a CEO to build his or her Launch Plan on the concept of brokering out the "function" of problem-spotter and problem-solver to other companies. COMPAQ Computers began much this way and many movies are now developed along these lines. This is the epitome of the virtual chaordic web.

Problem-Spotter and/or Problem-Solver but no CEO. This situation almost demands a spin-in strategy if these two Imagineers can't solicit a business building CEO to join them as a founder. What they need to do is find a larger company to purchase their idea, or form a partnership with the company to provide financing, production, and distribution. This, of course, is common with software start-ups.

Something More Than the Dream Team

Having more than the "Big 3" principals start the company is not necessarily good, although it's not automatically bad either. Robert Reich, a controversial but respected economist, made this interesting observation about the chaordic web organizational strategy of Knowledge/Creation businesses:

> Here, all that really counts is rapid problem-identifying and problem-solving— the marriage of technical insight with marketing know-how, blessed by strategic and financial acumen. Everything else—all of the more standardized pieces—can be obtained as needed. Office space, factories, and warehouses can be rented; standard equipment can be leased; standard components can be bought wholesale from cheap producers (many of them overseas); secretaries, routine data processors, bookkeepers, and routine production workers can be hired temporarily.

> In fact, relatively few people actually work for the high-value enterprise in the traditional sense of having steady jobs with fixed salaries. The inhabitants of corporate headquarters, who spend much of their time searching for the right combinations of solutions, problems, strategies, and money, are apt to share in the risks and returns of their hunt.

> With risks and returns broadly shared, and overhead kept to a minimum, the enterprise web can experiment. Experimentation was dangerous in the old high-volume enterprise because failures (like Ford's notorious Edsel) meant that the entire organization had to change direction—retool, retrain, redirect sales and marketing—at a huge cost. But experimentation is the lifeblood of the high-value enterprise, because customization requires continuous trial and error.

In the web, suppliers of standard inputs (factories, contract engineers, technicians, equipment, office space, routine components, bookkeeping, janitorial services, data processing, and so forth) contract to provide or do specific things for a certain time and for a specified price. Such arrangements are often more efficient than directly controlling employees. Suppliers who profit in direct proportion to how hard and carefully they do their jobs have every incentive to find increasingly efficient ways to accomplish their tasks.[40]

The Dream Team—More Than a Metaphor. The staffing goal of any emerging high-growth, high-value business is to have a core group of owners/leaders, each a primary Imagineer. Every traditional inside position should be an Imagineer-only position. If not, then the position should be considered secondary and outsourced if possible. There is no shortage of independent specialists for every secondary position. The inside positions that are ultimately considered primary become part of the company's "imagination works." One of the best examples, of course, is Walt Disney Company, where every employee is a "cast member." Each plays a "part" and wears a "costume." Being on duty means to be "on stage." You might say, "Well, of course Walt Disney Company had to be so imaginative, since it's in the entertainment business." Well, consider this: what Walt Disney has been selling (fun) and doing to produce it (imaginative innovations of everything) represent the archetypal Dream Team of the 21st Century. Being "Goofy" is in now, so let's get used to it.

3. THE PROMISES OF DISCIPLINE 2

Start-up businesses, by definition, don't have the luxury of showing investors a record of their past performances. The very nature of any start-up's business plan is to project or promise things that will take place in the future. Perhaps more attention should be given to the moral and spiritual nature of this promise by the leadership team. Two good things might happen: If entrepreneurs perceived their business plans as solemn promises or covenants, then more serious and sober plans might emerge. In turn, the investor community might respond in kind by taking a more serious look at these entrepreneurs and their aspirations. Perhaps a business plan should be in the nature of a contract. Business plans may not go this far, but where lawyers are concerned stranger things have happened.

The Promises of Discipline 2 are an attempt to answer two of the biggest questions investors have: "Who are these people?" and "What are they trying to become?" Your answers can be found in the three promises of Discipline 2:

1. This is our Destiny Path.

2. This is our Core Competency.
3. This is our Core Ideology.

We can examine how easy it is to express in summary form these promises. An example is shown below.

We are a high-knowledge/creation business that offers _____
                                                        HIGH VALUE OR HIGH VOLUME

products/services in order to achieve _____ . We aim for
                                       HIGH GROWTH (OR OTHER GOAL)

constant _____
               HIGH CHANGE (OR SOME OTHER GOAL)

and intend to provide _____.
                          HIGH RETURNS (OR SOME OTHER GOAL)

To accomplish this we have and will continue to develop the following core

competencies: _____ . We hold as sacred

these values: _____. Our purpose

is to _____ .
         CORE IDEOLOGY

EVIDENCE POINTS FOR YOUR IDENTITY
1. The "Paradigm Vision" Evidence Points

A Written Paradigm Vision Statement. Include this statement in the first part of the business plan—you might even place it on the cover page. (See Step 3 for a further discussion on business plan preparation.)

Strangers To The Industry. This Evidence Point goes against traditional thinking. When your leadership team is an outsider to the industry you're about to do business in, your investors will be paying close attention to your Paradigm Vision. Here's why:

- "We found no case in which a major advance, one that established a new trajectory for progress, came from a major firm in the industry." *James Utterback, one of America's foremost authorities on innovation*[41]

- "Indeed, the most dramatic innovations have occurred when the leaders emerged from a new sector." *Fumio Kodama, one of Japan's leading experts on the patterns of innovation*[42]

- "Strangers change paradigms." *The late Buckminster Fuller, one of the 20th Century's most revered futurists and innovators*[43]

2. The "Principals" Evidence Points

CEO + 1 + Plan. There should be a qualified CEO as part of the founders' team. Having at least one other Dream Team Imagineer as part of the founding team is important for winning investor trust. A recruitment plan for how and when the third member of the Dream Team comes on board is necessary.

P.R. Clippings. Industry articles written by or about the principals is helpful. Print has power.

Testimonials and Awards. Letters of recommendation, quotations and endorsements from influence makers in the industry, vendors, and customers are all useful. Include all awards that relate to the business or the skill of the leadership team.

Track Record. If your leadership team has been successful in the past with start-up enterprises, investors feel comfortable.

Two-Year Lockup. One way to convince investors that the leadership team is committed to the company is for them to agree not to sell their stock for a designated period.

Space is Open. Your Launch Plan and Growth Plan financial projections for the company must show that the size of the company and its activities have lots of room to grow. This makes it believable that "key superstar" talent can be brought in.

Plans for Succession. Include in your business plan a discussion of how the company will replace key team members if they leave the company.

Key Person Insurance. "Penciling-in" insurance in the financial forecast on the lives of valuable members of the team shows how important these people are.

3. The "Promises of Discipline 2" Evidence Points

Destiny Promise Description. Provide investors your decision about your Destiny Promise. It will be one of these two:

> The *high-value* promise is to be: A high-knowledge/creation, *high-value*, high-change, high-growth, high-return, high-relationship, high-learning, high-phenomena, high-stakeholder business.

> Or the *high volume* promise is to be: A high-knowledge/creation, *high-volume*, high-change, high-growth, high-return, high-relationship, high-learning, high-phenomena, high-stakeholder business.

Core Competency Description. A specific description in the business plan of your core competencies is a good start. The following items go a long way in proving the competency building promise of the company:

- *Education in the Budget.* The extent to which training and education are included in the budget is an indicator of the Dream Team's concern for skill improvement.
- *Originality.* This is a strong indicator of the leadership team's concern for the value and importance of core competencies.
- *Alignment.* Original and authentic descriptions of core competencies must be in alignment with the Destiny Promise.
- *Capable of Continuity.* In order for the descriptions of core competencies to be valid, they must, on their face, be capable of continuity and endurance through good and bad business cycles.
- *Commands Long-Term Investment.* Competencies that need a long-term perspective will give the impression of being solid and well thought out.
- *Significance.* The intensity of the impact on the core customer dictates how significant and meaningful your core competencies are.

Core Ideology Statement. An honest written statement detailing the values and purposes of the enterprise is crucial.

Leadership Cash Stake. Investors want the leadership team to play with a stake in the game. Real cash anted up by the leadership team is the right card here. This is the strongest indication of boldly loving one's destiny. Whatever monies have been spent to get the business this far should be documented.

Leadership Sweat Equity. Next to a cash stake, "sweat equity" is the best evidence of the leadership team's sincerity. Many investors will accept the "sweat equity for stock" or the conditional "earn in" formula for the leadership team's acquisition of "founders" stock. Nothing kills a financing quicker than an unwillingness to commit stock ownership and high salaries to targeted industry leaders who can round out the leadership team. Apple Computer, Inc. has been given credit for making over 100 employees millionaires. Now that's a stake worth working 80 hours a week for.

Resumes Speak Loudly. The resumes of the principals should scream out that "we were born and prepared for this challenge." The work histories do not necessarily have to be industry specific. In fact, long track records in the same industry can be a sign of paradigm following, rather than a potential for paradigm shifting.

Deferred Participation, or Low Starting Salaries. One of the strongest signs of a "destiny team" is that their current salary structures, or projected salary schedules, are moderate, deferred, or based on performance. This is a clear sign of the leadership team's commitment to something they love and are destined to do.

Long-Term Ambition. One of the most striking discoveries of Collins' and Porras' research was the average length of time the CEOs of the Visionary Companies remained in office—32.4 years. In our clinics and workshops, we ask the attendees this question, "How long do you envision being involved with your company?" Less than 1% of the participants answered, "More than ten years." Once again, we see the venture capital industry's influence at work. American entrepreneurs (including the ones in our seminars) believe the business building game is supposed to be a short, sweet ride. This attitude is not consistent with the Visionary Business Builder. Bear in mind that Sam Walton opened his first Wal-Mart twenty years after his first launch product—The Ben Franklin Five & Dime Store.

YOUR LAUNCH PLAN

Let's keep our eye on the ball. We are trying to raise capital. Investors want phenomenal companies, the kind that innovate. Let's remind ourselves that innovation can be established through short-term, evolutionary small steps as well as long-term, revolutionary NPLPs. Peter Drucker offers advice here when he says: "Effective innovations start small—they are not grandiose. . . . They require little money, few people and only a small and limited market."[44] Thank you, Mr. Drucker, for reminding us that to get into business and raise capital doesn't require us to have an NPLP right out the gate.

Here's the definition again of the Launch Plan: It is the specific plan that describes everything that the Visionary Business Builder will do until it reaches a point of profitability (usually a 6 to 24 month period of time). The Launch Plan is a short-term plan to get the company going and prove to investors the entrepreneurial skills of the management team and its capacity for Discipline 3's requirement to do well in the short run. A well conceived Launch Plan can provide a stable cash flow base, which can be an important antidote to the usually unpredictable market creation challenges for the company's new product initiatives of its Growth Plan.

4. THE PATH

The Launch Plan for the Visionary Business Builder takes one of several basic paths. Not surprisingly, the choice of path has a great impact on the business challenges facing both the company's leadership team and the company's investors. As an example, the Launch Plan path dictates a lot about the possible financing instruments and structures (which are discussed in full in Step 5). The three principal Launch Plan paths are:

- Incubate with permission
- Acquisition

■ The "Existing Paradigm Secondary Product/Service" (EPSP)

Incubate with Permission

This path basically involves the leadership team finding support and comfort in the arms of another company. This takes the form of traditional spin-outs or spin-ins. It also includes the situation where a full-time employee or consultant is given permission to keep his or her existing employment, but given permission to moonlight on the side as a Visionary Business Builder. Whatever the exact form the incubation takes, the key here is to have "permission" from the mother company to raise capital for a separate entity.

Acquisition

This path involves looking for an existing business to buy. It can often be easier to raise $3 million to buy an existing business than it is to raise $300,000 to start from scratch. The kind of business to purchase, and how to do so, will not be covered in this book. (There are many texts available that cover this subject.)

For the Visionary Business Builder, the acquisition of a business is always a stepping stone move. The acquired business is never the end in itself. The acquisition serves as a base camp. Its usefulness will depend on how well the leadership team uses the acquired business to meet the challenges posed by the rest of the Launch and Growth Plan chaordic web elements.

The "Existing Paradigm Secondary Product/Service" (EPSP)

This is the start from scratch, bold move of starting a business or regenerating an existing business. The focus here is that the success of the Launch Plan depends on the success of the company's first product/service. Being new, this product/service must always be offered to an existing market that is moving through an existing paradigm. Since the launch product/service is not a NPLP, it is something less and we call it the EPSP. The success of this EPSP rests on how well the leadership team develops the remaining Launch Plan chaordic web elements.

Illustrations 1-12A through 1-12E should be used when studying the next four Chaordic Web Elements that apply to the Launch Plan. These illustrations are based on the five stages of the PALC curve. They summarize for each of those stages the customers' needs, the NPLP companies' needs, the Visionary Business Builder's launch position strategies, the product/service strategies, the partner strategies, and the process dynamics that factor into a Launch Plan analysis.

ILLUSTRATION 1-12A:
EARLY MARKET palc ANALYSIS FOR LAUNCH PLAN

Customer needs	NPLP companies needs	Launch position "The special scout"	Product/service "The rifle"	Partner strategies "The silver bullet"	Process focus "The right boots"
Innovators want: • "Techie" things • Demos • Breakthroughs • Guru claims	To find the innovators Capital to sustain demos To have "far out" products/services	Business to business Attach to existing paradigm Buy an existing business tactic Licensing tactics	Advice Market research Capital Supply something Initiate industry claims	Outsource to key vendors everything but core activities Too early to partner with NPLPG company Offer credit	Bootstrapping High value management, marketing, sales, and infotech systems Keep only core / have capacity
Visionaries want: • Innovator references • First on board • Application specific • Breakthroughs • Trade press coverage • Product reviews	Enough segments of visionaries Have compelling killer application story High value — specific for customer "Systems Integrators" to alliance with Capital and credit	"Specialist provider of high value services" for NPLP companies needing visionary clients Available credit	Advice Market research Supply part of whole product to specific customers Being the systems integrator to a few niches Capital	Outsource to key vendors non-core activities Be exclusive vendor for a component of NPLP company's whole product concept Be the systems integrator masterminding the whole product web for specific customer segment Offer credit Be the "ring giver," even to the NPLP companies	Bootstrapping High value management, marketing, sales and infotech systems Keep only core / have capacity

ILLUSTRATION 1-12B:
The Chasm palc Analysis for Launch Plan

Customer needs	NPLP companies needs	Launch position "The special scout"	Product/service "The rifle"	Partner strategies "The silver bullet"	Process focus "The right boots"
There are few, if any, customers. The pragmatists of the Mainstream market are waiting.	Get whole product done fast Outsource to stay lean and mean R&D to determine Bowling Alley segments Capital and credit Cross Chasm fast	"Fast specialist provider of high-value services offering credit" *plus* Have to use us now to cross the Chasm ("The Silver Bullet")	Vendor for fast, whole product packaging Market research for Bowling Alley information Incubate a NPLP company (a "little fish" taking care of a "big fish")	Be the system integrator and do the prep work for Bowling Alley segments in advance of entrance there Keep outsourcing to key vendors Scope out and literally bring to the NPLP company a bunch of Bowling Alley clients Offer credit Position for power in contracts to exit Chasm as permanent component of Bowling Alley	Bootstrapping High value management, marketing, sales, and infotech systems Keep only core / have capacity If discovering NPLP —is it protected?

ILLUSTRATION 1-12C:
BOWLING ALLEY PALC ANALYSIS FOR LAUNCH PLAN

Customer needs	NPLP companies needs	Launch position "The special scout"	Product/service "The rifle"	Partner strategies "The silver bullet"	Process focus "The right boots"
Pragmatists want: • No downside risks • Other pragmatists buying • Whole product solution • Very high value	To make profits To find strong segments To get whole product to segments To be recognized as "standard" Good distribution alliances Capital and credit To sense the oncoming Tornado Maybe do an IPO in advance of Tornado To find paradigm shifters	"Specialist provider of high-value services" *plus* Permanent component for Tornado Be the R&D paradigm shifter for NPLP companies	Affordable services Find the segments for NPLP A high-value component to the whole product High value requirement of the "standards." Identify and distribute to segments Offer credit Good anticipator of Tornado	Outsource to vendors all non-core activities Be exclusive vendor in all contracts JV some of the segments, if your contribution is high value enough Be the "ring giver" in the segments to the NPLP companies Position for power in contracts to exit Bowling Alley as permanent component of Tornado Be exclusive R&D paradigm shifter for NPLP company	Bootstrapping High value management, marketing/sales, and infotech systems Keep only core / have capacity If discovering NPLP —is it protected?

ILLUSTRATION 1-12D:
TORNADO palc ANALYSIS FOR LAUNCH PLAN

Customer needs	NPLP companies needs	Launch position "The special scout"	Product/service "The rifle"	Partner strategies "The silver bullet"	Process focus "The right boots"
Pragmatists want: • Fair price • Business press to point the way • To know who the industry leader is • Retailers to tell them what to buy	Infrastructure alliance support High-volume capacity Institutionalized, commoditized whole product To design out Bowling Alley service providers Capital and credit	A major distribution vendor alliance or A major capacity component for fulfillment plus Exit Tornado as a permanent component ("The Silver Bullet") of the "club of companies" leading the paradigm	Affordable distribution support or Affordable capacity component Offer credit	Outsource to key vendors who can stay up to capacity Be exclusive vendor in all contracts Position for power as permanent component of Mainstreet Be exclusive R&D paradigm shifter for NPLP company	Bootstrapping High value management, marketing/sales, and infotech systems Keep only core / have capacity If discovering NPLP —is it protected?

ILLUSTRATION 1-12E:
MAINSTREET PALC ANALYSIS FOR LAUNCH PLAN

Customer needs	NPLP companies needs	Launch position "The special scout"	Product/service "The rifle"	Partner strategies "The silver bullet"	Process focus "The right boots"
Conservatives and laggards want: • Highest value *and/or* • Lowest prices	To find niche extensions *or* To find high-volume, low-price moves R&D help More distribution strategies like direct mail/cataloging To find paradigm shifters	"Specialist provider of high-value products/services R&D paradigm shifter	Affordable niche extension component Offer a NPLP company another NPLP idea	Outsource to key vendors all non-core activities Be exclusive vendor in all contracts Be exclusive R&D paradigm shifter for NPLP company	Bootstrapping High value management, marketing, sales, and infotech systems Keep only core / have capacity If discovering NPLP — is it protected?

5. THE POSITIONING

Being the Specialized Scout. The assumption, of course, is that the company does not have, as yet, a high change product/service at the level of a New Paradigm Lead Product. (If it did, this entire discussion of the Visionary Business Builder Message wouldn't be necessary, since the Great American Product/Exit Game Message would be available to attract venture capitalists.) So, where does the company start its positioning? To begin with, the Destiny Promise of Discipline 2 told investors a lot already. All that remains really is to identify a spot (position) in an existing, developing market paradigm to offer your product/service. It can even mean purchasing an existing business as a Launch Plan strategy for your first product/service. The market (or existing paradigm) will tell the Visionary Business Builder every time where in the market to start. Markets, not companies, tell investors what positions are possible.

Making Money, Not Markets. The Launch Plan's positioning description is about a quick and low-capital approach for offering a secondary product/service to an existing market that is already developing around a new paradigm. The use of a licensing strategy is often a good choice here. The Visionary Business Builder looks for pioneer companies that already have the "map" for the new territory. The Launch Plan does not have to concern itself with new market development plans and share of market plans. To do so would imply that the company's first product/service is in reality a high change innovation. Only high change products/services really go through the new market development process. "Egos" have to take a back seat to "brains" if the Visionary Business Builder wants to have the right positioning tactics for the Launch Plan. The smartest positioning role to play is that of a special scout, ready to help already daring pioneers who are trying to forge a trail into new territory. Purchasing an existing business that is already playing the role of a special scout in an existing paradigm is an excellent strategy.

Making High Value, Not High Volume. Launch Plans make more room for high value business market contributions than high volume consumer market contributions. Getting profitable quickly in the new economy is more a case of "brains" than "brawn." High-volume contributions are historically known for longer ramp-up times and capital-intensive, highly competitive, price-sensitive consumer markets. Entering a market as a high-volume player implies entering either a Tornado market or a Mainstream market. Since margins tend to narrow later in a paradigm's life cycle, a high-volume start-up company may be increasing its margin for errors. The odds favor high-value strategies for Launch Plans. Even a business with a superior high-volume idea, like Gateway 2000's idea for customized computer sales, is supported by a high value Launch Plan.

Making Love, Not War. High value Launch Plans imply customer inti-macy operations from top to bottom. The focus of the Launch Plan is not posi-tioning relative to competitors (making war). Winning a market-share race quickly in the at-large market is not the start-up game of Visionary Business Builders. This kind of hyper-competitive business environment will be expe-rienced by the Visionary Business Builder during the company's growth phase (Growth Plan) when its first try with an NPLP is in the Tornado (hopefully), but probably not before.

The Launch Plan's high value thrust will, in most cases, be directed at busi-ness customers who themselves have special needs dictated by the demands of the NPLP race they and their clients are on. The aim of the Launch Plan is to find a "position of dependent cooperation" with customers who have to leverage off your company's products/services to accomplish their goals.

High value specialization by the Visionary Business Builder is the best approach to insure a customer base that will not design your company out of its vendor plans as the NPLP companies keep moving through the PALC. (See the further discussion in the next section on Partners.)

Making High Margins, Not High Share of Customers. Launch Plans should strive for high-margin business. High-margin business can be found more often in the early markets of the PALC than in the later, mainstream mar-kets. The market development pressures on the NPLP companies in the early markets is usually so high that their vendor partners (one of whom should be your company) are in position to sustain premium pricing. Conversely, NPLP companies in the mainstream markets of add-on, price-sensitive niche exten-sions leave their vendors with little room for any premium pricing.

Another important element of positioning strategy is the matter of "share of customer." We've learned that "market share" should not be part of the Launch Plan, but what about "share of customers?" Don't high value, one client-at-a-time Launch Plans imply the need to maintain a long-term cus-tomer relationship for corporate growth? The answer is sometimes yes and sometimes no. It is at this point of planning that the stakes really go up and Visionary Business Builders with a Launch Plan must stay focused. Here's why: If, for example, the lead product/service is positioned well, the NPLP customer-company may continue its initial vendor relationship with your company long into the PALC. This permanency could mean substantial and stable revenues. Several such relationships could literally make up your entire future business. This kind of initial product/service permanency is dependent on how specialized and indispensable ("the Silver Bullet" factor) your lead product/service is to the NPLP company as it moves on through the PALC. Most "Silver Bullets" are of themselves the closest thing to a high-change innovation, only on a smaller paradigm basis. "The Silver Bullet" long-term relationship is the exception to the rule. The prevailing experience of most start-up companies is their initial product/service is not a "Silver Bullet" and thus it is phased or designed out over time by the NPLP company. So this kind of "share of customer" strategy, although attractive, is elusive.

Another "share of customer" strategy is to make follow-on offerings to a client. A follow-on, non-high-change product/service strategy inside the Launch Plan time frame of 6 to 24 months is a very poor idea. A Launch Plan has to stand or fall on the merits of the initial product/service. Essentially, "share of customer" through diversification/expansion of products/services, although highly tempting and seemingly logical for an installed customer base, is not the high road of Launch Plan innovation and growth. High-change innovation and corporate growth come from division strategies, not diversification. Also, any "share of customer" strategies should be reserved for Growth Plan strategies when the company is going after its own market development with its own NPLP.

6. THE PRODUCTS/SERVICES

Having the Rifle. Is it easier, faster and less expensive to make something for someone or to offer advice and sell it at a premium? As a rule, the right answer is to sell advice. Consulting type services should always be a top priority consideration for the Launch Plans' products/services. The essence of any Dream Team's work is ideas. Through proper outsourcing of non-Imagineering work, the Launch Plan's capital requirements and budget can be "lean and mean."

Since the positioning strategy is to meet the "special needs" of others, the high road for Launch Plan success is to find special knowledge/creativity customer needs that your company is uniquely qualified to meet.

The search for first product/service ideas by most start-ups usually begins by management declaring, "Here's what we do, let's go find someone who needs it." Launch Plan strategies ought to be more market-centric, with management asking itself, "Where is our opportunistic PALC? At what stage of maturity is it and where would our company uncover clients for high-value services that we can uniquely provide?"

Gaining knowledge of current paradigms pushing through the economy (and their players) will uncover new Launch Plan product/service ideas. Remember, the purpose of the Launch Plan is not to show to investors "fast track" opportunities; rather, it is simply to show immediate "cash track" opportunities, so the company is in a position to pay for its own way into the future (the Growth Plan). "Cash track" thinking is very innovative and the by-product of incrementalism at work. The visionary companies of Collins' and Porras' work are definite "cash trackers." For example, Hewlett-Packard, with all its profits, still follows a Launch Plan mentality. Here's how a Hewlett-Packard vice-president describes it:

> This philosophy of pay-as-you-go provides great discipline all the way down. If you want to innovate, you must bootstrap. It is one of the most powerful, least understood influences that pervades the company.[45]

Tracking PALC for the Cash. There is no magic formula or strategy for Launch Plan Product/Service offerings. Each company has its own research work cut out. The tool to use for this research analysis is the PALC curve of existing paradigms that drive the economy.

7. THE PARTNERS

Having "The Silver Bullet." Once the appropriately positioned product/service offering is determined, the next step in your Launch Plan chaordic web design is to develop strategic partner alliances. High value products/services, by definition, imply partner relationships with customers and vendors. The form of these relationships can go from joint venturing entirely new companies to informal, but exclusive, contracts. Illustrations 1-12A through 1-12E can be used to trigger partner planning ideas. Like products/services strategies, there is more than one way of approaching partner strategies.

An important consideration in Launch Plan partner strategies is the "permanency factor." "Permanency factor" relates to the chances of the company sustaining its exclusive vendor status with its NPLP customers as these customers keep advancing along the PALC. Most NPLP companies are highly dependent on smaller specialists for whole product development help when crossing the Chasm into the Bowling Alley. These same NPLP companies, when the Tornado phase starts blowing, try to rush to the market with a more hollowed-out, commoditized product/service offering. They attempt to "design out" as many adjunct vendor companies as possible, even though these alliances got the NPLP company through the Early Market and the Bowling Alley phases. This "design out" threat for the smaller Visionary Business Builder persists all the way through the Mainstreet phase. To stop this "design out" threat, the Visionary Business Builder must have "the Silver Bullet" component of the NPLP companies' whole product. However, proving to investors in advance that this "Silver Bullet" protection will exist in the future is a long shot projection.

8. THE PROCESSES

Wearing the Right Boots. The Launch Plan should have a certain "odor" to it. It should "smell" a bit like an old boot. With a "boot smell," the investors can get a stronger feel for what capabilities the Visionary Business Builder team has to bootstrap. Smart investors have respect for resourcefulness and frugality. Bootstrapping processes are an early way of life for Visionary Business Builders—it just goes with the territory. The topic of bootstrapping could fill an entire book.

Here's a sampling of companies that started out with less than $10,000 and lots of bootstrapping:

Hewlett-Packard	E. & J. Gallo Winery
Apple Computer, Inc.	Lands End, Inc.
Black & Decker Corp.	Marriott Intern, Inc.
The Coca-Cola Co.	Microsoft Corp.
Dell Computer Corp.	Nike, Inc.
Domino's Pizza, Inc.	United Parcel Service, Inc.[46]
Eastman Kodak Co.	

In addition to the "lean and mean" bootstrapping processes, investors may want to know about the high-value management, marketing/sales, information snd Internet based technology systems of the company during its launch phase.

The Launch Plan rarely has high-volume management, marketing and information technology systems. No matter where on the PALC curve the company decides is the appropriate place to enter the market and begin business, there is rarely a reason to try high volume business strategies. Launch Plans are supposed to be small, low-capital intensive, high-value moves.

The issue of "capacity" should also be addressed in the Launch Plan. For example, if the Visionary Business Builder is fortunate enough to have "the Silver Bullet" product/service be a "permanent component" of an NPLP company, capacity issues become critical at the time the NPLP company hits the Tornado of Mainstreet. How the Visionary Business Builder plans on creating its own capacity and vendor alliances is critical.

9. THE PROFITS/OWNERSHIP

Profits

Having High Stakes. Since the main objective of the Launch Plan is to design a quick path to profits, the investors want to know what your intentions are with these early cash flows. Is the company going to distribute profits, hold profits as retained earnings, or zero-out all profits by R&D expenditures?

Good investor relations begin with managing their expectations about cash flow. There is no rule of thumb to follow. One will never go wrong with a policy of retaining all profits for reserves, R&D, and other growth targeted expenditures. If you plan to do this, it is imperative that investors be made aware of this policy before they invest. The decisions made during "Step 5: Structuring the Financing," will also influence Launch Plan cash flow decisions.

Ownership

Having Generosity. Ownership issues are a major concern to investors. Not only do investors want a fair ownership stake for their investment, but they may (and should) desire that the company be "employee-owned" and "web owned." Like other areas addressed in this book, employee ownership has a wealth of information on it available elsewhere, so no attempt will be made to detail the strategies and structures of employee ownership. There is, however, one point about employee ownership worth mentioning. Dream Teams are not effective (and don't stay together for very long) without large and fair ownership positions. Investors and the Dream Teams they stake have to respect and appreciate each other's contributions. It takes two to tango. The investors' ideal structure would start the Dream Team low in equity ownership (or low valuation of stock if purchased "pre-cash investor" with cash or services) and accelerate equity ownership through performance benchmarks. The Dream Team's ideal structure would be a stock position for the investors redeemable at the election of the Dream Team or the company at the lowest rate of return possible. This is another obvious advantage of a profitable Launch Plan. Most structures rest between these two extremes.

When Do You Really Know What To Do? At Step 8 you will know if your ownership structures are acceptable to your investors or not. "Step 8: Testing the Market and List Assemblage," allows you to test the waters of all your business planning ideas before you "go final" with your offering campaign which is dealt with in Step 10.

10. THE PROJECTIONS/LIQUIDITY

Projections

Having the Secret Map. The Launch Plan's financial projections should have two separate reports: "The Time and Budget to Breakeven" and "The Time and Budget to Develop the NPLP."

The Time and Budget to Breakeven. This is the detailed financial forecast that covers the time before the company finally reaches a stable breakeven level. Every dollar to be collected and spent has to be identified and justified. Remember, the Visionary Business Builder message lets the Dream Team off the hook for leading with an NPLP, however, the investor pay-back is the Dream Team's responsibility for precise Launch Plan financial forecasts.

The Time and Budget to Reach the NPLP. The Launch Plan has to include the Dream Team's forecast about what will happen and how long it will take before the Growth Plan for the company kicks in. This, of course, implies the Growth Plan is built on the assumption of the company introducing its own NPLP and riding a paradigm wave as a lead company.

A company theoretically can achieve high growth through an extension of its Launch Plan strategy of support for other NPLP companies. This theory rests on the good fortune of the Visionary Business Builder having a "Silver Bullet" lead product/service that stays in demand for its NPLP company customers as they march on through the PALC. Such "Silver Bullet" opportunities present to investors a business plan that really takes the form and substance of the Great American Product/Exit Game Message.

Putting aside the "Silver Bullet" lead product/service situation, the Visionary Business Builder has to have a financial forecast that truly reflects the most likely scenario of how long the company can stay in business profitably until it begins its high growth off its first NPLP.

Liquidity

Investor liquidity planning is not a normal Launch Plan item for the Visionary Business Builder message. The Dream Team that purposely positions a Launch Plan for a business sale is communicating a confusing message. The very essence of the Visionary Business Builder message is a long-term business-building team at work. To project in the Launch Plan a short-term business sale is not consistent. Now if the Dream Team factors in an investor "buy-out" during the launch phase, that's totally different. There is no mixed message or negative implications with an investor redemption or buy-out arrangement.

During the launch phase, it is possible the company could begin planning for public registration of its stock. However, this kind of planning is not a normal occurrence for most Launch Plans. Taking the company public for investor liquidity is normally a strategy and event that occurs during the growth phase of the company.

A SUMMARY OF THE CHAORDIC WEB ELEMENTS USED IN THE LAUNCH PLAN

Visionary Business Builders position the company as a special scout to help pioneers (NPLP companies) navigate through new territories (the new PALC). The Dream Team takes the right rifle (product/service) to help protect the pioneers. The rifle could even be an existing business that the Visionary Business Builder purchases for its Launch Plan strategy. If lucky, the Dream Team has its rifle loaded with "Silver Bullets" (lead products/services) that are so important to the success of the pioneers' efforts that the Visionary Business Builder is indispensable for the pioneers' entire journey. At all times, the Dream Team uses appropriate boots (bootstrapping processes) and has a large stake in their company. This Dream Team always has the secret map (accurate financial projections) to navigate its launch phase.

EVIDENCE POINTS FOR YOUR LAUNCH PLAN

4. The Path Evidence Points (Launch Plan)

Path Descriptions. The business plan should describe the particulars of any incubator support. Naturally, if the Launch Plan path involves acquiring an existing company, then all the packaging that goes along with purchasing a business will be part of the business plan. If there is no business acquisition, then investors will turn to the following evidence points that relate to the EPSP path.

5. The Positioning Evidence Points (Launch Plan)

The business plan needs a thorough description of the positioning strategy. Referencing Illustrations 1-12A through 1-12E will be helpful. There are four parts to a positioning statement that are necessary for any investor to understand the Launch Plan's chances of success:

Existing Paradigm Description. What existing paradigm is the company entering? Here are three examples:

"We are entering the personal computer paradigm."
"We are entering the pen-based computer paradigm."
"We are entering the online children's education paradigm."

Existing PALC Entry Point. What stage of the existing PALC are you entering? Here are some examples, "We are entering the Mainstreet stage of the PC paradigm." "We are entering the early stage of the pen-based computer paradigm." "We are entering the Bowling Alley of online children's education paradigm."

NPLP Companies' Needs. Describe the target customers' companies and their needs that you intend to meet with your high-value product/service. Here are some examples: "There are fifteen PC software target companies. They are [*list names*]. These PC Software companies need an extended product line in order to open up a new niche Mainstreet market." (Be specific for each target company.) Another example, "There are ten companies racing to develop applications for pen-based computers. They are all in the Early Market phase of their market development." A final example, "There are twenty companies trying to enter the Bowling Alley of Mainstreet with online children's education. The needs of each company are as follows: [*list needs*]."

Launch Position. With target customers and paradigm-entry stage identified, your company can write a Launch Position. The description would go something like this, "We will position the company during the launch phase as a high value specialist provider of [*product/service*], with the expectation of being "the Silver Bullet" permanent component for the customer during the customers' [*Bowling Alley, Tornado, or Mainstreet*] phase of their PALC."

6. The Products/Services Evidence Points (Launch Plan)

Describe your high value products/services. Better yet, describe them for each candidate customer listed in the positioning statements. Are these products/services descriptions in alignment with the positioning statements? Describe for investors why the products/services may be a "Silver Bullet."

Product/Service Protections. Strive to secure the legal protections for your technologies and "success formulas" as early as possible. Service businesses need to spend whatever creative time and energy is needed to develop ideas and to describe their service business in components, processes, and formulas that can be called technologies. Investors like proprietary formulas and they want them developed early. All products and services have the potential for the protection afforded by patents, trademarks, service marks, and copyrights. Even companies offering the most mundane of services ought to strive for protection of their "success formula." A leadership team unwilling to protect its products or services by claiming a proprietary secret formula, innovation, or new standard, may be perceived as lacking the "fire in the belly" investors look for. The positioning of your company should germinate uniquely valuable ideas that are capable of protection: slogans, product descriptions, corporate names, market definitions, customer descriptions, product uses, training, and so on. Registration of patents, trademarks, service marks, and copyrights are the best form of protection. Corporate name reservation is also a good strategy.

A service business should be proud of its innovative practices and not afraid to use aggressive wordsmithing to develop creative slogans and short word phrases to capture its high value business practices. Proof of this courage is shown in a company's use of service marks in their corporate and product/service identity programs. A good example is the Ventana Companies. For years this venture capital firm sold its international investors on its unique concepts of a global working partnership. Ventana applied for a service mark for Global Working Partnership[SM] and increased its marketing efforts, through its investor relations efforts, to reinforce the idea that its unique global operating technologies are valuable for both its investor customers and the portfolio companies it invests in.

7. The Partners Evidence Points (Launch Plan)

Partner Profiles. Profile vendors as well as customers. Candidate vendors and customers should also be included. The form of these alliances should be explained as well as the substantive points of the relationship. Explain if they have an ownership stake in your company.

8. The Processes Evidence Points (Launch Plan)

Process Descriptions. The following items need a description in the Launch Plan: Bootstrapping strategies and tactics, high-value management, marketing, information and Internet based technology systems, and chaordic web outsourcing of non-core activities.

9. The Profits/Ownership Evidence Points (Launch Plan)

Launch Phase Profits and Ownership Statement. A statement should be made in the Launch Plan about what will be done with launch phase profits and ownership.

Profits for Growth Plan Funding. Growth Plans that attract start-up capital are usually built on the assumption that high corporate growth will occur when the company begins NPLPs. Determining how much capital will be generated from Launch Plan profits to fuel the R&D and development work for the company's NPLP is an important point of investor inquiry. It also provides another benchmark of planning. There may not be enough cash thrown off from launch phase activities to finance NPLP development. Thus, additional financing may be needed. This all needs to be discussed in the Launch Plan.

Ownership Structure Description. The "employee-owned" company should be the goal of the knowledge/creation company. If the company's long-term plan is to have only Dream Team members be employees, that's fine. The point is, will the Dream Team have a large, but fair, percentage of the company's common stock?

10. The Projections/Liquidity Evidence Points (Launch Plan)

Financial Projections. Launch Plan forecasts have to be detailed and footnoted. Every income and expense item must be explained. This financial forecast must cover a time frame that includes the "time to breakeven" and the "time to the NPLP."

Liquidity Description. Include a description of the Dream Team's longer-term plans about stock liquidity. The execution of most stock liquidity plans happens during the growth phase, but it doesn't hurt to mention company policy (if it has one).

YOUR GROWTH PLAN

The Launch Plan is the Dream Team's chance to manifest the first part of Discipline 3, namely doing well in the short term. The Growth Plan is the manifestation of the second part—doing well in the long run.

You will recall that the first three chaordic web elements were the "Paradigm Vision," the "Principals," and the "Promises of Discipline 2." They provide a good start for any investor's inquiry into the identity, longer-range plans, and potential of the company.

Let's define the Growth Plan again. It is less specific than the Launch Plan, but detailed enough to substantiate that management has done its homework. It can cover any time frame, but should never be less than 3–5 years. This Growth Plan shows investors the path toward the Paradigm Vision.

4. THE PATH

The Growth Plan is built on one or more of the following paths.

- "The Silver Bullet" path
- "The Spin-in" path
- The Acquisition path
- The NPLP path

One may argue that a specific Growth Plan path is not necessary if a profitable Launch Plan is reached. This argument fails when one brings to mind the real purpose behind the work on the Visionary Business Builder message: namely, winning investors' trust and confidence in advance of performance. There will not be a chance at deploying Launch Plan profits for growth if there is never a launch to begin with. So, we keep our eye on the ball and do all the required work—if we want to raise capital now.

"The Silver Bullet" Path. This path results from the good fortune of the Launch Plan's product/service being incorporated permanently into one or several NPLP companies' whole product as the NPLP companies move through the PALC. A "Silver Bullet" presents the potential for extraordinary corporate growth. In effect, such a Launch Plan transitions smoothly into the Growth Plan for the company. That's the good news. The bad news is this: During the launch phase, a company is never guaranteed a permanent long-term vendor relationship. A lot of chance and luck are usually necessary for the "Silver Bullet" effect. Therefore, the Dream Team and its investors should always expect Launch Plan "Silver Bullets" to be long-shot opportunities.

"The Spin-in" Path. This path finds the company looking specifically for a larger company to acquire a substantial (and most often, controlling) stake in the Visionary Business Builder company. The result of the transaction is a position of strength in resources and direction for both companies. The Visionary Business Builder usually acquires stock in the larger company in exchange for the Visionary Business Builder's stock. The growth of the larger company, with the support by its acquisition of the Visionary Business Builder, is now the focus of future growth by the investors. This "spin-in" path is a common path for software companies and venture capital backed companies. Many "spin-ins" also result from unprofitable Launch Plans. Profitable Launch Plan companies do not, as a rule, choose the "spin-in" path as their growth strategy. This is partly because such paths are not very predictable. They are also difficult to describe to investors at the outset. It's hard to initiate much excitement about this path.

The Acquisition Path. This path is the fast-track world of the mergers and acquisition markets. Largely a financial engineering game of monopoly-like proportions, it can be a solid path for growth. This path rests heavily on a Dream Team's ability to have close allies within the investment banking community who stake the Dream Team with the needed acquisition capital for the various "buy-out" targets. As a rule, a profitable Launch Plan would not normally provide enough chips to play the acquisition game.

A fine example of a company who has successfully exploited this path is Computer Associates. This company has grown through purchasing, at "rock bottom" prices, software companies languishing in the Mainstreet markets. Once acquired, these companies are right-sized for Computer Associates' core business of maintenance contracts.[47]

The NPLP Path. This path represents the centerpiece growth path for Visionary Business Builders trying to access private capital. The reason

ILLUSTRATION 1-13A:
EARLY MARKET PALC ANALYSIS FOR GROWTH PLAN

Customer needs	Growth position "The pioneer with the map"	Product/service "The gold"	Partner strategies "The ring giver"	Process focus "The right horse"
Innovators want: • "Techie" things • Demos • Breakthroughs • Guru claims	To find referring enthusiasts; To have enough capital; Trade press endorsement	Breakthrough quality; Intellectual property protection	Outsource as much as possible	High value management, marketing/sales and infotech systems; Keep only core processes
Visionaries want: • Innovator references • First on board • Application specific • Breakthroughs • Trade press coverage • Product reviews	To segment the visionaries; To have enough capital; Trade press endorsement	Killer application for segment; To create the standards	To find "System Integrators"; To use vendors wisely; To find distribution alliances; Determine "the Silver Bullet" partners	High value management, marketing/sales and infotech systems; Keep only core processes

ILLUSTRATION 1-13B & 1-13C:
CHASM palc ANALYSIS FOR GROWTH PLAN
BOWLING ALLEY palc ANALYSIS FOR GROWTH PLAN

Customer needs	Growth position "The pioneer with the map"	Product/service "The gold"	Partner strategies "The ring giver"	Process focus "The right horse"
There are few, if any, customers. The pragmatist of Mainstreet are waiting.	To expect downtime To research for Bowling Alley segments To have staying power To prepare for fast Chasm crossing	To complete high value whole product	Make alliances to complete whole product Make alliances for distribution Determine "the Silver Bullet" partners	High value management, marketing/sales and infotech systems Keep only core processes

Customer needs	Growth position "The pioneer with the map"	Product/service "The gold"	Partner strategies "The ring giver"	Process focus "The right horse"
There are few, if any, customers. The pragmatist of Mainstreet are waiting.	To expect downtime To research for Bowling Alley segments To have staying power To prepare for fast Chasm crossing	To complete high value whole product	Make alliances to complete whole product Make alliances for distribution Determine "the Silver Bullet" partners	High value management, marketing/sales and infotech systems Keep only core processes

ILLUSTRATION 1-13D & 1-13E:
TORNADO palc ANALYSIS FOR GROWTH PLAN
MAINSTREET palc ANALYSIS FOR GROWTH PLAN

Customer needs	Growth position *"The pioneer with the map"*	Product/service *"The gold"*	Partner strategies *"The ring giver"*	Process focus *"The right horse"*
Pragmatists want: • Fair price • Business press to point the way • To know who the industry leader is • Retailers to tell them what to buy	To have capacity in advance for high volume Recognition as the standards and industry leader Watching out for paradigm shifters	Commoditize the product/service wherever possible Lower the price	Strip away all but "the Silver Bullet" partners Partners who are high-volume specialists	High value management, marketing/sales and infotech systems Keep only core processes

Customer needs	Growth position *"The pioneer with the map"*	Product/service *"The gold"*	Partner strategies *"The ring giver"*	Process focus *"The right horse"*
Conservatives and laggards want: • Highest value *and/or* • Lowest price	Watching out for paradigm shifters Looking for niche extensions	Lowering price Segmenting for niche extension applications and improvements	Distribution partners who are high-volume specialists Partners and vendors who are niche high-value creators	High value management, marketing/sales and infotech systems Keep only core processes

should be obvious. This is the path that presents the picture of the rare and significant—the phenomenal. This is the path for the bold, sweeping, controversial promise by the Dream Team. This is the rule-breaking, paradigm-pioneering, path. The rest of the Growth Plan discussion will center on the NPLP path. In doing so, we will look at PALC one more time. This time we will look at PALC from the vantage point of how a company discovers and jumps on a new paradigm wave and seeks to develop a new market to become one of the NPLP companies. The Launch Plan was how the Visionary Business Builder tagged along as a secondary support company for the other NPLP pioneers. The NPLP Growth Plan is about how your company will become the new market maker. The NPLP path is the high road of innovation. It's the path *Fortune* magazine (June 1997) called the killer strategy path for increasing shareholder wealth. It's the path of how to boldly honor your destiny in the new economy.

Let's turn to the remaining chaordic web elements of the Growth Plan built on the NPLP path. These remaining chaordic web elements assume the company has already discovered a high change innovation in one or more existing paradigms that are doing well in the economy. This discovery of a high-change innovation could be the result of spotting a rule breaker (paradigm shifter) somewhere in the Bowling Alley or Mainstreet of a mainstream existing paradigm. This rule breaker could be a corporate insider or another company messing with current paradigm rules and practices. Regardless of the how, when, or why of this discovery, the Visionary Business Builder is now prepared to pioneer this innovation and develop a market. This market development process will move us once again through the PALC. Illustrations 1-13A through 1-13E should be referenced while studying the following material.

5. THE POSITIONING

During the Launch Plan, the Dream Team was a special scout for other paradigm pioneers. Now it's the Dream Team's turn to be the pioneer in its own Wild West show. Bold, gutsy, well-stocked Dream Teams will make the journey into the unchartered territory of new paradigms. This brings up the importance of making sure the territory is indeed new.

Breakthrough Territory. The premise of the NPLP path is the discovery of a NPLP. This is not a path of EPLP (Existing Paradigm Lead Product), or EPNP (Existing Paradigm, New Product), or EPOP (Existing Paradigm, Old Product), or NPOP (New Paradigm, Old Product), or even NPNP (New Paradigm, New Product). Brutal honesty by the Dream Team is a must. Any mistake here means a Growth Plan that finds the company launching growth in either existing markets or new paradigms dominated by other companies. Each case results in a high drama, glorified repeat of the Launch Plan. The Launch Plan has to be focused on entering existing paradigms and finding cozy cash track spots, allowing the Visionary Business Builder to be in business and have a launch pad for a shot at creating a new order. Growth Plans for emerging Visionary Business Builders' Dream Teams can't be about entering existing markets and out-muscling, outspending, and/or outwitting a cadre of ensconced bullies. It can't even be about entering a new paradigm as a new product to enjoy some kind of tag along ride. The NPLP path is about "new paradigm" and "lead product." Many books could be written about how to succeed in business with the other non-breakthrough paths. The point here is that by not having a message of a NPLP in the Growth Plan, you reduce your chances of attracting investors to even launch your company.

Having the Map. The NPLP growth path has to have the look and feel of the untraveled yellow brick road, leading to a dreamy emerald city of abundance where no human has ever been.

The ultimate position of power (whether real or just perceived) is to own or control the map leading to this emerald city. The pioneers having power are those that have scoped out ahead of time, with their advance scouts, the new territory. With map in hand, even larger companies can trust the smaller Visionary Business Builder daring to be the pioneer of the new paradigm. The old saying, "With no plan you're planning to fail," is an appropriate reminder. Chaordic webs form around a handful of companies that influence the market-share positions of everyone riding a new paradigm wave. Since the dynamics of power and influence shift at each stage of the PALC, it is imperative that the Dream Team have, in advance, a map of when and how to change its business strategies to maintain power and influence. Anticipation is a vital skill for the paradigm pioneer trying to stir up a gold rush. Illustrations 1-13A through 1-13E should be reviewed for the specific positioning strategies of each stage of the PALC.

6. The Products/Services

The map discussed above has to lead to a new pot of gold. There has to be gold in "them thar hills." In other words, there must be a New Paradigm Lead Product idea.

The New Paradigm Part of the NPLP Formula. The New paradigm idea is about how a new ecosystem or web of companies (a market) is about to take shape in the economy. Your company has to be a part of this new value network. I had a friend once who went on a ski trip with me in 1978. He brought one fat ski with bindings for two boots. He was funny, un-cool and alone. My friends and I failed to notice he was on a snowboard. We missed a huge paradigm about to snowball.

Four Kinds of New Paradigms. There are four kinds of innovation or change that can cause new paradigms to appear. These four are sustaining change, substitute change, discontinuous change and disruptive change.

Sustaining Change is any new paradigm that causes incremental changes to a prevailing technological trajectory. An example is accounting software that computes faster or has more functions. Generally, this kind of innovation will enhance old technology.

Substitute Changes are new paradigms that do not cause old ways (or technology) to disappear. A good example is snowboards. The skiing paradigm is still around and co-exists with snowboarding.

Discontinuous Changes are new paradigms that displace old ways of doing things. Personal computers displaced all sorts of ways of being in business and living. Networked computers are displacing single station computers. The Internet, as of the date of this book, threatens huge markets inside the Information Technology space. One can imagine that all information processing technology in the future will be linked together through a network protocol and over a universal network, the cost of which will very soon be free.

Disruptive Changes are new paradigms that co-exist with sustaining technology, but eventually can cause a discontinuity to occur in that sustaining technology which can disappear in the market. The history of how computer disk drive components became increasingly smaller and cheaper is a vivid example of disruptive innovation at work in a market. (48)

The Lead Product Part of the NPLP Formula. Creating a certain kind of Lead Product is just as important as the question—is there a new paradigm and if so, what kind or paradigm. There are three classifications of Lead Products—enabling, killer app and application. I will be using a strictly technology based application here, but non-technology based companies and industries can draw valuable inferences. After all, the new economy of knowledge/creation is going to build itself on top of the Information Economy, not along side it. We are all technology businessess, whether technology based or technology effected.

Enabling products are processes or technologies that the infrastructure of a market anoints as the "compatibility savior"—the standard that others build their products to adapt to or from. Another key feature of Enabling Lead Products is they have open and propietary architecture, resulting in high switching cost effects for users of the technology. The best example is the computer operating software of little known Microsoft.

Killer App products are processes or technology that provide a key link in the "whole product solution" or "adoption complexity solution" for a new paradigm's enabling or application Lead Product company. A good example was Visicalc spreadsheet software and then Excel spreadsheet software that was at first an adoption complexity solution for computer hardware and systems software makers during the early years of personal computer mainstreet market entry and later became a part of the whole product solution for Microsoft.

Application Lead Products are processes or technologies that do not possess enabling or killer app characteristics. Lead Products in this category win their status as "lead" through branding, first to market and quality based strategies. A good example is Amazon.com's effort to out brand and be first over Barnes & Noble in the Internet book sales space.

What do Investors Want? Venture capitalists seek companies with ideas about new paradigms based on substitute, discontinuous and sometimes disruptive new paradigms. Venture capitalists, up until the Internet rush of the late 1990's, sought Lead Products of a new paradigm that were "enabling" or "killer app". The Internet's new paradigm effect has ben so strong that many venture capitalists have thrown caution to the wind and invested even in application lead products. A key point for Visionary Business Builders to remember is that venture capitalists generally look for their preferred NPLP to be "right now" in a company's launch plan. Most Visionay Business Builder launches do not involve an NPLP—now, but rather a NPLP concept to be worked out carefully over time during the Growth Plan phase of the company.

7. THE PARTNERS

The Launch Plan's ultimate high-value partner strategies focused on the Dream Team's ability to create "the Silver Bullet" effect with partners. Power was made through the Visionary Business Builders' specialized services being irreplaceable by the NPLP companies. Often just one key "Silver Bullet" customer is enough. Now the NPLP Visionary Business Builder is able to win power through making sure that as many vendors, customers, and even competitors as possible are making money. Here is how Geoffrey Moore describes it:

> In short, the ringleader's power is a function of its ability to be a "ring giver." The focus of the leader's efforts must be to make sure that each partner in the alliance makes money, particularly in the

first few engagements. This money primes the pump for the partnership. Once the pump is running, it will feed itself, and the ringleader can sit back and reap the profits.[48]

Once again the importance of knowing the territory and having the map shows up. Being both pro-active and the initiator is the key to molding "ring giver" situations. The CEO of the Dream Team has to flex his or her strategic broker muscles.

8. THE PROCESSES

The specialized scouts of the Launch Plan had to show up with high value management, marketing/sales, information and Internet based technology systems, largely pieced together by bootstrapping.

The "lean and mean" capitalization and process strategies of the Launch Plan have to be replaced now with "smart," and sometimes even capital intensive, process strategies. The challenges and demands of the NPLP path require a different mind-set about processes. This is the usual spot where venture capitalists bring in the "growth management team," believing that the entrepreneurs that launched the company do not have the sophistication and experience to line up the right horses to play the growth game.

The Dream Team has their work cut out. Just knowing that processes change at each stage of the PALC should motivate the Dream Team to have a handful of consultants to help meet these challenges. The capital required to meet the projected capacity requirements of each stage of the PALC has to be carefully analyzed in advance. For example, moving from the Early Market to the Bowling Alley, in order to cross the Chasm, may require an infusion of capital if Launch Plan profits are not enough to fund the Growth Plan.

9. THE PROFITS/OWNERSHIP

Profits

As in the Launch Plan, investors want to know the company's cash management policy regarding profits. There are no rules of thumb recommendations. Each team has to balance investor expectations for current distributions with corporate growth demands for accessible capital. As a rule, the longer investors go without cash distributions, the higher their expectations go for some "paydays." Perhaps a policy of starting early continuous (but low to moderate) distributions is the best policy. Another worthwhile policy to pursue is one of nominal cash distributions with the aim of cash management targeted toward corporate growth at all times. While the company is privately held, management should be able to influence profit distribution policies quite well. Once public, management may have too much pressure from its investment bankers and market makers for more generous investor distributions.

R&D Allocations. As early as possible, the Dream Team needs to condition its current investors and future investment bankers about the size of the R&D allocation. Smart Dream Teams will strive for high R&D allocations. At a minimum, the R&D budget should be a line item equal to 5 to 15% of the entire corporate budget. In addition to its line item allocation, you should consider allocating 50% of profits to R&D.

Core Competency Building. Like the R&D war chest, the Dream Team needs to protect and nurture aggressively the core competency agenda. The acquisition and training components of this agenda are vital for the Knowledge/Creation enterprise. Investors need to know how important management considers this to be. Always include the appropriate line items for core competency building. Each company will have its own unique challenges to meet.

Ownership

A highly successful Launch Plan may allow the company to literally pay for its own growth. Should this happen, the early investors are spared the financial insults of dilution caused by future rounds of equity investment capital. In the event the best case scenario does not materialize, the growth agenda usually dictates corporate financing strategies of one sort or another. Careful advance planning by the CEO and his or her advisors and boards is obviously the right step to take. Part of this kind of long-range planning is taken up for the first time during Step 5 of the Investor Financing™ process. The business plan should discuss management's policy and plans about the likelihood of growth capital, how it will be accessed, and what ownership stake it will take. There are many possibilities and variables. Whatever you decide should be talked about in the initial business plan.

10. THE PROJECTIONS/LIQUIDITY

Projections

In the initial business plan the usefulness of a full financial forecast for the Growth Plan is questionable. This subject is hotly debated. Whether the team uses, or doesn't use, a complete financial forecast for the Growth Plan is not as important as the success or failure of the current Investor Financing™ challenges. Step 8 of the Investor Financing™ process will allow the CEO to find out the extent of investor interest for Growth Plan financial forecasts. Some investors may demand them, others could care less, knowing the Growth Plan forecast is a wild guess anyway. There are even some legal and accounting firms that refuse to "be named" in an offering if detailed Growth Plan financial forecasts are included.

Repeating the Promises of Discipline 2. What should be projected is what and how the Dream Team intends to passionately pursue the advancement of the Discipline 2 promises. The Destiny Promise, Core Competency Promise, and Core Ideology Promise deserve the Dream Team's careful forward thought and business plan discussion.

Liquidity and Exit

Many "financial return only" investors in emerging companies are quick hitters. They want to know when they will be able to sell their shares, who is likely to buy them, and what multiples the shares can command. These investors believe that the value of their stock may be directly proportional to the liquidity of their shares. They believe if they pick an emerging company, that investment success for them can hinge as much on how well the company does in the securities or merger and acquisitions markets as it does in its customer market. Visionary Business Builders hooking up with short-term "financial return only" investors are almost certain to enter the product/exit centricity zone. How eccentric the investors' expectations are can only be determined on a case by case basis (see Step 2).

In many countries, the investment community is conditioned to invest for the long term. But a large percentage of American investors who finance growth companies are "financial return only" and look toward their investments with an eye for quick profits. High returns, quick cash-outs, no-risk, and no-load opportunities are high on the investment-criteria list of many American investors. The Internet gold rush of the late 1990's has only exacerbated this. Don't be discouraged. If you have a Launch Plan that is solid, and your Growth Plan is exciting, then following the Investor Financing™ steps will lead you toward the huge market of stakeholders, strategic and long-term "financial return only" investors (visionary capitalists). The investor market is a big market, and like the ocean, is full of different fish.

Stakeholders, strategic investors, and long-term "financial return only" investors do have their concerns for stock liquidity and exit strategies. However, they are not as preoccupied with the immediacy of blockbuster first products and fast-track stock liquidity/exit.

The concepts of "liquidity" and "exit" are often misunderstood. It is very important to distinguish the two. "Liquidity" means that the investors' ownership stake (usually a stock certificate or Certificate of Ownership) is freely tradable. In the securities industry this means the stock or Certificate of

Ownership is not "legended." "Exit" is the event that triggers the end of the investor's involvement in the company or project. Often an event that gives rise to liquidity also provides an exit.

Liquidity. Step 5 describes the kind of planning necessary to show investors that their investments may have liquidity. The planning and effort invested in establishing your Liquidity Track will pay big dividends. You'll learn in Step 2 how it may be possible to secure a place for your inner circle of friends, relatives, and associates in almost any kind of offering you structure. Don't mistake your inner-circle response as indicative of the other investor sources. Since your Liquidity Track is a plan about future events, it is important to remember that you are, in effect, making a promise to do certain things. The cost and time of executing future financings must be weighed now. Don't promise something you're not convinced you can deliver.

Exit. Cashing-out can take the form of the company being merged or sold (or just some of its assets sold with the proceeds distributed to shareholders). It can also result in the company going through an initial public offering (IPO) of its stock. Of course this assumes that the IPO proceeds are used to purchase the stock of early-stage investors. A lesser form of cashing-out can occur when shareholders convert their initial shares into another class of stock. The following paragraphs describe some common strategies of Liquidity and/or Exit.

Stock Gets Registered. The company's assets are large enough, and/or enough shareholders exist, to qualify the stock for registration on an exchange. Investors then have liquidity, and if a market is made in the stock, then an exit is possible through the sale of the stock.

A favorite strategy is to provide very early-stage investors with the promise that the company will include a round of Investor Financing™ that will bring the number of shareholders in the company up to at least 300 shareholders. This is the number of shareholders that, when combined with NASDAQ's minimum size requirements of $4 million in assets, allows a company to "go on" the over-the-counter market, and thus enjoy free trading. If structured carefully, this later round of financing can be for less than 50% of the company's common stock so that the initial investors can still be in control of the company's destiny. In fact, this later financing round can be for a very small amount of money and a small percentage of ownership. The key here is to achieve the 300 shareholders requirement and the $4 million asset size requirement.

Company Goes Public. The company goes through the traditional initial public offering (IPO). Investors can have both liquidity and an exit if the use of proceeds from the offering includes the purchase of stock from the early stockholders.

Company Is Sold or Merged. Another company, or buyer, acquires the company. Investors have both liquidity and an exit.

Insider Buyback of Stock. The founders of the company or other earlier-stage investors buy the stock of early investors, or the company is structured in its early years to redeem the stock of early investors with various sinking and reserve account strategies.

LBO Financed "Going Public" Transaction. This is listed last because the leveraged buyout is probably least understood as an exit strategy for investors. In 1975 the total value of LBO's was only $1.3 billion. However, since 1988 this capital pool has invested an average of $100 billion per year to purchase publicly held stock.

A SUMMARY OF THE CHAORDIC WEB ELEMENTS USED IN THE GROWTH PLAN

Visionary Business Builders use the Growth Plan to describe for investors the race to the company's NPLP. Thus the Growth Plan positions the company as the pioneer with the map to the gold. Using the NPLP as the high-growth "path" for the company, the leadership team tells its investors that it has a Paradigm Vision for radically changing the way the company's customers will work, live, or play in the future. This is the high-change gold mine that investors are hoping for. Given this "path," the company has to prepare itself for the daunting challenge of shifting and/or pioneering a new paradigm. Being the lead company in a new web of companies trying to pioneer a new order requires the Growth Plan to be specific and bold as to what the company plans to do as the "ring giver" to vendors and distribution allies. The strategies to implement these plans need specific tactics for positioning at each stage of the PALC. Investors want to know the company's distributing and retained-earnings policies. They also want to see themselves and the leadership team having a fair ownership stake in the company. Lastly, the Growth Plan must address the company's strategies for investor liquidity through business sale, stock redemptions, or going public.

EVIDENCE POINTS FOR YOUR GROWTH PLAN

4. The Path Evidence Points (Growth Plan)

Describe the first path of growth for the company. It will be one or more of the following:

   ■   "The Silver Bullet" from Launch Plan Path

- "The Spin-in" Path
- Acquisition Path
- NPLP Path (see the description template below)

The _____ for _____

       PRODUCT / SERVICE   YOUR MARKET OR OPPORTUNITY ENVIRONMENT

will be so _____ that no _____

        MOST ATTRACTIVE PRODUCT FEATURE   CUSTOMER / MARKET

will be able to resist _____ one. Everyone in _____

        OWNING / HAVING   YOUR MARKET

will have one. The _____ will have disappeared.

        OLD PARADIGM

If the NPLP Path is selected, then the evidence points which follow should be included in the description.

5. THE POSITIONING EVIDENCE POINTS (GROWTH PLAN)

Describe the new paradigm lead product/service. For example:

Who is the Paradigm Shifter and Pioneer? Describe who in the industry was the shifter responsible for the new breakthrough solution to its problems. If applicable, describe how your company is to be a pioneer or shifter. What other companies are acting or going to act soon as pioneers?

6. THE PRODUCTS/SERVICES EVIDENCE POINTS (GROWTH PLAN)

Describe the products/services. Are they high-value or high-volume based? How high—be specific (e.g.: knowledge based or self-fulfillment based)? Describe the current stage of your company's NPLP. Is it at concept, seed, or product development? If it is at product development, is it at alpha (in-house) or beta (in market)?

Products/Services Protections. Describe the legal protections to be taken to protect your future NPLP ideas for your company.

Other Products/Services Categories of the New Paradigm. Describe the various kinds of products/services categories other companies may show up with to ride the new paradigm wave. List the names of these companies, if possible, and indicate when they may show up with their products/services. Will they make attempts at NPLP or EPSP?

7–8. THE PARTNERS AND PROCESSES EVIDENCE POINTS (GROWTH PLAN)

Describe the PALC stage the company is currently in with its NPLP. Then describe for investors what you have done, or plan to do, at each stage of the PALC. Illustrations 1-13A through 1-13E will be a helpful guide for these plans and descriptions. Obviously the Early Market, Chasm, and Bowling Alley stages will be more descriptive and specific than the Tornado and later stages. Include in your discussions the strategies for positioning, product/service (whole product concepts), and of course, partners and processes.

9. THE PROFITS/OWNERSHIP EVIDENCE POINTS (GROWTH PLAN)
Include a discussion of R&D and core competency funding through cash flows and profits. How does the Growth Plan of the company impact the future ownership structure?

10. THE PROJECTIONS/LIQUIDITY EVIDENCE POINTS (GROWTH PLAN)
Include financial forecasts for 5–10 years. Also include the plans the company has for developing and improving along the Destiny Promises of Discipline 2, namely, the core competency agenda, and the strengthening of the core ideology and its implementations. A description of the company's liquidity path is important. If any consultants or investment bankers are involved, describe them and their roles.

DISCIPLINE 2: BOLDLY LOVE YOUR DESTINY
The simple essence of raising capital is to do what you love to do and do it *boldly*. Young Bill Gates and his Lakeside buddies loved writing code for the C-Cubed computer they shared during high school. The universe has richly blessed and supported Gates, but he had to boldly honor and nurture this one oddball thing he uniquely loved to do—writing code.

Imagine an investor, upon seeing the young Gates, staking him with money to make those early years easier. What would that investor be worth today? Spotting bold destiny players is the simple essence of venture investing. If you can enhance the signals of bold destiny for your investors, you're on the right track. That's what this Discipline is centrally about. Your designs for your phenomenal company have to start with an introspective look at yourselves. You and the other principals explain more about the why of your future success than anything else. You and your associates are the chromosomes that investors want to put under a microscope. Through the lens of this microscope hints of phenomena can be seen. Evidence of rare and significant commercial potential may be discovered. Glimpses of the kind of business builder (Product/Service Specialist, Traditional, or Visionary) are seen. Traditional investor and money raiser due diligence starts with product or structural capital centricity. Better that it start with people (human capital) centricity.

Business builders must be in love with their gifts. Doing so they are whisker-close to answering for investors why they exist as a business—their destiny. The only sure chance the start-up company has at matching its inspiration with the long road of implementation is to have congruity between corporate direction and the destiny of the individual members of the company's leadership team. This is the start of the Human Capital agenda, and the start of finding the Intellectual Capital potential of the enterprise. Self reckoning at deep levels must precede smart corporate positioning. Yet this is often overlooked and, in doing so, can make an Investor Financing™ very difficult.

Having healthy Investor Financing™ chromosomes (i.e., people in touch with their own unique destiny) requires deep personal awareness and self honesty. The destiny of the company hinges on each member of the leadership team applying the axiom, "Know thyself first," and always proceeding from their God-given strengths. The Chinese philosophy of Taoism illuminates this by holding that the cycle for obtaining long life and good fortune rests on the sequence of "Be ➡ Do ➡ Have."

All the fuss and confusion about what you should do as a company and how you should develop the markets for your first products/services gives way to clarity by first focusing on "who you are," "your being," and "your personality."

What you've done as a company can be understood from objective profit and loss statements and cannot be debated. The "what you are going to do" can be described through strategies and financial forecasts and can be argued about and challenged by investors. However, "who you are" and "what you're becoming" doesn't even show up on the new IC measurement systems, and thus, can only be understood through perception. Investors have to get a feeling about the rarity and significance of "who you are" and "what you're becoming." They will perceive you as either exciting or not. Investors will take the time to pour over your business plan if they are first excited into action by the leadership team itself.

This Discipline of the Visionary Business Builder model demonstrates to investors "who you are." To convince them that you have this Discipline, you need to follow the strategies and evidences detailed earlier in this Step that show them what it is you love doing and how bold you are about your fate.

DISCIPLINE 3: FANATICALLY HOLD TWO OPPOSED IDEAS AT THE SAME TIME AND REMAIN FUNCTIONAL

Visionary Business Builders can be accused of schizophrenia. Here's why: Collins and Porras found that visionary companies live with seemingly contradictory forces or ideas at the same time.

So How Does This Relate to Raising Capital? Plenty! Smart investors looking for Visionary Business Builders will demand entrepreneurs who can engineer short-term profitability and visionaries who can be the architects of new paradigm shifts and/or pioneering. If this is possible, why should investors expect less? If you want to provide evidence to investors, employees, and vendors that you're a Visionary Business Builder, there is no better place to start than by providing evidence of these two extremes: Entrepreneurial Excellence—Now, and Paradigm Pioneering—Someday.

THE "ENGINEER A LAUNCH PLAN INTO YOUR BUSINESS PLAN" STRATEGY

If the would-be Business Builder wants to attract capital with his Visionary Business Builder message, it is critical that he or she focus on engineering— as part of the business plan (see Discipline 1)—a "Launch Plan" that describes how, when, why, and how much will be done by the company in the next 6–18 months *along with the financial performance that will result* from these actions. This Launch Plan is the future period of time the company is prepared to go toe-to-toe on with investors, with substantiating data, studies, results, and performance to back up these immediate predictions. It is the description of immediately accessible resources and of the planned deployment of activities by the company that will result in the company making immediate progress with its first products/services.

THE "IMAGINE A PARADIGM VISION INTO YOUR BUSINESS PLAN" STRATEGY

A business plan with a low-impact Launch Plan is difficult to reconcile with claims by the leadership team that they are a talented, motivated bunch. It takes the Paradigm Vision to tie it all together. The intended investor response should be, "So this is why these extraordinarily talented people are throwing themselves totally into this company."

Having a Paradigm Vision affords the leadership team a great chance at opening with that bold, sweeping, and controversial opening claim that conveys the perception that a phenomenal enterprise is in the making. More importantly, this activity is the other extreme and opposite of "Entrepreneurial Excellence—Now," thus completing this third Discipline of Visionary Business Building.

DISCIPLINE 4: PASSIONATELY PRESERVE THE CORE AND DRIVE FOR PROGRESS

This Discipline is, according to Collins and Porras, the "essence" of a visionary company!

PRESERVING CORE IDEOLOGY

The values and purposes of the Visionary Business Builder—his or her philosophy and ideology—never change. Your company's Paradigm Vision, strategies, culture, goals, products/services, competencies, compensation structures, partners, and just about everything else changes, but not your Core Ideology.

DRIVE FOR PROGRESS

The visionary companies of Collins' and Porras' research had a deep, inner, compulsive—almost primal—drive for progress, attitudes, and behaviors. This drive for progress consists of all the goals, dreams, innovations, patience, sacrifice—all the "doingness" to manifest the company's destiny. According to Collins and Porras, the drive for progress should be an incurable itch. There is no finish line for Visionary Business Builders.

Management teams of fast-track companies playing the Great American Product/Exit Game generally look forward to cashing out in a few years after start-up. Visionary Business Builders, on the other hand, never see an end in sight. Perhaps that's why the CEOs of the visionary companies of Collins' and Porras' research were at the helm an average of 32.4 years. This, of course, violates a prevailing attitude in many academic, venture capital, and entrepreneurial circles that a CEO who starts a business is probably the wrong CEO for the company's growth phase and the wrong CEO for its renewal phases.

Collins and Porras summarized the interplay between Core Ideology and Drive for Progress this way:

Core Ideology	*Drive for Progress*
Is continuous and stable	Continually changes
Is like a fixed stake	Constantly moving
Limits directions to those consistent with Ideology	Expands the possibilities
Clear content	Can be content-free
A conservative and deliberative act	Can lead to radical innovation

THE DESIGN "PASSIONATELY PRESERVE THE CORE AND DRIVE FOR PROGRESS" INTO YOUR BUSINESS PLAN STRATEGY

Talk comes cheap and investors know it. The best chance the start-up company has for manifesting this Discipline is to incorporate into the business plan many tangible, specific ways the company can preserve its Core Ideology and Drive for Progress. Believe it or not, a Launch Plan that is simple, not capital intensive, gets the company profitable quickly, and secures a platform for the business plan, is an excellent manifestation of this Discipline.

DISCIPLINE 5: SYSTEMATICALLY INNOVATE

Visionary companies "try a lot of stuff and keep what works." This, according to Collins and Porras, is one of the defining Disciplines of visionary companies. This Discipline permitted these visionary companies to make progress (even survive at times) with small, incremental steps, often in the form of quickly taking advantage of unexpected opportunities that eventually mutate into major paradigm shifts. In short, the Visionary Business Builders are always entrepreneurial and always on the high change road. The visionary companies of Collins' and Porras' research were purposeful about these "things" that caused new ideas—what the authors called "purposeful accidents." The lesson is that innovation can be systematized.

This last Discipline then is the manifestation of this "basic process" of innovation methodology: Systematic Innovation. This is the lifeblood of the Visionary Business Builder, because both high-value and high-volume enterprises require continuous high change if the expected high growth is to materialize.

DISCOVER IT—DIFFUSE IT

Systematic Innovation has two parts. First are the processes (trying a lot of stuff) that lead to the discovery of new ideas. (Maybe even new paradigms that can make major high-change shifts.) Second are the processes that diffuse the new idea (keep what works—the markets accept it). Although Leonardo da Vinci drew some of the first pictures of helicopters and submarines, he never cashed in. Visionary Business Builders know that the commercial value of any high-change innovation is dependent on their ability to get the idea to market and have it accepted as close to schedule and proforma as possible.

THE PARADIGM ADOPTIVE LIFE CYCLE TOOL (PALC)

The context of Systematic Innovation has a useful analytical tool. The earliest form of this was the Adoption Life Cycle. When combined with the principles governing the field of paradigms (whose serious study began with the work of Thomas Kuhn in the 1960s) we have what I have chosen to call the Paradigm Adoptive Life Cycle tool. As explained earlier in this Step, PALC allows us to construct a useful context or landscape for analyzing both the discovery and diffusion of high change innovations and the new paradigms they start and move.

CONCLUSION

Step 1 demands rigorous honesty. Doing Step 1 thoroughly assures the very best chance of finding capital.

In our national clinics and workshop programs we find that attendees come with the belief that raising their capital depends primarily on their implementing new and different strategies and tactics. In our training we show the necessity for the CEO to first change the company's overall theory about launching and financing their business. It is well established that real improvement and change comes about as a result of changing one's theories and philosophies.[50] New strategies and tactics are useful to have, but pale in comparison to the performance power generated through utilizing the highest and most appropriate theory and philosophy. Step 1 explores the Visionary Business Builders theory for launching and financing the growth businesses of the 21st Century. It is a simple theory with a compelling track record of performance for business builders and investors alike. Although simple in theory, it will usually be difficult in practice due to the conventional thinking of most American entrepreneurs and their advisors and educators. Hopefully the fire in the soul of this country's business builders will be hot enough to motivate them away from old paradigms. The demands of the new Knowledge/Creation Economy are making us all painfully aware that there is no escape from the need to change old paradigms.

We are now ready to go on to Step 2 and survey the sources of capital.

SURVEYING INVESTOR FINANCING™ SOURCES AND APPROACHES

Step 1

STEP 2

Step 3

Step 4

Step 5

Step 6

Step 7

Step 8

Step 9

Step 10

2 *In the U.S. alone, there is over $90 billion invested in start-up enterprises every year.*
—U.S. SMALL BUSINESS ADMINISTRATION

Step 2 is your opportunity to learn about the investor landscape. Learning about this landscape now will make the rest of the Investor Financing™ steps easier to implement. This step is a survey of the available *sources* and *approaches* to access investor capital that will give you the information you need so that you can later determine which source(s) and approach(es) are best for you.

You might see the information in this step as the most important part of this book. If it's the meat of the meal for you, then that's fine. However, don't lose sight of the fact that all the steps are interdependent and all are required for the Investor Financing™ process to work. If you don't complete each step thoroughly, the action ideas in each step may not produce the outcome you're hoping for in "Step 10: Executing the Offering Campaign." The steps are demanding and they take some time. Your Investor Financing™ will be the toughest financing you'll ever have to make. Just remind yourself that your competitors are having an equally difficult time accessing their capital. If Investor Financing™ was easy, everyone would be doing it.

Step 2 is a "study and learn" step. It does not ask you to take any action—it only asks you to learn.

IT'S LIKE FISHING

If you think about it, all of the fish that you eat comes from only five *sources*: streams, rivers, lakes, oceans, and commercial fish tanks. If you want to add some fish to your diet, you have to decide which *approach* you're going to use to get it: either you go out and catch the fish yourself, or you buy fish (generally at the supermarket) that has been caught by professionals who fish for a living. If you decide to catch the fish yourself, you have to decide which *tactics* you're going to use to find the fish: you can rely on "hot" tips about where the fish are biting, you can research the history of where fishing has been good, or you might use electronic means to help find the fish (sonar, etc.). Finally, you have to decide which *tools* to use to catch the fish: the tackle and bait. Similarly, Step 2 is the survey of the five *sources* of investors and the two basic *approaches* used to reach your capital sources: the do-it-yourself Direct Placement Approach and the professional Money Raiser Approach. In Step 6 the *tactics* you will use to find the *sources* and the *tools* you can use to reach them are identified and discussed.

THE WAY THINGS ARE

Step 2 describes the way investors and money raisers, for the most part, think and behave. The way things are. As of the late 1990s, the investment behavior and business building paradigm of most of the American business community (the Great American Product/Exit Game) is not the Visionary Business Builder paradigm. You need to keep this in perspective during your planning. The design of a Phenomenal Message for the Investor Financing™ process is a delicate and hard-fought-for task. You have to balance ideal theory with practical solutions. Deals have to get done.

INVESTOR FINANCING™ SOURCES

There are five *sources* of Investor Financing™: The venture capital market, the strategic corporate investor market, the business angel market, the adventure stockholder market, and the soon arriving Visionary Capital market. These markets are uniquely distinct and separate from one another, but at the same time they share certain characteristics, traits, and players.

   Investor Motives and Business Builder Types. Each of the five sources of investor capital stems from one (or more than one) of the three kinds of investor motives. For example, in one deal a venture capitalist can have a stakeholder motive (emotional commitment) and a financial return motive. On another deal this same venture capitalist can be investing with strategic motives as well as financial return motives. In addition, the investor and money raiser sources have players who may be more comfortable with one kind of Business Builder over another. For example, some business angel investors may prefer a Product/Service Specialist opportunity to a Visionary Business Builder opportunity.

SOURCE 1: THE VENTURE CAPITAL MARKET

Definition: Venture capital is a source of Investor Financing™ that is invested primarily for financial investment reasons in high-risk business endeavors with the Great American Product/Exit Game message.

   The venture capital market is listed first out of respect for the major role this industry has played in America. Without the venture capital industry, America would not have many of its new technologies or new advances in science and medicine. Venture capital grabs the front page of the newspaper because it has historically taken big risks with entrepreneurs and their promises of major advancements and contributions to society. Venture capitalists are also more visible than the other capital sources because they are more organized as a group. They have their own trade organizations, directories, trade journals, trade analysts, and trade conferences.

For an excellent look into the history and development of the venture capital industry, read *Venture Capital at the Crossroads* by William D. Bygrave and Jeffry A. Timmons. Here is an excerpt:

> . . . [Venture capital] has played a catalytic role in the entrepreneurial process: [the] fundamental value creation that triggers and sustains economic growth and renewal. In terms of job creation, innovative products and services, competitive vibrancy, and the dissemination of the entrepreneurial spirit, its contributions have been staggering. The new companies and industries spawned by venture capitalists have changed fundamentally the way in which we live and work.

Consider the following examples:

- In 1957, American Research & Development (ARD) invested $70,000 for 77% of the common stock of a new company created by four MIT graduate students. In 1971, that investment had grown to comprise $355 million in common stock in Digital Equipment Corporation (DEC), which today is a world leader in the computer industry, with one of its founders, Kenneth Olsen, still at the helm.
- In 1975, Arthur Rock, in search of innovative concepts "that change the way people live and work," invested $1.5 million in the start-up of Apple Computer, Inc. At Apple's first public stock offering in 1978, that investment was valued at $100 million.
- After monthly losses of $1 million and more for twenty-nine consecutive months, a new company that launched the overnight delivery of small packages turned the corner. The $25 million invested had a valuation of $1.2 billion when Federal Express issued its stock to the public for the first time.[1]

HOW BIG AND ACTIVE IS THIS MARKET?

Because the venture capital market generates a lot of press, many people believe that it is larger than it actually is. There are approximately 700 venture capital firms in America. According to ADS Financial Services, Inc., the U.S. venture capital market is a pool of funds of over $58 billion.[2] However, the venture capital industry only invests approximately $4 billion each year in start-up companies. That may sound like a lot, but it's actually only 4% of the estimated $100 billion of investor capital annually invested in start-up companies in America from all sources. Less than 2,100 businesses each year receive funding from the venture capital community. Only 15% of these are start-up companies. That means that less than 320 new start-ups each year are funded by venture capitalists. In 1991, venture capital firms invested just $60 million in only 47 start-ups, according to Venture Economics, publishers of *Venture Capital Journal*.[3] Venture Economics reported that in 1992 there were 79 corporate venture capital subsidiary financings. In 1992, according to Coopers & Lybrand of Boston, the average age of companies receiving their first round of venture capital was 5.8 years.[4] However, between 1985 and 1989 the average age was 1.9 years.

It is estimated that 99% of the business plans submitted to venture capital investors are turned down. They invest less than 35% of their capital in deals requiring less than $1 million, and less then 15% into financing under $500,000. In 1993, according to *Inc.* magazine, nearly 60% of the venture capital was concentrated in a select group of "funds" with $100 million or more each—the so-called megafunds.[5]

VENTURE CAPITAL MYTHS

- *Venture capitalists are only interested in high-tech manufacturing or medicine.* Wrong. Retail or other service businesses are also acceptable if the "future-value impact" is high.[6]
- *Venture capitalists want control of your company.* Wrong. They want you to run your business, and so long as your business plan is being met, you stay in control.[7]
- *Venture capitalists only do start-ups.* Wrong. In fact, one of the biggest complaints against the venture capital industry is that it doesn't do enough start-ups. The word "venture" is derived from the word "adventure," and a lot of entrepreneurs wish venture capitalists would be far more adventuresome.[8] Venture capital investments seem to go in cycles. For a year or two the venture capitalists will aggressively invest in early-stage companies, then they back off and seem to limit themselves to later-stage financing such as bridge, mezzanine, and LBO financing.
- *You need an introduction.* Wrong. However, an introduction certainly helps. Using the right approaches, tactics, and tools that are presented in Step 2 and 6, will help insure that your deal gets looked at.

THE TYPES OF VENTURE CAPITALISTS

The venture capital community is basically comprised of the following types:

- *Venture capital firms.* These are usually privately held companies that raise their money through the formation of limited partnerships. The owners of these firms are very good promoters as well as experienced business people. These firms tend to invest in early-stage companies within industries that the leadership team or owners of the firms are familiar with. The capital sources for these firms are institutions, pension plans, corporations, and high net worth individuals. They will often take the role of "fund manager" and parcel out an allotment of partnership units to some of the other venture capital groups described here.

- *Venture capital subsidiaries of banks.* There are approximately seventy of these firms. These organizations tend to be managed by conservative managers. They tend to look for later-stage companies which fit their "low-risk management" profile.

- *Small business investment companies (SBIC's).* The federal government, as well as many state and local governments, have seed funds to invest in local companies that have good prospects for generating jobs. Most of them (approximately 180) target manufacturing businesses, although some will invest more broadly.

- *Venture capital subsidiaries of major corporations.* These companies, as a rule, combine financial investment reasons with strategic investment reasons. There are approximately eighty of these corporations.

- *Institutional investors.* These organizations tend to be managed by conservative managers. They tend to look for later-stage companies which fit their "low-risk management" profile.

- *Investment banks, law firms, and family funds.* This represents a small percentage of the venture capital available for investment. Their investments are sporadic, and in the case of investment banks, tied into other "core" services.

- *Product development partnerships sponsored by wirehouse firms.* Many Wall Street securities firms sponsor R&D partnerships that provide product development financing for companies.

WHERE TO FIND VENTURE CAPITALISTS

The good news is that, unlike the other sources of investors, there are directories and associations to help you locate venture capital firms.

THE NEEDS OF VENTURE CAPITALISTS

In order to access investor capital for your company you must satisfy the needs of your target investors. If you meet their needs, you get their money. This

Here are some useful addresses:

National Venture Capital Association
1655 North Fort Meyer Drive, #700
Arlington, Virginia 22209
(703)351-5269

Western Association of Venture
    Capitalists
3000 Sand Hill Road, Building 1, #90
Menlo Park, California 94025
(412)854-1322

*Pratt's Guide to Venture Capital
    Sources*
Venture Economics Inc.
40 West 57th Street, Suite 802
New York, New York 10019
(212)765-5311

International VentureCapital Institute
Box 1333
Stamford, Connecticut 06904
(203)323-3143

For information on government-affiliated venture capital firms:

National Associations of Small
    Business Investment Companies
1156 15th Street, #1101
Washington, D.C. 20005

Association of Small Business
    Development Centers
1050 17th Street, N.W., #810
Washington, D.C. 20036
(202)887-5599

section identifies the needs of venture capitalists and the information that they need to know about you and your company.

The Messages They Relate To. Venture capitalists, almost without exception, are only attracted to the Industry Superstar, Profitable Company, or Great American Product/Exit Game message.

Familiarity Index Rating. This indicates the investor's level of knowledge about and relationship with the company and its industry. In "Step 6: Creating the Capital Relations™ Plan," a full explanation of the Familiarity Index is given. Reference should be made to that section of this book. Illustration 6-1 defines the Familiarity Index Ratings. Venture capitalists, as a rule, need the highest Familiarity Index Rating of 6 (or at least 5), if they are going to invest in an early-stage enterprise.

Location of Operations. The specific location is not critical, but it does make sense for you to research venture capital firms in your area first. Venture capitalists will be able to monitor your business and communicate with your leadership team easier if you are located nearby. They like that.

Growth Track. The bigger your growth potential, the better. Your "future-value impact" is more believable if your market is large and your perceived chance of a large market share is high. Venture capitalists' first choice are companies projecting sales of $50 million to $100 million within five to ten years. They love to see forgiving and rewarding economies, such as gross margins of 40–50%, early positive cash flow, break-even sales, and 10% or more profits after tax dividends.

Return on Investment. Venture capitalists want to see cumulative returns in the range of 25–50% per year once they cash in. Ideally they want a return equal to ten times the investment within five years, and price earnings ratios of 15:1 or more.

Exit Time. Venture capitalists want to get out as fast as they can. Prior to 1985, it was not unusual for most of the venture capital community to expect five- to ten-year holding periods before they could cash out. Since 1985, the expected holding time has been shortening. For example, *Business Week*, in their July 19, 1993 issue, profiled the one to two year Exit Track record of venture capitalist D. Blech & Company, located in New York.[9] This kind of early exit is not normal, but it's a trend sign worth watching. If there is no planned exit, venture capitalists will not be interested in your company.

The Leadership Team. To venture capitalists, people are very important. A strong team, evidenced by a strong track record, is essential. If you don't have a full team, but you have a hot idea or product, the possibility exists that a venture capitalist will help you build your leadership team.[10] When venture capitalists say they'll back you, they're referring to your leadership team, not your company.

Industry. Although science and medical industries grab the headlines, don't be discouraged if you're not in one of these high-profile industries. There is venture capital money available for almost any industry.[11]

Types of Products/Services. Venture capitalists will look at any kind of product/service. They prefer New Paradigm Lead Products (NPLP). They will invest in evolutionary products/services or knock-off substitutions with a strong added-value twist so long as they perceive an NPLP is in the making. They want blockbuster breakthroughs.

Proprietary Nature of Product/Service. Venture capitalists want the protection that patents, trademarks, copyrights, service marks, secret formulas or processes, franchise licenses, or know-how provide. They will make an exception to this if your company has a "first with the most" competitive strategy. If not, they expect your company to have at least a 12-month lead time, and a monopoly position for as long as possible.

Psychological Needs. Venture capitalists are managed by real people who have personal as well as corporate needs. Being a powerful, highly "promotion oriented" group, venture capitalists tend to have fairly strong egos. They also like to fancy themselves on the leading edge. Your company, and the promise your NPLP offers can be positioned to appeal to the emotional or personal needs of the venture capitalist.

Product/Service Development Stage. These investors prefer that other investors take the risk on concept stage and seed stage financing. Venture capitalists will invest at the product or market development level.

Stage of Company Growth. The venture capital community swings in and out of cycles. At one moment they emphasize early-stage companies. The next year they only want to finance mature companies. The most desirable situation is for your business plan to show your company already making money, even though it is still in the early stages of developing the full potential of the product/service (or its market).

Liquidity Track. Venture capitalists want liquidity within three to six years. Your business plan has to incorporate a thorough discussion of your liquidity track. As far as venture capitalists are concerned, your "future-value impact" depends largely on the strength of your liquidity track.

Exit Track. Your liquidity track, exit time, and exit track have to mesh with each other. Your business plan can't promise that your company will be sold (the exit track) in year 3 (the exit time), if you're planning a NASDAQ small-capital market registration that can't be completed before year 4.

Presentation Documents. Be ready with your business plan and executive summary when you approach a venture capitalist. Most of them will want to study your executive summary before they agree to study your business plan.

Ownership. Venture capitalists are in the business of upside opportunities generated through their courage in providing capital to a new or growing business. They usually expect some share of ownership for the capital they put at risk. According to a San Francisco-based research firm, VentureOne, stage 1 companies (see Illustration 2-1) have to give up at least 30% of the company for every $1 million needed from venture capitalists—assuming the targeted investment return is feasible. VentureOne also determined in their research that stage 2 and 3 companies give up an average of 8–15% of equity ownership per $1 million invested. Stage 4, 5, and 6 companies give up to venture capitalists 5–6% of equity ownership per $1 million invested.

Let's look at an example of how ownership of a company might be divided up. Our hypothetical venture capital firm, FastCapital, Inc., is prepared to invest $1,000,000 in ForSure, Inc., a stage 2 (development) NPLP company. FastCapital, Inc. expects a 48% annual return to justify its early-stage investment risks. ForSure, Inc.'s business plan states that in year 5 the company can be sold or go through an IPO. The "future-value impact" and financial projections need to substantiate that the company will have a certain value.

Here's a range of values that the company might have in year 5, and the corresponding percentage of ownership that would have to be given up to the venture capitalist:

	Projected value of ForSure, Inc. in year 5	Percent of company to be allocated to FastCapital, Inc. in year 1
Scenario 1	$7,000,000	100%
Scenario 2	$14,000,000	50%
Scenario 3	$21,000,000	33%

Venture capitalists want to control enough voting stock of early-stage companies to be able to gain control of the company if the leadership team fails to perform. They are not adverse to structuring leadership team "earn-ins" or granting warrants to the leadership team in order to allow the leadership team the right to be in control after they've proven themselves.

Number of Co-Investors. Venture capitalists like to take positions with other investors in the companies in which they invest. However, "the more the merrier," is not necessarily the right tune to play. The best formula is to have luminary or influential investors as part of the investment group. Investors with "clout" make the other investors feel safer, more prestigious, and/or lucky. A venture capitalist in Phoenix might be heard to say, "Boy, we got in on a deal with Forstmann, Little & Co. out of New York.

Types of Financing. The venture capitalist's first choice in financing is, by far, a bridge financing round to get the company in position for an IPO. Beyond that, any type of financing is a possibility, depending on which part of the cycle the venture capital community is currently in.

Leadership Team Involvement. Venture capitalists expect to fill a certain number of the board of directors seats. Although venture capitalists do not want the responsibility of day-to-day leadership team positions, they can fill these roles if they have to.

Warrant and Future Underwriting Rights. If your company is seeking early-stage financing, your venture capital investors will negotiate for warrants on your company's stock, and seek anti-dilution protection. Venture capitalists are attracted to companies that can use their services for future financing. The "right of first refusal" to do the next round of financing is usually expected.

Due Diligence Time Requirements. Ask for the venture capitalist's due diligence checklist (if they use one). You'll need to allow one to four months for the venture capitalist to check out your deal, before an investment is made.

One way of finding out the current investment criteria of the venture capital market is to attend one of their regional conferences. You can get information about these conferences from Venture Economics, Inc., whose address and phone number are listed earlier.

Illustration 2-1 summarizes the needs of venture capitalists.

SOURCE II: STRATEGIC CORPORATE INVESTORS

Definition: A business (usually a corporation) that invests in another company for reasons other than pure financial investment.

In Step 4 strategic associations will be analyzed with the aim of showing you how other companies can help you overcome various weaknesses that

ILLUSTRATION 2-1:
PROFILE OF VENTURE CAPITALISTS' NEEDS

	Most desired	Acceptable	Unlikely
Message they relate to	Industry superstar Profitable company GAPE	Industry superstar Profitable company GAPE	Visionary Business Builder
Familiarity Index	6	5	Under 5
Location of operation	Home office in same city National market	Home office in same region Regional markets	Home office out-of-state Local market only
Growth track	Shows $50–100 million sales in 5 years	Shows $25–50 million sales in 5 years	Shows less than $10 million sales in 5 years
Return on investment	40%	25%	Under 20%
Exit time	2–3 years	5–7 years	Over 10 years
Leadership team	Full team with all qualities	Partial team with most qualities	One-man show with no plans for team
Industry	High-tech manufacturing Life science	Low-tech manufacturing and other service	Dying industry

ILLUSTRATION 2-1: (CONTINUED)
PROFILE OF VENTURE CAPITALISTS' NEEDS

	Most desired	Acceptable	Unlikely
Type of product/ service	NPLP	Evolutionary or substitute niche	Revolutionary with no market or "Me too"
Proprietary products and services	Absolute protection with patents, etc.	No protection, but "first with most" andmonopoly evident	No protection, not "first with most" no monopoly
Psychological needs	Leading edge Ego boost	Socially responsible	"Same old thing"
Product/service development level:			
Concept			X
Seed			X
Product Devel.		X	
Market Devel.		X	
Static	X		
Stage of company growth:			
1. Research			X
2. Development		X	
3. Losing money & proven dist.		X	
4. Breakeven	X	X	
5. Profits — need capital	X	X	
6. Profits — need major expansion	X	X	
7. IPO / Sale			X
Liquidity Track	Stock exchange in 3–6 years	Stock exchange in 5-10 years	No public trading foreseeable
Exit Track	IPO almost guaranteed	Sale of business	None planned
Presentation Documents	Executive summary Business plan	Executive summary Business plan	Executive summary only
Ownership	As much as needed for projected return and control of company if management fails	As much as needed for projected return and control of company if management fails	Minority position in a private company. Not on liquidity track for for IPO

ILLUSTRATION 2-1: (CONTINUED)
PROFILE OF VENTURE CAPITALISTS' NEEDS

	Most desired	Acceptable	Unlikely
Number of co-investors	6–10 Prestigious investors	3–5	1
Financings:			
Seed			X
Development		X	
Expansion	X	X	
Bridge	X	X	
LBO	X	X	
Acquisition	X	X	
Turnaround		X	
Refinance			X
Direct participation offerings			X
Leadership team involvement	Board of directors Partner	Board of advisors	No position
Warrants and future underwriting	Must have	Would like to have	Not offered
Due diligence time	90 days	60 days	30 days

your company might have. It will be explained that with all three kinds of associations (strategic relationships, strategic alliances, and strategic joint ventures) one party may invest in the other. This is known as a strategic investment.

HOW BIG AND ACTIVE IS THIS MARKET?

No one knows exactly. Estimates range from $10 billion to $20 billion annually. Here are some examples of large companies making strategic corporate investments in smaller companies:

- Between 1988 and 1992, IBM invested over $100 million in fifteen smaller software development companies. The ownership stake IBM purchased ranged from 2% to 40%.[12]
- Bausch & Lomb made twenty-seven strategic investments in 1991. In a ten-year period they made 145 strategic investments in start-up companies.
- Dow Jones, publishers of the *Wall Street Journal* formed a $6 million venture capital fund in 1992.[13]

- ▪ Advent International, a venture capital management company, was hired by thirteen international corporations to direct their strategic investments.[14]
- ▪ In the health-care field it is reported that there are over 550 strategic alliances a year involving direct investments by larger companies into smaller companies.[15]
- ▪ Price Waterhouse & Co. reviewed 500 software start-up companies and found that two-thirds of them got some form of financial help from larger companies.

WHERE TO FIND STRATEGIC CORPORATE INVESTORS

There are several ways to locate prospective strategic corporate investors. One way is to use corporate directories. The *Direct Placement Approach* requires a lot of cold calling and fact finding. You should have realistic expectations about this investigative process. Here are some recommendations from Washington Researchers Publishing to help you in your quest:

1. *It's an art.* Discovering information about companies is an art, not a science. Success is greatly dependent upon the creativity, imagination, and skill—artistry, if you will—of the researcher.
2. *It's a people business.* The most complete, current, and insightful information about companies usually is in the minds of individuals, not in published or computerized sources. The clever researcher can tap this information reservoir of industry/company watchers and participants.
3. *Balance reliability and cost.* When accuracy of intelligence is crucial—when costly decisions are to be based on the information—intelligence gatherers must scrutinize, examine, and evaluate the data, whether obtained from an individual, a published or unpublished document, or a data base. Seek to corroborate every answer with other informed sources.

Venture capital directories can also be used to find potential strategic corporate investors. These directories include the professional venture capital managers, as well as companies that have, in recent years, established venture group subsidiaries. For example, Raytheon, Xerox, IBM, Motorola, Upjohn, Kodak, and a host of smaller companies will be listed in these directories.

WHO TO CONTACT WITHIN THE COMPANIES

There is no quick and easy method of finding the right person; thorough searching and persistence will yield the best results.

The following is a list of the most common guides to directories:

Directories in Print
(2 volumes, annual with supplements)
Information Enterprises
Gale Research, Inc.
835 Penobscot Building
Detroit, Michigan 48226
(313)961-2242 or (800)347-4253

Guide to American Directories
(biannual)
B. Klein Publications
P.O. Box 8503
Coral Springs, Florida 33075
(305)752-1708

Trade Directories of the World
(annual loose-leaf service with monthly supplements)
Croner Publications, INc.
34 Jericho Turnpike
Jericho, New York 11753
(516)333-9085

The following is a list of the most common corporate directories:

Dun's Directory of Service Companies
Dun's Marketing Services
Three Sylvan Way
Parsippany, New Jersey 07054
(201)605-600 or (800)526-0651

Million Dollar Directory
(5 volumes, annual)
Dun's Marketing Services
Three Sylvan Way
Parsippany, New Jersey 07054
(201)605-600 or (800)526-0651

Standard & Poor's Register of Corporation, Directors and Executives
(3 volumes, annual with 3 supplements each year)
Standard & Poor's Corporation
25 Broadway
New York, New York 10004
(212)208-8000

Reference Books of Corporate Managements
(4 volumes, annual)
Dun's Marketing Services
Three Sylvan Way
Parsippany, New Jersey 07054
(201)605-600 or (800)526-0651

Macmillan Directory of Leading Private Companies
(annual)
R.R. Bowker/National Register Publishing Co., Inc.
3004 Glenview Road
Wilmette, Illinois 60091
(707)445-2210 or (800)323-6772

Thomas Register of American Manufactures and Thomas Register Catalog File
(26 volumes, annual)
Thomas Publishing Co.
One Pennsylvania Plaza
New York, New York 10119
(212)290-7343; orders only, (800)222-7900, ext.200

The following directories allows you to search for current financial information about public companies:

Moody's Manuals
Moody's INvestors Service, Inc.
99 Church Street
New York, New York 10007
(212)553-0495 or (800)342-5647

Standard & Poor's Corporation Records
(7 volumes, loose-leaf, with a daily news section)
Standard & Poor's Corporation
25 Broadway
New York, New York 10004
(212)208-8000

Standard & Poor's Stock Reports
Standard & Poor's Corporation
25 Broadway
New York, New York 10004
(212)208-8000

The Market Guide Over the Counter Stock Edition
(quarterly service)
Market Service Corporation
49 Glen Head Road
Glen Head, New York 11545
(516)759-1253

Wall Street Transcript
(weekly)
Wall Street Transcript Corporation
99 Wall Street
New York, New York 10005
(212)747-9500

The job titles of those responsible for the selection process of strategic investments are often one of the following:

Directors of:

Corporate Planning	Business Development
Strategic Development	Business Alliances
New Enterprises	Mergers and Acquisitions

Small- and medium-sized companies may not have someone with such a specialized position, but if the company has been involved in strategic investments and alliances, someone is a decision maker. The person you're looking for may be found in the marketing department, or the R&D division, or in the office of the executive vice president.

FOREIGN STRATEGIC CORPORATE INVESTORS

Don't be afraid to think globally. Foreign companies may provide excellent opportunities. Your search can begin with the Foreign Service Commercial Officer in the U.S. Embassy of the country you're targeting. The U.S. Department of Commerce's International Trade Association has a listing of their sixty-five foreign offices. Other helpful sources are U.S. banks, foreign banks doing business in the U.S., and trade associations and their publications. Foreign trade missions exist in many countries and coordinate their activities with foreign trade mission headquarters in New York, Los Angeles, and Washington. Keep your eye out for the activities of world trade centers. These organization have operations in many U.S. cities and abroad. Watch closely the activities of your competitors and companies in parallel industries: they may be up to something overseas that you can coattail off of or associate with. There are venture capital firms that concentrate some of their efforts abroad. For example, the Ventana Companies, a venture capital firm in California, has over fifty-five strategic corporate and governmental investment partners in fifteen countries.

Here is a list of the most commonly used foreign company directories.

Principal International Businesses
(annual)
Dun & Bradstreet International
Three Sylvan Way
Parsippany, New Jersey 07054
(201)605-6000 or (800)526-0651

Who Owns Whom
(annual)
Dun's Marketing Services
Three Sylvan Way
Parsippany, New Jersey 07054
(201)605-6000 or (800)526-0651

Standard Directory of Worldwide Marketing
R.R. Bowker/National Register
Publishing Co., Inc.
3004 Glenview Road
Wilmette, Illinois 60091
(708)445-2210 or (800)323-6772

THE NEEDS OF STRATEGIC CORPORATE INVESTORS
The needs of these investors fall into two basic areas: their strategic business needs and their financial investment needs.

STRATEGIC BUSINESS NEEDS
PALC Revisited. Finding companies that may have strategic reasons to invest in your company begins with your insight in existing paradigms at work in the economy. Who are the companies involved in current paradigms? What are their challenges? What help can you provide? How mature are the paradigms? The PALC is the tool for answering these questions. A thorough

understanding of both Disciplines 1 and 5 is essential for uncovering potential strategic corporate investors.

Low-Cost Acquisition. Your company may be an intended target of acquisition by a larger company. If this is the larger company's motive, it will generally invest a small stake and option-out or receive warrants for more stock which can be exercised later, if it feels your company, and their needs, match.

Training Ground. By striking a relationship with your company, and hinging its investment on the right to have its managers and staff "in your house," the larger company can use your company as their "entrepreneurial training ground."

Pick Up the Slack. Your company may offer the larger company an opportunity to keep some of their staff (whom they would otherwise have to let go), or to sublease to you unused office or plant space. Downsizing, for large companies, carries a painful price tag. Your company can help soften the downsizing blow.

Technology on the Run. Earlier you learned that a lot of the technology of most businesses, especially service businesses, is embedded in their employees. Larger companies don't like the prospect of its knowledge-rich employees leaving. It's common for a large company to invest in the start-ups of departing employees as a form of technology retention. This is known as "spinning-out" a business.

FINANCIAL INVESTMENT NEEDS

Large companies don't just throw their money around. Regardless of any compelling strategic business need of theirs that your company meets, they will still handle their investment decisions carefully. Their financial investment needs closely parallel the "Most Desired" venture capital or business angel needs. (You should refer to Illustrations 2-1 and 2-7 for the venture capitalists' and business angels' needs profiles.)

SOURCE III: BUSINESS ANGELS

Definition: A business angel is usually an individual financial investor (as opposed to a strategic investor) who invests in an enterprise directly (instead of through money raisers). He or she will accept a small group of other investors joining in the deal and is not a passive investor in the company.

HOW BIG AND ACTIVE IS THIS MARKET?

Each year at least 1,000,000 new businesses make a go of it. As mentioned earlier, venture capitalists in some years invest in less than 400 start-ups. Who invests in the other 999,600 start-up companies? The Small Business Administration sought to answer this question in 1984, and retained a

Tennessee firm, Applied Economics Group, Inc., to help them. Five years later Robert J. Gaston, the president of that company, published the results in a book titled, *Finding Private Venture Capital For Your Firm*.[16] This section of the book will rely heavily on the findings of this study, which will be referred to as the "SBA Study."

According to the "SBA Study," each year more than 490,000 of the 720,000 business angels in the U.S. commit an average of $25 to $56 billion to 87,000 new companies. This represents up to 267 times the annual investment activity of the venture capital industry, and up to 18 times the dollar amount invested.

Here is what the "SBA Study" found: Of the $56 billion invested each year, $32 billion is straight equity and the other $24 billion is in the form of loans and guarantees. The amount of capital committed in any one year can go as high as $82 billion or as low as $32 billion. Most encouraging is the fact that each year, another $20 billion is available from the 720,000 business angels that is untapped. So the business angel market may be as large as $82 billion. The "SBA Study" claims that 1 of every 250 people is a possible business angel. This means, if your home town has 250,000 residents, then at least 1,000 business angels are in your backyard. The average business angel investment is $37,500, with the largest in the SBA study being $800,000.

BUSINESS ANGELS VS. VENTURE CAPITALISTS

Don't confuse these two groups. There are some important differences in their investment behavior. Remember the credo, "clarity leads to power." Before you design your Capital Relations™ program (Step 5) and Offering Campaign (Step 7), you must clearly understand the differences among the various investor sources, so that you can decide on the right source for your needs.

Illustration 2-2 depicts the differences between business angels and venture capitalists.

THE TYPES OF BUSINESS ANGELS

By definition, a business angel is an individual who supplies risk capital or other financial arrangements to new or growing businesses, generally without the aid of a commissioned money raiser.

Many people assume that anyone with a net worth of over a $1 million automatically falls into the business angel category. However, even though there are approximately two million people in the United States who have a net worth of over $1 million, there are, at the most, only one million business angels; and less than half of those actually invest in any given year. So it's clear that not every millionaire is a business angel. (An interesting aside can be mentioned here. American millionaires have an average annual income of

ILLUSTRATION 2-2:
THE INVESTMENT BEHAVIOR OF BUSINESS ANGELS VS. VENTURE CAPITALISTS

Business Angels...	*Venture Capitalists...*
Accept more deals (20% acceptance rate).	Don't accept many deals (1% acceptance rate, at most).
Love local companies.	Want regional or national companies.
Have more capital than deals.	Have more deals than capital.
Have no formal trade associations or clubs.	Highly organized.
Are very private people (shun spotlight).	Are very public people (love spotlight).
Offer one source financing (equity and debt from one place).	Can offer one source financing.
Use their own money.	Are money managers for institutions, pension funds, partnerships, etc.
Tend to rely on inner circle for deals.	Look for deals everywhere and from everyone.
Make small investments ($37,500 average).	Make large investments. (Rarely invest less than $500,000.)
Accept small offerings/placements (72% of their deals are under $500,000.)	Accept large offerings/placements. (Only 15% of their deals are under $500,000.)
Accept private offerings, not public offerings.	Accept mainly private placements, but also some public offerings.
Love start-up companies.	Scared of start-up companies.
Are emotional investors.	As a rule, are real number crunchers, besides being "people oriented."

Illustration 2-2: (continued)
THE INVESTMENT BEHAVIOR OF BUSINESS ANGELS VS. VENTURE CAPITALISTS

Business Angels...	*Venture Capitalists...*
Are active in company (4 out of 5 are active as employees, consultants, and/or members of the board of directors.	Only company activity is membership on board of directors—as long as the leadership team performs well.
Avoid money raisers (and the commissions money raisers charge).	Investors rely on their money managers and general partners.
Are numerous (approximately 720,000)	Are scarce (700 nationwide)
Perform due diligence quickly (1 to 2 weeks)	Perform due diligence slowly (1 to 4 months)
Are located in your backyard (1 angel for every 250 people).	May not be located in your city.

$130,000, while the average annual income of American business angels is only $90,000.) [17]

Although not all millionaires are automatically business angels, they are all potential business angels. Because of this, it will be useful to look at two profiles.[18]

Illustration 2-3 is a demographic profile, and Illustration 2-4 is a psychographic profile of American millionaires.

Illustration 2-3:
DEMOGRAPHIC PROFILE OF AVERAGE AMERICAN MILLIONAIRES

I. **GENERAL INFORMATION**
   1. The average age is 57. Only 10% are under 40.
   2. Grew up in middle or working class families (80% are first-generation millionaires).
   3. Attended some college (15% dropped out by 12th grade).
   4. Approximately 60% are men.
   5. Generally white (40% are WASPS).
   6. Drives an older American car (60%).
   7. Dresses moderately.

ILLUSTRATION 2-3: (CONTINUED)
DEMOGRAPHIC PROFILE OF AVERAGE AMERICAN MILLIONAIRES

II. HOME LIFE

1. Over 80% are married. Many to their high school or college sweethearts.
2. Small families. Two grown children is average.
3. About half of America's millionaires live in working.or middle class neighborhoods. The rest live in nicer neighborhoods.
4. Both husband and wife often work. (The wealthier they are, the less likely the wife is working.)

III. BUSINESS

1. Millionaires are paid for performance. They are generally self-employed (only 16% work for someone else).
2. The gross revenues of most of these companies is between $500,000 and $10,000,000 per year.
3. Average family income is $130,000, but can range from $30,000 to over $1 million.
4. They may have only one part-time employee, or provide jobs for up to 100 people. It depends a lot on the nature of the business.
5. There are only three ways that business owners can get rich in America:
    a. Carve out a *narrow market niche* and charge *premium prices* for their products/services.
    b. Develop a *unique application* of a mundane process or product that has a *broad market*.
    c. *Superior management* can squeeze extra profits from any market.

ILLUSTRATION 2-4:
PSYCHOGRAPHIC PROFILE OF AVERAGE AMERICAN MILLIONAIRES

I. GENERAL ATTITUDE

1. Have a tremendous need for power, control and approval.
2. Don't feel rich and do not flaunt their wealth.
3. They are frugal bargain hunters.
4. Defer gratification today to create a better tomorrow.
5. Have a nose for opportunity and are good at getting and processing information.
6. Independent thinkers who believe in their own decision making abilities
7. Politically conservative.

ILLUSTRATION 2-4: (CONTINUED)
PSYCHOGRAPHIC PROFILE OF AVERAGE AMERICAN MILLIONAIRES

II. ATTITUDE TOWARD MONEY

1. Highly money motivated and prefer money over material things. (They believe money can buy happiness, love, acceptance, security, etc.).
2. Hate paying taxes.
3. Favor direct ownership of assets they can control such as their own businesses or real estate.
4. Aggressive growth-oriented investors and are very interested in increasing their wealth. (They are willing to take controlled risks.)
5. A small minority favor defensive investments.
6. Seek to minimize their personal financial exposure in business and investment deals. (Like to use Other Peoples' Money to enhance their own wealth.)

III. TOP PRIORITIES

1. Business or career success.
2. Financial security for their families.
3. Maximizing returns from their careers and their investments.
4. Providing an excellent education for their children.

IV. BIGGEST FEARS

1. The IRS and taxes.
2. Their children ending up as failures.
3. Losing all of their money and power (particularly strong among people who grew up in poverty).

BUSINESS ANGELS ARE ACCUMULATORS

People wealthy enough to be considered potential business angels fall into one of two categories. They are either accumulators or preservers. You want to steer clear of the preservers and seek out the accumulators. Retirees and inheritors are most likely to be preservers, and they are not, as a rule, business angels. Business angels can be divided into five career categories:

- Business owners
- Key executives
- Self-employed professionals
- Sales and marketing professionals
- All others (including entertainment and sports personalities)

It is important to know the emotional trigger of these five career categories. Business angels decide to invest on emotion, and then justify their decision by looking at your numbers. Nearly 70% of all business angels are business owners, 20% are sales and marketing professionals, and the other categories make up the remaining 10%. As a rule, business angels are twenty years older than the CEO of the company they invest in. Later, in Steps 6 and 7, when your first Capital Relations™ program and Offering Campaign Plan are being developed, you will want to incorporate into your planning the distinctions shown in the following illustration.

ILLUSTRATION 2-5:
THE CAREER CATEGORIES AND EMOTIONAL TRIGGERS OF BUSINESS ANGELS

Business angel category	Emotional trigger
Business owners	Power / Control / Profits
Key executives	Security / Agency power
Self-employed professionals	Ego / Bragging rights
Sales and marketing professionals	Freedom / Profits
Other (including entertainment and sports)	Varies widely

WHERE TO FIND BUSINESS ANGELS

Since there are no business angel associations or directories, it is difficult to compile a list of qualified persons. The discussion of *tactics*, and *tools*, in Step 6 will be your guide for finding these angels. Lately there have been a number of venture capital "clubs" and "networks" popping up around the country. In addition, there are several computer-based matchmaking services. For example, in 1993 the Missouri State Department of Economic Development formed a matchmaking network called the Confidential Investors Network, Inc. to match business angels with entrepreneurs.[19] Some of these clubs and networks are legitimate, while others are fly-by-night operations. The addresses below may be helpful.

Clubs:

Association of Venture Clubs
235 East 100 South, Suite 300
Salt Lake City, Utah 84110-3358
(801)364-1100

Networks:

Venture Capital Network
Box 882
Durham, New Hampshire 03874
(607)862-3558

The Needs of Business Angels

Not surprisingly, the needs of business angels differ from those of venture capitalists. On the one hand, venture capitalists tend to flock together. In other words, at any one time, the investment criteria of the majority of venture capital firms are the same. Business angels, on the other hand, have diverse needs.[20] They carry a mixed bag of idiosyncrasies and prejudices. Nevertheless, the following information can serve as your guide to understanding the needs of the business angel market.

The Messages They Relate To. Business angels relate easiest to the Industry Superstar, Profitable Company, and the Great American Product/Exit Game messages. However, they are smart enough and open enough to listen and respond to the Visionary Business Builders message if it is presented well.

Familiarity Index Rating. Generally business angels need a Familiarity Index Rating of 3, 5, or 6 (see Step 5). Business angels definitely need to personally know the leadership team, or at least know a great deal about them (see Step 6).

Location of Operations. Business angels, as a rule, want to be able to drive over and see your leadership team in action. It's fine if your market is more than local, but business angels like to be close to you.

Growth Track. Like venture capitalists, business angels invest in companies with a sizable market. Your company should be able to generate sales fast, and your market should either be historically stable or have recently become exciting. Business angels are quick to spot trends and will take a chance to invest in a new trend if they believe you're set up to capitalize on it fast and to quickly get out with cash. But they are not interested in "short-lived fads."

Return on Investment. Business angels shoot for an annual return in excess of 20%. They are not much different than venture capitalists on how much they expect to make. However, business angels will usually accept a lot more risk than venture capitalists.[21]

Exit Time. Until the American investor market becomes enlightened about the advantages of investing in Visionary Business Builders, your business plan needs to show a strong likelihood that the business angel will be able to exit, cash-out, or have a high cash flow within five years. Although they will accept a higher risk of loss than venture capitalists, they expect you to plan an exit through a sale of your business, a merger, or another round of financing.

The Leadership Team. Business angels, like venture capitalists, need a leadership team that makes them feel confident that promises will be kept.

Industry. Business angels are not picky about industries. What they are more concerned with are these questions: Is your deal exciting? Will it make money? Are you experienced and qualified? Business angels will look at a deal in any industry that answers these questions positively.

Types of Products/Services. Business angels love the NPLP, but will look at any type of product/service, if your "success formula" is clear and believable and either your market niche is deep or you are creating a new market. There is no escaping the organizational work of Step 1. Your idea has to pop out and be both exciting and attainable. "Me-to" products/services put business angels to sleep.

Proprietary Nature of Product/Service. Like venture capitalists, business angels expect you to protect what can be protected. (See the earlier discussion of this topic in the venture capital section of this chapter.)

Psychological Needs. As a rule, business angels are people who have already made their mark in the world at least once or twice. Having done so,

ILLUSTRATION 2-6:
PSYCHOLOGICAL NEEDS OF BUSINESS ANGELS

Psychological needs	*Your response*
Need to avoid boredom.	Your deal must excite them.
Feels "over the hill."	They can still contribute.
Wants to contribute more to society	Added value. Social responsibility.
Would like to sit on an outside board of directors.	Put them on your board of directors.
Feels bad that children didn't turn out well.	You can be the kind of child they never had.
Feels bad that their business has not been sold.	Buy or merge your business with theirs.
Greediness.	Your deal is going to make them money.
Afraid of dying.	Your deal will give them a reason to live. They're needed.
Feels grateful for having had a good life.	Help others have a good life. Share with you but not fully retiring.
Wants to take care of their child.	Your company has a place for their child.
They haven't had any fun yet.	Your company will be a fun place for them.
Feel they were not acknowledged enough during their career.	You make them feel important—just like a "king".

they possess many personal qualities that can be capitalized upon. Also remember that business angels are usually at least twenty years older than the CEOs of the companies they invest in. Illustration 2-6 presents a list of some of the psychological tendencies of business angels that you might encounter and what you can do to capitalize on them.

Product/Service Development Level. Business angels will take chances. They probably won't consider concept level deals, but seed and development level deals are acceptable. Where else can they find the thrill? The earlier the development level, the higher the balance sheet should be to justify their investment risk.

Stage of Growth. One of the best things about business angels is that they are eager to finance start-up operations. Like venture capitalists, business angels find businesses desirable that are breaking even financially, even though they are still in the stage of the basic development of their product/service potential.

Liquidity Track. Business angels want liquidity when they can get it. It will help you to construct a logical and aggressive Liquidity Track. Keep in mind that less than one half of one percent of the businesses in this country are publicly-held. You have to keep a watchful eye for every opportunity to register your company on the ever expanding securities exchanges.

Exit Tract. Some business angels have the same requirements as venture capitalists. Your exit time and your exit track have to mesh with each other.

Presentation Documents. Business angels, like venture capitalists, want to see your business plan and your executive summary. Whether or not you use a private placement memorandum depends on many factors. A complete discussion of compliance with securities laws is not the aim of this book.

Ownership. Business angels take the position that "cash talks" and that they deserve every bit of ownership that they can negotiate for. However 85% of the business angels in America expect to end up in a minority position in the companies they invest in. Smart business angels know from experience that the leadership team has to have an incentive to do a good job. There must be enough on the table for everyone. Leadership team "earn-ins" and "flip flopping" of ownership percentages are attractive to business angels. Business angels like the leadership team to earn the right for their control and stake. (See the discussion on "Current Financing Instruments" in Step 5.)

Number of Co-investors. The "SBA Study" discovered that business angels most often invest in deals when there are no more than four other investors. Who the other investors are is important to business angels. Most business angel financing (82%) are under $500,000.

Types of Financing. Business angels prefer to invest in deals where there is a "thrill with the ride." They like to take on the risks associated with early-stage financing. And while venture capitalists are not interested in direct participation offerings (discussed in Step 5), business angels are great candidates for them. Business angels prefer simple and straightforward offerings.

Leadership Team Involvement. Unlike venture capitalists, four out of five business angels participate in the companies they invest in. Their involvement ranges from board membership, to "as needed" consulting, to staff employment (one out of five business angels become full-time employees).

Warrants and Future Underwriting Rights. Business angels naturally like to receive whatever future rights the company is willing to give them. Warrants on stock and inexpensive options are attractive. Later steps will explain the considerations that go into deciding what to offer to business angels.

Due Diligence Time Requirements. One of the main advantages of business angel financing is that they tend to be quick to respond. Since they have no fiduciary responsibilities (except to themselves), they can perform due diligence a lot easier than venture capitalists. Even business angels who invest from their own corporate pension plans (which implies a certain fiduciary responsibility), generally move due diligence along quickly.

Illustration 2-7 summarizes the needs of business angels.

ILLUSTRATION 2-7:
PROFILE OF BUSINESS ANGELS' NEEDS

	Most desired	Acceptable	Unlikely
Message they relate to	Industry Superstar Profitable company GAPE	Visionary Business Builder	A poorly presented Visionary Business Builder message
Familiarity Index	6	3 or 5	1,2,4
Location of operation	Local	Local home office Regional markets	Home office more than 50 miles away
Growth track	Shows $5–10 million sales in 5 years	The profit is real, regardless of sales volume and growth	Stagnant industry
Return on investment	25+%	20+%	Under 15%
Exit time	2–3 years	5–7 years	Over 10 years
Leadership team	Full team with all qualities	Partial team with most qualities	One-man show with no plans for team
Industry	High-tech Life science	Almost anything	Dying industry

ILLUSTRATION 2-7: (CONTINUED)
PROFILE OF BUSINESS ANGELS' NEEDS

	Most desired	Acceptable	Unlikely
Type of product/ service	NPLP	Evolutionary, revolutionary, or substitutes	"Me too"
Proprietary products / services	Absolute protection with patents, etc.	No protection, but "first with most" and monopoly evident	No protection, not "first with most" and no monopoly
Psychological needs	"I get to contribute" and "Make money"	"Make money" and socially responsible	Low return and "Same old thing"
Product/service development level:			
Concept			X
Seed		X	
Product Devel.	X		
Market Devel.	X		
Static		X	
Stage of company growth:			
1. Research		X	
2. Development	X	X	
3. Losing money & proven dist.	X	X	
4. Breakeven	X	X	
5. Profits — need capital		X	
6. Profits — need major expansion		X	
7. IPO / Sale			X
Liquidity track	Stock exchange in 3–10 years	Sale of business	No public trading and weak exit track
Exit track	IPO almost guaranteed	Sale of business or high cash flow	None planned
Presentation documents	Executive summary Business plan	Executive summary Business plan	Executive summary only

ILLUSTRATION 2-7: (CONTINUED)
PROFILE OF BUSINESS ANGELS' NEEDS

	Most desired	Acceptable	Unlikely
Ownership	As much as needed for projected return and control of company if management fails	Will take minority positions with voting control	Minority position without voting control
Number of co-investors	1–3	3–15	Over 15
Financings:			
Seed		X	
Development	X		
Expansion	X		
Bridge			X
LBO			X
Acquisition	X		
Turnaround		X	
Refinance			X
Direct participation offerings		X	
Leadership team involvement	Board of directors	Consultant Employee	None offered
Warrants and future underwriting	If offered	None	If offered to some investors and not them
Due diligence time	60 days	30 days	7 days

SOURCE IV: ADVENTURE STOCKHOLDERS

Definition: An adventure stockholder is an entity or individual who makes a passive investment in an enterprise, either directly or indirectly (through a money raiser), and is usually one of many investors in the business.

HOW BIG AND ACTIVE IS THIS MARKET?

As we discussed earlier, the venture capital community invests in less than one half of one percent of the new businesses each year, and business angels invest in about 14%. Where does the remaining 85+% of America's new businesses get their financing from? The answer is by no means clear. A large percentage is either self-financed or bank financed. Another large percentage is financed through the strategic corporate investor market and the adventure stockholder market. How much is actually invested by the adventure stockholder market is pure speculation.

A conservative estimate is that this market invests at least as much as the business angel market. If so, the adventure stockholders market would be investing at least $85 billion annually. However, there are a great many more adventure stockholders than there are business angels in the United States. We can infer that the total size of the adventure stockholder market, in terms of available dollars to invest, is three to five times the size of the business angel market. It would not be unreasonable then to estimate the size of the investing adventure stockholder market to be $200 billion strong.

THE TYPES OF ADVENTURE STOCKHOLDERS

Almost every breathing person or active corporation is a potential adventure stockholder. This market is the largest investor market segment in terms of the number of participants. The "Affluent American Market" is growing seven times faster than the household population.[22] Finding adventure stockholders is easier than finding business angels (how to do this is discussed in Step 6). Many adventure stockholders are retired business angels—that is, they are people with money who want to be more passive with their investments than they were while active as business angels. Another type of adventure stockholder is the private trust/corporation that is often domiciled in a foreign tax haven (offshore) with an appointed United States manager. This is a very low profile source of investor capital.

As a rule, these investors look for emerging companies on a fast track for an IPO offering. One kind of offering they find attractive is a warrant offering entitling them to the right to purchase common stock slightly below the market or asking price. These investors want companies that price the IPO offering at $5 or above so the stock can be used for margin account transactions.

There are also two types of corporate adventure stockholders. The first are the LBO associations structured as limited partnerships with insurance companies, pension funds, and family funds. These syndicated pools prefer mature companies that are usually already public. The second type of corporate adventure stockholders are insider or buyers groups who want to take companies private by buying out the existing stockholders. Corporate adventure stockholders are not interested in early-stage companies, so the rest of this discussion will focus primarily on individual adventure stockholders.

Individual adventure stockholders, like business angels, are either accumulators or preservers. If possible, you want to market to adventure stockholders who are accumulators. Accumulators have worked hard to make their money and they invest it to enhance their financial position. Preservers are either inheritors of their money or retirees, so their motives tend to center around safety and "coupon-clipping" activities.

Adventure stockholders fall into the same five career categories that were identified for business angels in the last section:

- Business owners
- Key executives
- Self-employed professionals
- Sales and marketing professionals
- All others (including entertainment and sports personalities)

Adventure stockholders invest on the basis of emotion even more than business angels do, so it is important to know the emotional triggers for each of the career categories as shown in Illustration 2-8.

ILLUSTRATION 2-8:
THE CAREER CATEGORIES AND EMOTIONAL TRIGGERS OF ADVENTURE STOCKHOLDERS

Adventure stockholder category	Emotional triggers
Business owners	Profits
Key executives	Security/Agency power
Self-employed professionals	Ego/Bragging rights
Sales and marketing professionals	Freedom/Profit
Other (including entertainment and sports)	Varies widely

Keep in mind that the biggest differences between a business angel and an adventure stockholder is that the latter expects to exert little control over his or her investment and generally invests as part of a large group—in fact, the more the merrier—and they do invest through money raisers.

WHERE TO LOOK FOR ADVENTURE STOCKHOLDERS

As you might expect, there are no directories, networks, or associations that focus exclusively on adventure stockholders. The venture clubs, listed in the business angel discussion, have both business angel and adventure stockholder members. Also the financial services industry has developed lists of potential investors, all of whom are potential adventure stockholders.

The following list of brokers can help you select lead lists. Remember, 5% of America's households control 50% of the personal wealth in this country.

Business Lists:	Consumer/Residential Lists:
American Business Information 5711 South 86 Circle Omaha, Nebraska 68127 (402)593-4600	Metro Mail 901 West Bond Street Lincoln, Nebraska 68521 (402)475-4591
Dun & Bradstreet Three Sylvan Way Parisppany, New Jersey 07054 (800)526-0651	R.L. Plok 4850 Baumgartner Road, Suite 200 St. Louis, Missouri 63129 (314)894-3590
Investor Profiles P.O. Box 838 New York, New York 10010	

THE NEEDS OF ADVENTURE STOCKHOLDERS

As you'll learn later in this step, Investor Financing™ is done either through the Direct Placement Approach or the Money Raiser Approach, or a combination of both. As a rule, venture capitalists and business angels are only accessed through the Direct Placement Approach, whereas strategic corporate investors and adventure stockholders can be accessed through either approach.

The profile of adventure stockholder needs, listed below, is to be used when you are using the Direct Placement Approach. (If you plan to use the Money Raiser Approach, then the profile of money raisers needs, which appears later in this step, should be incorporated into your planning for accessing adventure stockholders.)

The Message They Relate To. Like business angels, this group is conditioned for the Industry Superstar, Profitable Company, and Great American Product/Exit Game messages. Also like business angels, they are smart enough to listen to a well-presented Visionary Business Builder message.

Familiarity Index Rating. For early-stage companies, adventure stockholders need a Familiarity Index Rating of 3, 5, or 6 (see Step 6).

Location of Operations. Adventure stockholders are not as sensitive as business angels about the locations of your operations. But it does make sense to look for adventure stockholders in your own area first.

Growth Track. Adventure stockholders, like the other investor sources, prefer to invest in companies with a sizable market. Your company should be able to generate sales fast, and your market should either be historically stable or appear ready to take off.

Return on Investment. An annual return of 20% is acceptable to most adventure stockholders, particularly if your company is at growth stage 3 or later. If you have a growth stage 1 or 2 company, then you should plan on showing a 30+% annual return.

Exit Time. Just as with venture capitalists and business angels, your business plan needs to show a strong likelihood that your adventure stockholders will be able to exit or cash-out within five years.

The Leadership Team. Adventure stockholders, like the other investor sources, need a leadership team that makes them feel confident that your promises will be carried out.

Industry. It doesn't matter too much to adventure stockholders what industry you're in. They will look at deals in most industries—if your deal is exciting, if it will make money, and if you're experienced and qualified.

Types of Products/Services. Adventure stockholders will look at any type of product/service.

Proprietary Nature of Product/Service. Like the other investor sources, adventure stockholders expect you to protect what can be protected.

Psychological Needs. Unlike business angels, adventure stockholders are not, as a rule, financially independent. They will not necessarily be older than you and your leadership team. (See Illustration 2-9.)

ILLUSTRATION 2-9:
PSYCHOLOGICAL NEEDS OF ADVENTURE STOCKHOLDERS

Psychological needs	*Your Response*
Don't want to be active.	You provide a passive investment opportunity.
Do·not feel "over the hill.	They can start contributing.
Want to contribute more to society.	Added value. Social responsibility.
Very busy with their own business affairs.	Don't put them on your board of directors.
Greediness.	Your deal is going to make them money.
Need to take care of family.	Your company builds their worth.
Need freedom.	Don't ask them to help you.
Need to have their financial consultant look at deal.	You will give their consultants whatever they need.

Product/Service Development Level. Adventure stockholders, as a rule, take fewer chances than do business angels. These investors prefer that other investors take the risk on concept or seed level financing. However, if your company can convey a powerful Great American Product/Exit Game message and you're at the product/service level or market development level, there is a good chance that money raisers can obtain adventure stockholders to invest in your company.

Stage of Company Growth. Adventure stockholders may not be as aggressive as business angels, but if you have a strong NPLP story, adventure stockholders will even invest in a company at growth stage 1 or 2.

Liquidity Track. Adventure stockholders want liquidity when they can get it. It will help you to construct a logical and aggressive liquidity track.

Exit Tract. Adventure stockholders have the same requirements as venture capitalists and business angels. Your exit time and your exit track have to mesh with each other.

Presentation documents. Be ready with your executive summary, business plan, and, in most cases, a private placement memorandum. Securities compliance will be a major issue in most adventure stockholder financing. When accessing adventure stockholder capital, plan to ask for less money from each stockholder than you would if you were dealing with business angels.

Ownership. There isn't a rule of thumb for how much ownership, if any, that you'll have to give up. But "Step 8: Testing the Market" will allow you to determine what will be necessary.

Number of Co-investors. "The more, the merrier," is the appropriate attitude when approaching adventure stockholders. They derive comfort from knowing that a lot of investors support the company. Compliance with securities laws will, in some cases, limit the number of investors that you may have in your current offering if it is a private placement.

Types of Financing. Unlike the situation for the other investor sources, any kind of financing can be structured for adventure stockholders, especially if you're approaching adventure stockholders through money raisers. You'll find that one of the strengths of money raising firms is that they can work with any type of financing. This will be discussed in detail later in this chapter in the section on money raisers.

Leadership Team Involvement. As we've said, adventure stockholders want to remain passive. They want you to run the show. All they want are their dividends, their profits, and their reports.

Warrants and Future Underwriting Rights. Like the other investor sources, adventure stockholders naturally like to receive whatever future rights the company is willing to give them. If you're approaching adventure stockholders through money raisers, you'll find that they will be very concerned about the nature of the warrants and future underwriting rights they can negotiate for. They want dilution protection if possible.

Due Diligence Time Requirements. If you are using the Direct Placement Approach to access adventure stockholders, you will find that their due diligence time will usually be controlled by their financial advisors (CPAs, attorneys, financial consultants, etc.). When approaching adventure stockholders through money raisers, you'll find that the length of time it takes for due diligence is directly tied to policies and requirements of the money raisers themselves.

Illustration 2-10 summarizes the needs of adventure stockholders.

ILLUSTRATION 2-10: PROFILE OF ADVENTURE STOCKHOLDERS' NEEDS			
	Most desired	*Acceptable*	*Unlikely*
Message they relate to	Industry Superstar Profitable company GAPE	Visionary Business Builder	A poorly presented Visionary Business Builder message
Familiarity Index	6	3 or 5	1,2,4
Location of operation	Local	Home office in the region	Home office and operations more than 200 miles away
Growth track	Growth Plan shows $50–100 million in 5 years	The profit is real regardless of sales volume and growth	Stagnant industry
Return on investment	25–30%	15–20%	10%
Exit time	2–3 years	5–7 years	Over 10 years
Leadership team	Full team with all qualities	Partial team with most qualities	One-man show with no plans for team
Industry	High-tech Life science	Almost anything	Dying industry
Type of product/ service	NPLP	Evolutionary, revolutionary, or substitutes	"Me too"

ILLUSTRATION 2-10: (CONTINUED)
PROFILE OF ADVENTURE STOCKHOLDERS' NEEDS

	Most desired	Acceptable	Unlikely
Proprietary products / services	Absolute protection with patents, etc.	No protection, but "first with most" and monopoly evident	No protection, not "first with most" and no monopoly
Psychological needs	Passive and and "Make money"	"Make money" and contribute	No profit likely
Product/service development level:			
Concept			X
Seed			X
Product Devel.		X	
Market Devel.		X	
Static	X		
Stage of company growth:			
1. Research		X	
2. Development		X	
3. Losing money & proven dist.		X	
4. Breakeven	X	X	
5. Profits — need capital		X	
6. Profits — need major expansion		X	
7. IPO / Sale	X	X	
Liquidity track	Stock exchange in 3–6 years	Stock exchange in 5-10 years	No public trading and weak exit track
Exit track	IPO almost guaranteed	Sale of business or high cash flow	None planned
Presentation documents	Executive summary Business plan Private placement memorandums	Executive summary Business plan Private placement memorandums	Executive summary only
Ownership	As much as needed for projected return and control of company if management fails	Whatever their advisors say is ok.	Whatever their advisors say is not ok.

ILLUSTRATION 2-10: (CONTINUED)
PROFILE OF ADVENTURE STOCKHOLDERS' NEEDS

	Most desired	Acceptable	Unlikely
Number of co-investors	15–20	20–100	3–5
Financings:			
Seed		X	
Development		X	
Expansion	X	X	
Bridge			X
LBO		X	
Acquisition			X
Turnaround			X
Refinance		X	
Direct participation offerings	X	X	
Leadership team Involvement	None	Board of directors	Employment
Warrants and future underwriting	If offered	None	If offered to some investors and not them
Due diligence time	60 days (120 days for money raisers)	30 days	10 days

SOURCE V: THE VISIONARY CAPITAL MARKET

Definition: Visionary Capital is a source of Investor Financing™ that is invested for financial and/or strategic reasons in Visionary Business Builders.

The Visionary Capital market is listed last because, as of the date of this book's publication, this market has not yet emerged. Most of the information about the sector is conjecture—an educated guess about the future.

What could be more appropriate for the new economy than to have a source of capital that is in step with it? Even if the new economy were not rewriting so many business rules, the old economy of information was still in need of a new source of capital. Here is how *Fortune* magazine described the situation in 1995 in an article titled, "Who Will Feed the Start-ups?":

> For a glorious three decades, American Venture Capitalists did a lot of good for the economy, while also doing very well for

themselves. Arthur Rock and Tom Perkins (Kleiner, Perkins, et al), among others, got famous and rich helping start and build high-tech stars like Intel, Apple Computer and Genetech. But now, the company creation machine that has been the envy of the world is sputtering. There's even a question whether organized Venture Capital is the best way to finance a start-up. If Steven Jobs (of Apple Computer fame) walked into a Venture Capitalist office today, he would have no chance of getting financed.[23]

So we think the timing is perfect as the millennium approaches to suggest that a new market sector, or even industry, should emerge to finance the Knowledge/Creation Economy. What the venture capital industry did for the Information Economy, the Visionary Capital industry will do for the new economy.

A New Trade Group. Although still a guess, odds are great that the Visionary Capital industry will be formalized, yet carry on in an informal basis. Look for a formal Visionary Capital trade association by 2005. We envision that by then, enough capital market infrastructure will have formed, and enough emerging businesses will give credit to the Visionary Business Builder model, for their financing and growth success.

Who Will Play. Venture capitalists will show up for two reasons: 1) they may feel guilty for abandoning start-ups in the mid- to late-1990s, and 2) venture capitalists will awaken to a new world beyond the Information Age investing model of product/exit centricity. They will find exciting and promising the prospects offered by the Visionary Business Builder.

Business angels, strategic corporate investors, and adventure stockholders will show up even before the venture capitalists. Why? Because there will be thousands of entrepreneurs teaching and preaching the tidings about the Visionary Business Builder paradigm. There will be a conversion in this country by a significant percentage of the private investor community—although not by all. The converted will awaken to the logic and reasonableness of the Visionary Business Builder model. They will be inspired by the tight fit this new model has in the new economy. Once the theories, principles, and practices of the new economy are accepted and widespread, the Visionary Business Builder model will seem like it's been around forever. In point of fact, the heart and soul of this model has been with us for a while; it just took two determined researchers—Jim Collins and Jerry Porras of the Stanford Graduate School of Business—to lock onto the reality and make it visible for the rest of us to see and use. Even the traditional banking community may join in, once they fully accept the challenge of lending on the important assets of

Intellectual Capital. When they do, the Visionary Business Builder model will be an indispensable part of their underwriting model. It has to be, since the Visionary Business Builder model defines the profile of success in the new economy. The Institutional investor markets may be playing as well. The 1990s trend of institutional investors allocating an ever larger percentage of their investments to alternative investments may continue. Alternative investments will continue to include start-ups.[24]

Where to Find Visionary Capitalists

At the time of this book's publication, there are no trade associations, clubs, or networks for visionary capitalists. Not yet anyway. The author and his associates will have this information when it surfaces. Until then, visionary capitalists will be any investors that are fortunate enough to have the foresight to invest now in a Visionary Business Builder. It is the challenge for these business builders to teach, coach, and sell investors on the validity of investing in this new model. It will be the entrepreneurs themselves who will create this new capital sector. Just like the birth of the venture capital industry thirty years ago, the Visionary Capital industry will be spawned by courageous, forward thinking ex-entrepreneurs and ex-business builders.

The Needs of Visionary Capitalists

The Message They Relate To. visionary capitalists will listen to Visionary Business Builders.

Familiarity Index Rating. Like the Visionary Business Builder model itself, and its Human Capital centricity, visionary capitalists will need a Familiarity Index Rating of 2, 3, 5, or 6. visionary capitalists will need to know personally, or know about, the management team.

Location of Operations. The location of operations will not be critically important. The closer the better, but it's not a deal-breaking point.

Growth Track. visionary capitalists will concentrate on high growth, not fast growth that venture capitalists favor. The Launch Plan will be very important and a strong Growth Plan will be a necessity.

Return on Investment. visionary capitalists will be satisfied with the Launch Plan forecasting a positive cash flow so the company can pay for its own way into the future. The Growth Plan will indicate the size of the potential new market/industry. Since there will be no financial forecasts with the Growth Plan an inference by the investor will have to be made.

Exit Time. This is not an issue for the Visionary Capitalist.

The Leadership Team. visionary capitalists will want the "Big 3" in place. The Evidence Points in the business plan will have to convince the investors that the five disciplines of the Visionary Business Builder are present.

Industry. This is not an issue. Visionary capitalists will be attracted to Industry Superstars because they know that these kind of business builders can change paradigms.

Types of Products/Services. Not an issue. Visionary capitalists just want an NPLP that can drive a successful Launch Plan.

Proprietary Nature of Product/Service. Visionary capitalists expect you to protect as much of the structural capital components of your Intellectual Capital as possible.

Psychological Needs. Since visionary capitalists are really an evolutionary development of the other investor sources, the psychological needs remain the same.

Product/Service Development Level. The Launch Plan product/service development level is immaterial so long as the Launch Plan reflects a breakeven or profitable company in twelve to twenty-four months. The development level of the product/service for the Growth Plan is irrelevant. What is relevant is the existence of a Paradigm Vision.

Stage of Growth. Visionary capitalists will go with early-stage companies if the Launch Plan is solid and there are lots of Evidence Points in the business plan.

Liquidity Track. Visionary capitalists want liquidity when they can get it, but it is not a condition of their investing.

Exit Track. Visionary capitalists take the approach that their exit should be at the same time that the management team and/or the majority shareholders leave.

Presentation Documents. Business plans and executive summaries are important. Whether or not a private placement memorandum is necessary depends on the securities compliance issues involved.

Ownership. A fair stake is all they ask for. What is most important is the leadership team's percentage of ownership and how they "earned it." Venture Capitalists love leadership teams with a high stake paid for in cash or real sweat equity. They also love leadership teams that have "earn-in" formulas and "legended stock."

Number of Co-Investors. Smart visionary capitalists will enjoy the comfort of a crowd. The quality of the co-investors is critical to visionary capitalists.

Types of Financing. Visionary capitalists prefer to invest in deals where there is a "thrill in the ride." They will like early-stage start-ups. Direct Participation Offerings will be acceptable, especially if attached with warrants, options, or conversion to common stock rights.

Leadership Team Involvement. The smart visionary capitalists will stay out of the management team's way. These investors make themselves available as a resource only when asked.

Warrants and Future Underwriting Rights. These are very attractive to visionary capitalists.

Due Diligence Time Requirements. This will vary depending on the size of the Visionary Capitalist's firm. The smaller the firm, the better the chances are for a fast look and approval.

Illustration 2-11 summarizes the needs of visionary capitalists.

Illustration 2-11:
Profile of Visionary Capitalists' Needs

	Most desired	Acceptable	Unlikely
Message they relate to	Visionary Business Builder	NPLP Profitable company	Industry Superstar GAPE
Familiarity Index	6	2,3,5	1 or 4
Location of operation	Location not critical, but local preferred	Local home office Regional markets	Doesn't matter if rest is OK
Growth track	High growth	Fast growth	Low growth
Return on investment	Paradigm Vision and compnay breaks even in 12 months	Paradigm Vision and company breakeven in 24 months	No Launch Plan or Paradigm Vision
Exit time	Not an issue	Not an issue	Not an issue
Leadership team	"Big 3" with all qualities	Partial team with most qualities	One-man show with no plans for team
Industry	Not an issue Loves strategies	Almost anything	Dying industry
Type of product/ service	NPLP	High value	High volume
Proprietary products / services	Absolute protection with patents, etc.	No protection, but "first with most" and monopoly evident	No protection, not "first with most" and no monopoly

ILLUSTRATION 2-11: (CONTINUED)
PROFILE OF VISIONARY CAPITALISTS' NEEDS

	Most desired	Acceptable	Unlikely
Psychological needs	"I get to contribute" and "Make money"	"Make money" and socially responsible	Low return and "Same old thing"
Product/service development level:			
Concept			X
Seed		X	
Product Devel.	X		
Market Devel.	X		
Static		X	X
Stage of company growth:			
1. Research		X	
2. Development	X	X	
3. Losing money & proven dist.	X	X	
4. Breakeven	X	X	
5. Profits — need capital		X	
6. Profits — need major expansion		X	
7. IPO / Sale			X
Liquidity track	Stock exchange in 3–10 years	Sale of business someday	No public trading and weak exit track
Exit track	Same time as management or majority investors	Sale of business	Different time than management or majority investors
Presentation documents	Executive summary Business plan	Executive summary Business plan	Executive summary only
Ownership	As much as needed for control of company with majority investors if management fails	Will take minority positions	Minority position without vote

ILLUSTRATION 2-11: (CONTINUED)
PROFILE OF VISIONARY CAPITALISTS' NEEDS

	Most desired	Acceptable	Unlikely
Number of co-investors	10–35	3–10	1–2
Financings:			
Seed		X	
Development	X		
Expansion	X		
Bridge			X
LBO			X
Acquisition	X		
Turnaround		X	
Refinance			X
Direct participation offerings		X	
Leadership team involvement	Board of directors	Consultant Employee	None offered
Warrants and future underwriting	If offered	None	If offered to some investors and not them
Due diligence time	60 days	30 days	7 days

INVESTOR FINANCING™ APPROACHES

The next area to survey consists of the two basic approaches that can be used to get closer to your targeted investor source. The Direct Placement Approach involves the CEO working directly with investors, while the Money Raiser Approach involves the CEO working with money raisers (either financial firms or individuals) who represent the investors, and who generally earn a commission or fee for raising capital for the business. These two approaches set the context for your Capital Relations™ program and the tactics and tools that will be used to complete your Offering Campaign. At the outset you should be aware that early-stage companies that are successful in attracting money raisers are companies that also undertake their own Direct Placement efforts. Money raisers feel a lot more comfortable if a company has investors of its own in the deal.

Both of these approaches require special knowledge and skill. Which approach you use will be determined by the Investor Financing™ source you are seeking funding from, as well as a number of other factors that will become clear as you work your way through the Investor Financing™ steps. For example, you have already learned that business angels, as a rule, do not invest through money raisers. This is because business angels don't like to invest in deals that have "loads," or commission charges, on their investments. It is obvious then that you will use the Direct Placement Approach when accessing business angels and venture capitalists. Either approach can be used when accessing strategic corporate investors or adventure stockholders.

THE DIRECT PLACEMENT APPROACH

Don't Be Afraid. Many business people have not had experience in asking people to invest. It's quite natural for them to be nervous, cautious, or even intimidated by the process. However, to be successful in accessing investor capital, the CEO must take on the responsibility of presenting the company and the offering.[25] One valuable by-product of these ten steps is that your confidence will increase significantly, because you will have done your homework. In fact, you might even discover that selling your deal was one of the most exciting and rewarding experiences that you've ever had.

Get Those Skills. The sections in Step 6 on tactics and tools will show you some of the best ways to implement the Investor Financing™ approaches that you've chosen and will give you a repertoire that you can draw on as you develop your Offering Campaign (Steps 7 and 10). However, this may not be enough. If you are inexperienced, you may need to study the techniques used by the best financial product sales professionals.

"Road Shows" and "Dog and Pony Shows." If you thought that you could avoid making presentations to investors by working through money raisers, you're wrong. Money raisers can help you locate investors, but they expect you to be the spokesperson for the company. Even national wirehouse firms like Merrill Lynch require the principals of the firms they fund to make presentations in front of their stockbrokers and investors. These kinds of presentations are called in the business "road shows" or "dog and pony shows."[26]

Showing Money Raisers How To Sell Your Deal. Money raisers will need help in understanding how to sell your company and its offering to their investors. It may sound ridiculous that money raisers, who are usually getting paid healthy fees and commissions, have to be taught how to sell your deal, but it's true. Keep in mind, that no one knows your business as well as you do. Most investors are likely to be motivated more by emotions than they are by facts, so it's up to you to show your money raisers how to sell the deal. You must convey to the money raisers the components that make up your Phenomenal Message and the emotional triggers that will generate a positive response from investors.

THE MONEY RAISER APPROACH

Using the Money Raiser Approach can involve many different kinds of people and firms. The term "money raiser" is a generic term referring to intermediaries that find your investors. These money raisers are often referred to as "the gate keepers of capital." The process of raising investor capital through money raisers is also known as "the investment banking process." So, we will begin the discussion of the Money Raiser Approach with a discussion of investment banking.

Traditional Investment Banking. When a company needs to access investor capital, it can turn to the investment banking community. The term "investment banking" is used very loosely within the financial community. Its meaning can range from "what Wall Street firms do," to such narrowly defined tasks as consulting on a business plan, undertaking a specific underwriting or merger and acquisition search, or performing risk management or fund management. In this book the term "traditional investment banking" means the process of raising investment capital for companies within the public markets. This includes the process of floating securities in the primary markets, and trading securities in the secondary markets. In these processes it is expected that the investment bankers will have a role in setting up standards, conducting due diligence, and establishing prices for the underwriting process in the primary market. They will also broker trades and make markets in the secondary markets.

Non-Traditional Investment Banking. Investment banking is evolving rapidly. More and more firms are hanging out shingles saying they do investment banking. A firm that calls itself an investment banker may seem to you to be a money broker or a business broker.

Regardless of what some of the money raisers call themselves, keep in mind that the money raiser market for investor capital includes many players besides those who call themselves "investment bankers."

Two Worlds. Money raisers fall into two classifications: one group is known as "the securities licensed money raisers" who are regulated by the National Association of Securities Dealers (NASD), and the other group is "the non-securities licensed money raisers." The difference is meaningful because what you can or can't do may be dictated by the securities regulations (or absence thereof) that the money raisers have to operate under. For example, the NASD Rules of Fair Practice prohibit a NASD licensee from participating in an offering where non-NASD licensed money raisers participate and receive commissions. If your Offering Campaign has the potential to use securities licensed and non-licensed money raisers, then you'll need to structure the non-licensed money raisers' compensation in the form of consulting fees, finders fees, or stock payments. You should consult with your attorney about this.

How Big Is the Money Raiser Market?
Securities Licensed Money Raisers. Illustration 2-12 depicts the different kinds of securities licensed money raisers. The NASD reports that there are over 5,400 broker/dealer and stock brokerage firms throughout the United States. All of these firms have one or more sales representatives. The broker/dealers generally refer to sales representatives as "reps," while the stock brokerage firms call their sales representatives "account executives." Only 20% of these firms have more than 100 sales representatives. A few have a great many—Merrill Lynch, for example, has 12,000 sales representatives.

In America, there are over a half million people who carry a NASD license. If every rep averages 100 clients then there are 50,000,000 potential adventure stockholders just from this money raiser segment alone.

The estimated number of securities licensed money raisers in the United States is listed below:

- 500,000 reps (individuals with a securities license)
- 30,000 branch offices of stock brokerage and broker/dealer firms
- 5,000 traditional and an unknown number of non-traditional investment bankers
- 80 independent direct participation offering wholesale firms
- 435 boutique stock brokerage wholesale/market makers
- 100 independent due diligence firms
- 17,000 money manager firms
- 250,000 insurance agents with a securities license

ILLUSTRATION 2-12:
SECURITIES LICENSED MONEY RAISERS

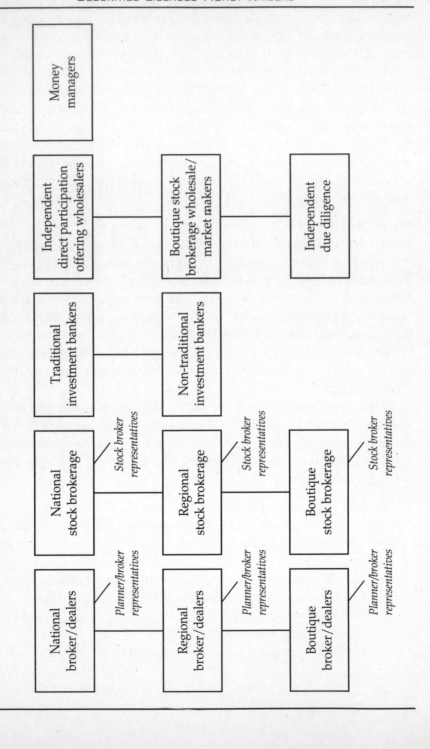

Non-Securities Licensed Money Raisers. Illustration 2-13 depicts the different kinds of non-securities licensed money raisers. The best available estimated number of non-securities licensed money raisers in the United States is listed below:

- An unknown number of LBO Associations (leveraged buyout)
- 20,000 pension advisors/administrators
- 950 fee-only financial planners
- 7,500 registered investment advisors
- 1,000,000 insurance sales people (237,000 of them working full time)
- 3,000 business brokers
- 1,300,000 licensed real estate brokers and agents
- 18,500 companies in the mortgage brokerage business
- 20,000+ business/management consultants
- An unknown number of non-traditional investment bankers
- 800,000 attorneys (of which 30% are specialists in tax, business, or estate planning)
- 318,000 CPAs (with the A.I.C.P.A.)
- 30,000 tax preparers (enrolled agents)
- An unknown number of bookkeepers
- An unknown number of venture and investor clubs
- An uncountable number of money finders.

ILLUSTRATION 2-13:
NON-SECURITIES LICENSED MONEY RAISERS

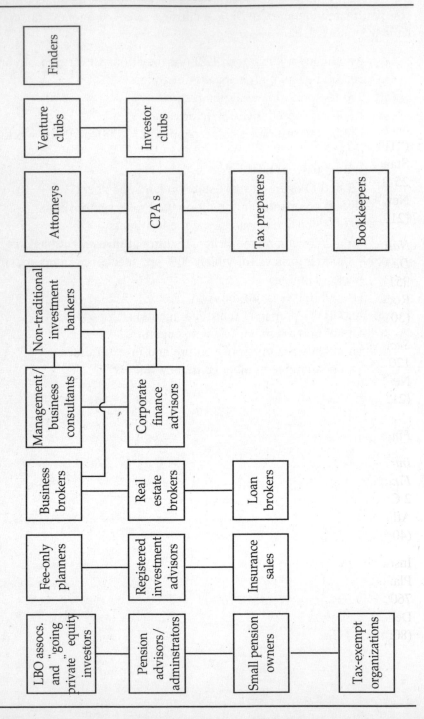

WHERE TO LOOK FOR MONEY RAISERS

Securities Licensed Money Raisers:

National, regional, and boutique stock brokerage and broker/dealer firms

Securities Dealers of North America ("The Red Book") Published by Standard & Poor's Corporation
25 Broadway
New York, New York 10004
(212)208-6500

National Association of SEcurities Dealers
9513 Key West Avenue
Rockville, Maryland 20850
(301)590-6500

Securities Industries Association
120 Broadway, Suite 35
New York, new York 10271
(212)608-1500

Financial planners (the reps):

International Association of Financial Planners
2 Concourse Parkway #800
Atlanta, Georgia 30328
(404)395-1605

Institute of Certified Financial Planners
7600 East Eastman Avenue, #301
Denver, Colorado 80231
(800)282-7526

Investment bankers:

Regional Investment Banking Association
600 Center Avenue, Suite 1220
Highland Park, Illinois 60035
(708)433-5800

Independent wholesalers:

National Association of Financial Wholesalers
2361 Campus Drive, Suite 204
Irvine, California 92715
(714)955-2788

Independent due diligence:

Alliance of Securities Consultants
425 Market Street, #2835
San Francisco, California 94105
(415)512-3591

Money managers:

Association for Investment Management Research
5 Boar's Head Lane
Charlottesvlle, Virginia 22903
(804)977-6600

Association of Investment Management Sales Executives
4380 Georgetown Square
Atlanta, Georgia 30338
(404)455-8923

Non-Securities Licensed Money Raisers:

Leveraged buyout associations and "going private" equity investors:

Pratt's Guide to Venture Capital Sources
Venture Economics Inc.
40 West 57th Street, Suite 802
New York, New York 10019
(212)765-5311

Pension advisors/administrators:

Directory of Pension Funds and Their Investment Managers
Published by Money Market Directories, Inc.
P.O. Box 1608
Charlottesville, Virginia 22902
(800)446-2810

For a profile of 3,000 European funds:

Pension Funds and Their Advisors
Published by Money Market Directories, Inc.
P.O. Box 1608
Charlottesville, Virginia 22902
(800)446-2810.

American Society of Pension Actuaries
4350 North Fairfax Drive
Arlington, Virginia 22203
(703)516-9300

Pension owners:

Directory of Pension Sunds and Their Investment Managers
Published by Money Market Directories, Inc.
P.O. Box 1608
Charlottesville, Virginia 22902
(800)446-2810.

Tax Exempt Organization:

Directory of Tax-Exempt Organizations
Published by Money Market Directories, Inc.
P.O. Box 1608
Charlottesville, Virginia 22902
(800)446-2810.

Fee-only financial planners:

National Association of Personal Financial Advisors
1130 Lake Cook Road, #150
Buffalo Grove, Illinois 60089
(708)537-7722

Registered investment advisors:

Directory of Registered Investment Advisors
Published by Money Market Directories, Inc.
P.O. Box 1608
Charlottesville, Virginia 22902
(800)446-2810.

SECURITIES LICENSED MONEY RAISER PROFILES

One way or another, most money raisers are in the business of advising people about their money and investments. As a rule, business angels work by themselves and not through commissioned money raisers. It's important to remember that money raisers usually represent adventure stockholders. On occasion a money raiser can help you locate and make a deal with a venture capitalist, strategic corporate investor, or Visionary Capitalist. Therefore the entire discussion earlier in this step on sources should be reviewed. Whatever you would have to do to sell directly to one of them, is exactly what your money raiser has to do. This is why it is so important that you try to raise a large percentage of your funding yourself through the Direct Placement Approach. An Offering Campaign balanced between a Direct Placement Approach and a Money Raiser Approach usually provides optimum results. Money raisers for early-stage companies don't want their clients to be the only investors in on the deal—they want the leadership team to directly place their own investors in the offering as well.

National Broker/Dealers. These are the large broker/dealers who usually have 300 or more licensed reps per firm. These reps are financial planners and investment counselors that operate very independently. As a rule, they office everywhere but the home office of the broker/dealer. Most of these firms have so-called corporate finance departments. However, they do not concentrate on corporate financing. Instead, they provide their reps with financial products such as annuities, insurance, partnership products, and mutual funds. You need a selling agreement to raise capital through a broker/dealer. A selling agreement is the contract between the firm and your company which gives you the right to market your offering to the reps in their firm. Selling agreements are given after a company passes the due diligence process used by the broker/dealer.

A national broker/dealer may be brought in as part of a selling group put together by a national or regional stock brokerage firm who is acting as a lead underwriter or broker/manager for an offering. National broker/dealers are not, as a rule, in the business of being the dealer/manager of a corporate securities offering, especially for an early-stage company. To get the attention of a national broker/dealer you would have to have very strong sponsorship (reps who want to sell your deal) of ten to thirty reps who carry clout in the firm. A limited selling agreement (permission to sell through selected reps of the firm) is possible.

It is virtually impossible to get a list of reps from the home office of national broker/dealers until you have a signed selling agreement for your offering. After you sign this agreement, the real marketing starts with the influential reps in the firm through whom you want to sell your offering. (See a further discussion of this in "Step 6: Creating the Capital Relations™ Plan.')

Since these firms already sell a lot of partnership products, direct participation offerings should be the structure of first choice (see Step 5). In addition, since these firms have a broad base of reps, it may be in your best interest (and theirs) for you to consider structuring your offering as a Staying-Private Public Offering™ (Step 5), rather than a private placement, regardless of whether or not the structure is a corporate offering or a direct participation offering.

Regional Broker/Dealers. These firms operate statewide, or at most in a few states. Typically they have between 100 and 300 reps. Reps like working for these firms because they have more influence at the home office than they do in the national firms. This bodes well for you, since a strong rep sponsorship can mean a selling agreement for you (either full or limited). Direct participation offerings are very popular with these firms (see Step 5). So are small Staying Private-Public Offerings™.

It is not uncommon for regional broker/dealers to have corporate finance departments and investment banking subsidiaries or affiliates. These firms definitely want warrants, stock options, rights of first refusal on later financing, etc., to pay them for their efforts.

If you're seeking an early round of financing, your best bet for securing a selling agreement is for you to raise the first two-thirds directly from other sources, or through other money raisers, and then ask the broker/dealer to raise just the last third of your offering. (In the industry this is called "doing the last third.') If your Financing Sequence Plan (see Step 5) calls for subsequent rounds of financing, then a winning strategy is to ask them to "do the last third of the offering," coupled with giving them the right of first refusal on the next financing round. (This is called "doing the last third plus exclusive rights on next round.')

Like the national broker/dealers, lists of the reps of the regional broker/dealers are difficult to come by. The real action is to find the right reps who carry clout with both the home office and other reps in the company. By securing strong rep sponsorship you'll have enough momentum to carry you through the due diligence process at the home office. Be prepared, once you have a selling agreement, to coordinate the entire Offering Campaign yourself. Regional broker/dealers are notoriously inefficient in managing these campaigns.

It is perfectly acceptable to have more than one selling agreement. Your Offering Campaign Plan may require you to "sign on" three or four broker/dealers to sell your offering.

Boutique Broker/Dealers. As a rule, these firms operate in only one part of a state. They usually have fewer than 100 reps. They are small for a reason: reps believe they get more service and have more influence at the home office of a smaller broker/dealer. Obviously, this is a perfect scenario for the small corporate offering. Rep sponsorship is absolutely necessary.

These firms like to do private placements, direct participation offerings, and early-stage deals. Small Staying-Private Public Offerings™ are very useful for boutiques, since the smaller investors of their reps get a chance to invest in exciting, early-stage opportunities.

These firms, as a condition to signing a selling agreement, insist on warrants and options on your stock, and the right of first refusal to do later rounds of financing. Boutiques tend to be a little stronger than regional broker/dealers in helping you push your Offering Campaign through the firm's reps. Definitely consider offering "doing the last third plus exclusive rights on next round"—these firms appreciate this strategy.

National Stock Brokerage Firms. These firms, sometimes called "wirehouses," do not normally participate in financing America's small business community. If your company is to be considered for a deal, your financing request must be in excess of $10 million. If you have some contacts in wirehouse firms, use them to introduce you to investment bankers, or other stock brokerage firms (either regional or boutique). The one exception to this observation about wirehouses is the on-again, off-again activity of their Product Development Partnerships. For example, as of year end 1993, Paine Webber Development Corporation had structured and arranged the financing for product development programs that have provided technology companies with approximately $2 million to develop new products.

Regional Stock Brokerage Firms. These firms are in the market to finance regional companies and to participate in the selling groups of national stock brokerage firms' underwritings. These firms may act as lead underwriters on smaller, local offerings.

When dealing with regional stock brokerage firms you want to try to get account executive support (sponsorship) prior to contacting the home office's corporate finance department. However, this must be arrived at indirectly, since most of these firms will be very "put off" if you directly solicit their account executives first. Instead, sponsorship should be sought through your attorney, CPA, or corporate finance advisor.

Regional stock brokerage firms are excellent at helping you push your Offering Campaign through their branch offices. These firms want to "move" products quickly and to do a volume business. (This kind of attitude does not exist in the broker/dealer firms.) They will do "best efforts" and "firm commitment offerings." Definitely consider offering "doing the last third plus exclusive rights on next round."

Boutique Stock Brokerage Firms. There are more boutique broker/dealers firms than there are boutique stock brokerage firms. It's very difficult to tell in advance if a particular boutique stock brokerage firm emphasizes stocks or concentrates on being a financial planning firm. The way to find out is to ask the senior management of the firm. Even small boutiques carry an active corporate finance department. Sponsorship by reps or through your attorney, CPA, or corporate finance advisor is vital.

In the mid-1980s, a hybrid type of consulting practice emerged known as broker/planners. The strategy of these boutique firms is to entice financial advisors (reps) into joining their firms by offering them more controlled stock brokerage support, plus a loose and independent financial planner type of structure.

These firms want to see ideas for new and exciting products/services. They will support local early-stage companies. They want in on the action in the form of rights of first refusal on subsequent financing, warrants, and options on stock. These firms only do "best efforts" offerings. Definitely consider offering "doing the last third plus exclusive rights on next round."

Traditional Investment Bankers. These are the firms that have the investors for your deal in their hip pocket. Their investors range from institutions to individuals. Each firm has carefully cultivated its investors over an extended period of time, and the relationships they have are usually hard earned and highly coveted.

Increasingly, the firms within the traditional investment banking community are concentrating their efforts in specific industries. Although there will always be upper-tier firms who can finance almost any type of deal, the rest of the firms want industry-specific deals. They also want deals in excess of $5 million, and they usually stay away from early-stage companies. The major exceptions to this are investment bankers working in very specific industries. They can spot the new innovators and feel confident in assessing the risks. Their investors expect them to find early-stage opportunities.

Traditional investment bankers love bridge financing prior to an IPO, and they love to be the dealer/manager on IPOs. They prefer to work on a "best efforts" basis, but may do a "firm commitment" underwriting. Your attorney,

CPA, or corporate finance advisor is the best person to approach these firms. Cold mailings are virtually useless.

Non-traditional Investment Bankers. These may actually be one of the other money raiser firms profiled here. In addition to their core business they like to offer investment banking services on the side.

These firms only work on a "best efforts" basis. There are a lot of top quality firms who can get the job done. Which ones are they? Since there is no rating service, be sure to talk to their past clients before you make a deal. Your best strategy for locating a trustworthy firm is to rely on your attorney, CPA, or corporate finance advisor for recommendations. When you've made your selection, be ready to give warrants, options, and rights of first refusal. Definitely consider offering "doing the last third plus exclusive rights on next round."

Independent Direct Participation Offering Wholesalers. These are unique firms, usually very small, with one or two principals who specialize in representing your company's offering. They concentrate on direct participation offerings such as limited partnerships and tenancy in common debt instruments. They are the ones you hire to locate the right broker/dealers and stock brokerage firms. They also fill the role of executing your Offering Campaign Plan. In effect they are the go-between for your company and the money raisers. Direct participation wholesalers, as a rule, already have staff who will do the "dog and pony shows," and also motivate and service the reps to get your offering sold.

To attract a good direct participation offering wholesaler, you'll need to meet their fee schedules which will be based on a 2 to 3-1/2% commission, plus expenses, plus draw against the commissions. Independent direct participation offering wholesalers are prevalent in the partnership and mutual fund markets where there is continuous product presence. However, if you can work out an excellent compensation plan for an independent direct participation offering wholesaler, he or she may be the key to finding the right reps with the right broker/dealer or stock brokerage firm.

One possibility worth trying is to locate a busy and successful independent direct participation offering wholesaler, and offer a finder's fee for "names only." That is, the wholesaler will supply you with only the names of the money raiser firms he or she thinks best suited to your deal. Then, you follow up with the marketing. Definitely consider offering "doing the last third plus exclusive rights on next round."

Boutique Stock Brokerage Wholesale/Market Makers. Many of the smaller NASD licensed stock brokerage firms (with between thirty and fifty reps) specialize in making markets in the stocks of smaller public companies. These firms concentrate their efforts in taking public early-stage companies. Taking advantage of the new Small Business Regulation of the SEC (SB-2), passed in 1993, these firms are able to wholesale and form syndicates with other smaller NASD stock brokerage firms to fund smaller IPO's. There may be an interest in these firms to fund a Staying-Private Public Offering™, if the company is positioning itself to "go public" soon. Most of these firms are located in New Jersey, New York, Colorado, Texas, and Florida.

Independent Due Diligence Firms. In the early 1980s a new kind of business emerged in the financial community, known as independent due diligence firms. They are hired by various money raiser firms, such as boutique broker/dealers, and stock brokerage firms, to help them with their due diligence processing.

There are not a lot of these firms around, but it can be worth the effort to track one down, because they are excellent "gate keepers" to the money raiser firms they service. Often these firms are hired by companies seeking an "introduction" to a money raiser firm.

The best way to make a deal with one of these firms is to first find one or two of them with money raiser clients who are right for your deal. Then do the best job you can to negotiate the right to make a pre-sell test with the firm's reps. Doing this gives your company the opportunity to see if there is enough interest to move ahead with its proposed offering.

Money Managers. Listed last under the category of securities licensed money raisers are those firms and individuals hanging the shingle of "money managers." This is a broad group from Wall Street's mutual fund managers to Main Street's financial planners wearing money manager hats. These are conservative investors that, as a rule, only invest in the securities of public companies or government securities. This is not a money raiser source for emerging companies or private placement.

NON-SECURITIES LICENSED MONEY RAISER PROFILES

LBO Associations and "Going Private" Equity Investors. This group of players is increasing its activity and influence in the investor capital marketplace. LBO associations are structured as limited partnerships with money managers, venture capital firms, or investment bankers as the general partner. The limited partners are typically pension funds, insurance companies, mutual funds, and family funds. These money raisers provide capital for the leadership team or outsiders to purchase the publicly traded stock of stockholders which can result in a public company "going private" when the number of shareholders falls under 500. The company then does not have to comply with the SEC's public company reporting requirements. Since 1988,

LBO associations have averaged over $50 billion of financing each year. Although not a prime source of capital for emerging stage 1-4 companies, they are nevertheless a large source of capital that should be watched. There are some who are predicting that the LBO association money raisers will continue their trend of taking private many more public companies.[27]

Pension Advisors/Administrators. There are over 20,000 independent pension advisors/administrators in America. Some of these firms and individuals perform third-party administration for pension plans. Others are actually under contract to make investment decisions for pension plans. Third-party administrators usually belong to their own local trade group. Third-party administrators are a good source of leads to smaller businesses and their pension plans. Many of your potential business angels and adventure stockholders will be small business owners, and their investments will be made through their pension plans. The third-party administrator will help process the paper work between your company and the pension plan of your investor. The most common form of pension plans for smaller businesses is the "Self-Directed Business Pension Plan." This kind of plan allows the participants to make their own investment decisions. The third-party administrators make sure that the ERISA rules are complied with.

Pension advisors are individuals or firms that have been selected to direct the investments of a pension plan. As a rule, larger corporate pension plans hire advisory or money management firms to be their investment advisors. These advisors are generally licensed as register investment advisors with the SEC.

Small Pension Owners. Hundreds of thousands of businesses in America have established pension plans. Normally these plans are administered by either CPAs or third-party administrators. The investment decisions are made by the company. If the owner of the business controls most of the stock, then the owner, in effect, controls the investment decisions. Many smaller corporate pension plans have "self-directed" features which allow their employees to select their own investments.

Tax-Exempt Organizations. There are over 10,000 of these organizations, foundations, and companies, and they have many billions of dollars under their control. There are 2,500 larger organizations, that have investable assets of over $5 million. The investment parameters of tax-exempt organizations are tightly controlled by law. Generally they do not invest in private companies.

Fee-only Financial Planners. In the mid-1980s, a small group of players in the financial planning industry came forth who wanted to avoid what they saw as a conflict of interest when financial planning firms collected commissions on the sale of financial products. This group has come to be known as fee-only financial planners. They formed their own institute in 1981.

There is both good and bad news if you make a deal with one of these fee-only financial planners. The good news is that these firms have some very affluent investor clients who lean heavily on their financial planners for advice. The bad news is that the planners tend to be conservative in working with their clients, and try to avoid "pushing" specific products.

The best approach is to win the attention, and then the trust, of these planners. Then hope that they will at least introduce you to their clients. Don't ask the planner for a strong recommendation, and don't expect, or even ask, the planner to do a formal due diligence. The planners believe that if they were to do a due diligence on your offering, they would be opening themselves up to liability because they no longer would be impartial advisors to their clients.

Registered Investment Advisors. There are over 7,500 firms and individuals who register with the SEC as registered investment advisors. They can be the very reps who hang their license with the broker/dealers and stock brokerage firms already profiled. These people and firms may even call themselves investment bankers. There are also many financial consultants and celebrity/sports managers who carry a registered investment advisor license. The independent ones are good money raiser contacts.

Insurance Salespeople. The one million plus insurance agents in the United States are potential money raisers for investor capital. The first thing you need to do is to ask the insurance agent if he or she has a securities license. If they do, then you know that they are a rep for a broker/dealer, and that you'll have to secure a selling agreement with that firm. It's not a good idea to try to get an agent to sell your offering if it has not been approved for sale by the agent's broker/dealer or stock brokerage firm. (This is called "selling away.")

It might pay to investigate the possibility of paying a finder's fee to the insurance agent if this would be acceptable to the agent's broker/dealer. This issue probably cannot be handled by the agent's insurance broker alone. You will have to consult with the broker/dealer directly.

If the insurance agent does not have a securities license, then your best tactic is to offer a finder's fee for an introduction to the agent's clients.

Business Brokers. These people can be an excellent source of investor capital. As we will discuss in more detail in Step 6, one tactic that can be used to locate investor capital is to find "money on the move." Business brokers know firsthand who is about to become liquid with cash from the sale of their business. They can be good finders of business angels and strategic corporate investors.

To motivate a business broker to present your deal to his or her clients, you may have to try many of the tactics discussed in Step 6. If a business broker has a securities license, then you must deal with the broker/dealer's due diligence and selling agreement issues.

If you're acquiring an existing business as part of your business plan, and you're using a business broker to help consummate the purchase, you may make use of the fact that the broker will only receive a good paycheck from the deal if the deal goes through. So it is to his or her advantage to help you find investors.

Also, if your company is on a fast Exit Track, and you find a powerful business broker, then you might make a deal with the broker to give him or her the future listing of the sale of the company in exchange for the broker helping you find the initial investors you need.

Real Estate Brokers. Like business brokers, real estate brokers and agents (Realtors) can be excellent potential money raisers. If your company has real estate acquisition needs, then it will be to the Realtor's benefit to help you find investors. An increasing number of Realtors have securities licenses. In fact, Century 21 has an entire division devoted to licensing Realtors in securities. Remember that if they do, their broker/dealer will have to be dealt with just the same way as previously discussed in these profiles.

If you can't work out a deal with the Realtor, don't forget the possibility of simply offering him or her a finder's fee.

Loan Brokers. Generally loan brokers have as many clients as real estate brokers. They are also in a position to know when their clients are going to come into some cash through a refinance or a loan payoff. Many loan brokers carry securities licenses. So remember that their broker/dealer will have to be dealt with.

Many of the direct participation offerings (DPOs), discussed in Step 6, can be made to fit the "comfort zone" of loan brokers. If your company is structuring a debt offering or a DPO, then you may be able to add credit enhancers along with real property to the structure, and then rely on the loan broker to find the capital.

Management and Business Consultants. This is a large and diverse group of people and firms who work directly with business owners. Like business brokers, these consultants have access to strategic corporate investors, business angels, and adventure stockholders. A well-connected consultant may be encouraged to help you find your investors if he or she is awarded a healthy employment contract with your company in addition to the finder's fee.

If these consultants carry a securities license, then their broker/dealer will have to deal with it. This can be a blessing if the broker/dealer is a regional or boutique firm and the consultant can sponsor you within the firm for your selling agreement. If you can do this, then you will have fifty or so reps looking for investors for your company.

Keep in mind that many business/management consultants call themselves investment bankers or represent that they perform investment banking services, so don't be misled by the name.

Corporate Finance Advisors. This is a group of individuals or firms that may also go by the name of business/management consultants or investment bankers. (It can sometimes be very difficult to ascertain the exact specialty of these people because of the interchangeability of the names used in the financial community.) A corporate finance advisor should, at the very least, understand very quickly all the points brought up in this book.

These professionals generally charge by either the hour or the project. If they indicate that they can fund your deal, then get down to the bottom line and discuss how, who, and when. Talk to their past clients.

Try your best to structure their fees on the back end of the funding as a "success fee." A good corporate finance advisor should be able to facilitate getting your company into the doors of the right money raisers (broker/dealers, stock brokerage firms, or investment bankers). If they do, your company should pay them a success fee of at least 1%. Do not ask for the corporate finance advisor to be paid by the money raisers. You want your corporate finance advisor to be able to win friends among the money raisers, and nothing turns off legitimate money raisers more than someone asking them to "share" or "cut" their normal fee structures. This is a bad way to start a search for investor capital.

Attorneys. If your offering can be structured to involve the money raiser market, you may want to give serious consideration to using the services of your attorney. If you have an attorney who is well connected, why not have him or her pave the way and get you in the door. Tax and estate planning attorneys are often asked by their clients for leads about investment opportunities. Such attorneys can be strong allies. Always offer a finder's fee to these professionals. Let them decline if they have a professional or ethical problem over taking a fee for finding investors.

CPAs. Your selection of a corporate CPA can include the requirement that the accounting firm help you find strategic corporate investors, adventure stockholders, or business angels.

H.D. Vest Financial Services, Inc. of Dallas specializes in licensing CPAs in securities. This firm is very aggressive in helping CPAs diversify their practice by including financial product sales. As of 1993, almost 4,500 accountants across the country have acquired their securities license and "hung" it with H.D. Vest. They represent 1.5 million investors, and according to *Forbes* magazine this translates into investments of $100 billion.[28]

Tax Preparers and Bookkeepers. Think of all the adventure stockholders in the files of the hundreds of tax preparers and bookkeepers in your city. These people are perfect money raisers for smaller offerings. Many real estate syndicators share office space with these money raisers just to get access to their clients. Their clients can be making five to ten investments each year, and may well want something more exciting than mutual funds to invest in. Be sure to pay these money raisers the full "pay-out" (commission) on your offering. Any securities licensing issues are largely their problem, not yours.

Venture and Investment Clubs. If your city has these clubs, then they can be a great source of investors. Just show up at the meetings, mix, and get to know the members.

Finders. Last, but not least, is the category known as finders. This includes anyone you come in contact with who can steer you to an investor. Every Offering Campaign Plan should include an action plan involving finders. Potential finders are everywhere: centers of influence, past clients, friends, all of the money raisers listed above, employment search funds, CEOs, syndicators, priests and ministers, etc.

Many state securities laws permit finder's fees, while others have tight restrictions. The generally accepted litmus test is "so long as your finder does not negotiate, sell, or broker the securities, then the payment of the finders fee is legitimate." A foolproof way of avoiding ethical or legal problems is to *never* give a finder a prospectus, private placement memorandum, or business plan. How can they sell your deal if they don't have any documents to present?—so the argument goes. Another strategy to help avoid compliance problems is to structure your finder's fee to be slightly less than the full commission pay-out that you're using on the offering (see Step 5). This helps legitimize your argument that your finders did not exceed their bounds.

Illustrations 2-14 through 2-17 summarize the characteristics and needs of the most important kinds of money raisers.

ILLUSTRATION 2-14:
PROFILE OF BROKER/DEALER AND STOCKBROKERAGE FIRMS:
CHARACTERISTICS AND NEEDS

	National	Regional	Boutique
Number of reps	Over 300	100–300	1–100
Type of placements	"Firm," "best efforts," or "all or nothing"	"Best efforts" No "all or nothing"	"Best efforts" No "all or nothing"
Kinds of deals:			
Size	Over $20 million	Over $3 million	Over $150,000
Devl. level of prod./serv.	Static	Market devl. or later	Seed level or later
Growth stage of company	5 or 6	4, 5, or 6	' 2, 3, 4, 5, or 6
Private	Yes	Yes	Yes
Public	Yes	Yes	Yes
Kinds of investors	Adventure stockholders	Adventure stockholders, some business angels	Adventure stockholders, some business angels, some Visionary Capitalists
Due diligence:			
Costs	$5,000+	$1,000+	$500+
Time	Several months	2 months	1 month
Type of funding instruments	Equity, debt	Equity, debt, DPO	Equity, debt, DPO
Selling agreement considerations	Non-accountable allowances	Non-accountable allowances, warrants, rights of first refusal	Non-accountable allowances, warrants, rights of first refusal
Commission payouts	3–8%	3–10%	3-15%
Accounting	Big 6	Local	Local
Legal	Major	Local	Local
Leadership team	Full team with all qualities	Full team with all qualities	Partial team with great qualities
Wholesaler needs	Yes	Yes	Yes

ILLUSTRATION 2-14: (CONTINUED)
PROFILE OF BROKER/DEALER AND STOCKBROKERAGE FIRMS:
CHARACTERISTICS AND NEEDS

	National	Regional	Boutique
Presentation documents	Due diligence kit; PPM or offering circular; business plan; executive summary; collateral sales literature	Due diligence kit; PPM or offering circular; business plan; executive summary; collateral sales literature	Due diligence kit; PPM or offering circular; business plan; executive summary; collateral sales literature
Types of financings:			
Bridge	X	X	X
LBO	X	X	X
Acquisition	X	X	X
Turnaround	X	X	X

ILLUSTRATION 2-15:
PROFILE OF SECURITIES LICENSED FINANCIAL CONSULTANTS (REPS):
CHARACTERISTICS AND NEEDS

	Stock brokers	Commission financial planners	Professional money managers
License hangs with	Stock brokerage house	National, regional, or boutique broker/dealer	National or regional broker/dealer
Freedom to sell	Only what home office approves	Only what home office approves	Only what home office approves
Have their own boutique broker/dealer	Sometimes	Sometimes	Sometimes
Selling tendency:			
Innovators	X	X	
Early adapters	X	X	
Late adapters	X	X	X
Laggards	X	X	X
Devl. level of produce/service	Same as their broker/dealer	Same as their broker/dealer	Same as their broker/dealer

ILLUSTRATION 2-15: (CONTINUED)
PROFILE OF SECURITIES LICENSED FINANCIAL CONSULTANTS (REPS):
CHARACTERISTICS AND NEEDS

	Stock brokers	Commission financial planners	Professional money managers
Growth stage of company	Same as their broker/dealer	Same as their broker/dealer	Same as their broker/dealer
Average size of client's investment	$5,000 to $20,000	$5,000 to $50,000	$5,000 to $5,000,000
Presentation documents	PPM or offering circular; business plan; collateral sales literature	PPM or offering circular; business plan; collateral sales literature	PPM or offering circular; business plan; collateral sales literature
Portfolio strategy motive	From none to diversification	From none to diversification	Diversification and safety

ILLUSTRATION 2-16:
PROFILE OF INVESTMENT BANKERS:
CHARACTERISTICS AND NEEDS

	Large investment bankers	Boutique investment bankers
Who they are	Divisions of large national and regional stock brokerage and financial service firms	Small independent firms
What they do	Underwrite stock issues by purchasing the stock from company and selling it to the public	Don't purchase stock, but do charge up-front fees
Types of underwritings	"Firm," "best efforts," or "all or nothing"	"Best efforts" only
Types of placement	Generally only public	Private or public
Kinds of deals: Size	Over $3 million	Over $500,000
Devl. level of prod./serv.	Market development or later	Seed level or later
Growth stage of company	2, 3, 4, 5, or 6	2, 3, 4, 5, or 6

ILLUSTRATION 2-16: (CONTINUED)
PROFILE OF INVESTMENT BANKERS:
CHARACTERISTICS AND NEEDS

	Large investment bankers	Boutique investment bankers
Kinds of investors	Own funds, their institutional investors' funds, and the funds from large "blind" pools of adventure stockholders	Sometimes their own funds, marketed to investors and other money raisers
Qualifications to look for in investment bankers	Reputation; experience in pricing the stock and selling it; research capability on the industry and company; distribution capability; market-making capability in order to make an OTC market, so long and short positions can be taken to ensure liquidity and price stability	Reputation; experience in pricing the stock and selling it; research capability on the industry and company; boutique market distribution; coordinate well with larger underwriters; advice capability
What they cost	Fees structured in the offering O & O costs. Generally 3% of offering funds for syndicate services. Generally 8–10% on retail underwriting commissions. Warrants and rights of first refusal	Generally 3–5% on distribution to other "selling" firms or brokers. Generally 8–10% on retail underwriting commissions from their own investors. Warrants and rights of first refusal
Leadership team	Full team with all qualities	Partial team with superstar qualities
Wholesaler needs	They do it	They are supposed to do it
	Large investment bankers	Boutique investment bankers
Presentation documents	Due diligence kit, discussion documents: term sheet, business plan, and executive summary; they will want to use their counsel for PPM or offering circular	Due diligence kit, discussion documents: terms sheet, business plan, and executive summary; they may want to use their counsel for PPM or offering circular

ILLUSTRATION 2-17:
PROFILE OF DIRECT PARTICIPATION OFFERING WHOLESALERS:
CHARACTERISTICS AND NEEDS

Who they are	Individuals or firms who are well-connected in the broker/dealer market, the stock brokerage market, and the investment banking community
What they do	Contract with a company to do their best job to find investment bankers, broker/dealers, or stock brokerage firms to participate in a selling group for an offering
Types of underwritings	"Best efforts" only on DPOs
Types of placement	Public and private DPOs
Kinds of deals: Size *Devl. level of* prod./serv. *Growth stage of company*	 $500,000+ Seed level or later 2, 3, 4, 5, or 6
Kinds of investors	Other broker/dealers and stock-brokerage firms, rarely investors direct
Qualifications to look for in a wholesaler	Reputation and experience in securing quality selling agreements with key broker/dealers and stock broker firms; research capability, with understanding of the company and industry; distribution capabilities; advice capability; and, most important of all, knows the other money raisers
What they cost	From monthly draws of $5,000 plus expenses, or 3 points to straight commission of 2–5% plus credit draws
Leadership team	They want a superstar team with as full a team as possible
Presentation documents	PPM or offering circular; business plan; collateral sales literature; videos; others

CONCLUSION

The final word is that there is no final word. The world of Investor Financing™, and its cast of characters, is forever changing. What is certain is that you must take Peter Drucker's advice seriously when he says that, "your #1 job is to access capital for your company." It's a constant process, requiring vigilance to stay on top of the Investor Financing™ process. The two basic Investor Financing™ approaches—the Direct Placement Approach and the Money Raiser Approach—will probably not change, but the players and practices are constantly changing.

Raising money is like most sales processes: you first determine the needs of your customers and then you meet those needs. This step should have provided you with enough information so that a picture is developing in your mind of which sources and approaches are most appropriate for your financing needs. Just as businesses in today's Knowledge/Creation Economy must market their products/services with laser pinpoint accuracy, you must target the investor capital market very precisely. Shotgun, "willy nilly," "let's throw a big bag of tricks against the wall and hope something sticks" marketing campaigns don't work anymore. This step has provided a survey of a big market with many players with many needs. Your study of this step, combined with an honest assessment of your Chaordic Web strengths and what kind of Phenomenal Message you have (Step 1), should help you identify which investor sources are right for you company.

"Step 6: Creating the Capital Relations™ Plan" explains the theory on how to find your targeted investor sources, and then how to gain their attention and win their trust. But first, your next step is to structure the first draft of your business plan.

DEVELOPING THE BUSINESS PLAN

Step 1

Step 2

STEP 3

Step 4

Step 5

Step 6

Step 7

Step 8

Step 9

Step 10

3

We are drawn into intimacy by possibilities rather than realities, by the promise of things to come rather than proven accomplishments, and perhaps by seduction.

— THOMAS MOORE

Having completed the first two steps of the Investor Financing™ process, you are now ready to develop the first draft of your business plan. Notice that this is only the first draft. You will return to make revisions to this draft twice more during the Investor Financing™ process: once in Step 7 and again in Step 9. The aim of Step 3 is to get your Phenomenal Message down on paper. Having surveyed the investor sources and approaches during Step 2, you should have an idea about the kind of investor who will be reading your business plan once it's completed.

ELEMENTS OF THE BUSINESS PLAN

THE CONTENTS

Step 1 detailed the importance of a Visionary Business Builder having both a Launch Plan and a Growth Plan. These two items form the core of your business plan. (A company fortunate enough to have a NPLP could, of course, try to use the Great American Product/Exit Game message, in which case their business plan will be different than that described below, which is based on the assumption a Visionary Business Builder's message is being deployed.)

The Visionary Business Builder's Business Plan should include the items listed in Illustration 3-1.

ILLUSTRATION 3-1:
CONTENTS OF VISIONARY BUSINESS BUILDER BUSINESS PLAN

- Cover page
- Table of contents
- Non-disclosure agreement
- Glossary of terms
- Executive summary
- Paradigm Vision description
- Principles description
- Promises:
   Destiny path

- Core competency
- Core ideology
- Launch Plan:
   Path description
   Positioning description
   Product/service description
   Partners description
   Processes description

ILLUSTRATION 3-1: (CONTINUED)
CONTENTS OF VISIONARY BUSINESS BUILDER BUSINESS PLAN

- Launch Plan
  Profits/ownership description
  Projections/liquidity
  description
- Growth Plan:
  Path description
  Positioning description
  Product/service description
  Partners description
  Processes description

Profits/ownership description
Projections/liquidity
  description
- Funding requirements
  analysis
- Risk analysis
- Appendices:
  Photographs
  Market studies
  Competitor studies
  Miscellaneous

THE GOAL OF THE BUSINESS PLAN

The goal of the business plan is to win the attention and trust of your strategic associates, investors, and/or money raisers, so they will invest, and/or raise capital, for your company—nothing more, nothing less. The leadership team, under the direction of the CEO, and with the *help* of the Funding Team, develops the business plan. The CEO and a professional business plan preparer (or a financial writer) can write the final version of the business plan.

BULLET-PROOF YOUR BUSINESS PLAN

Stay on Channel WIFM. Investors want to know "What's in *It For Me*?" Always keep your antenna pointed to your investors' channel—their needs and desires. Your thorough understanding of investor sources, approaches, and Capital Relations™ planning (Step 6), is your starting point in developing the skills necessary to write from the investors' perspective. If you have entrusted a consultant to prepare the final version of the business plan, make sure that he or she really understands the material in Steps 2 and 6.

Use of Evidence Points. In the section on Discipline 1 in Step 1, a detailed description was given of the importance of Evidence Points, which are used to substantiate the existence of the five disciplines of a Visionary Business Builder. Be sure to include in your business plan as many of these Evidence Points as possible.

Be Honest. If investors, money raisers, advocate messengers, or investor infrastructure members find any blatant distortions of facts, figures, or quotes, you're dead in the water.

Don't hide relevant information. If you have failed in the past, admit it. Investors know your past failures can be the price you pay for your future successes. Similarly, if you're in a financial straight jacket right now, don't try to hide it; just explain how your company is going to get out of it.

The speculative part of your Paradigm Vision can be (and should be) grand. But keep in mind the fine line between optimism and fantasy. If you're not sure how potential investors will react to the future points of view of your business plan, the market testing in Step 8 is aimed at keeping you from shooting yourself in the foot when you prepare the final version of the business plan in Step 9.

It is wrong, and very risky, to try to fool investors, money raisers, advocate messengers, and infrastructure members with your financial projections. If you're tempted to stretch, fudge, or outright "cook your books" on historical performance, remind yourself that if you do, you'll be committing fraud, and that could land you in jail.

Investors don't like to see significant deviations from industry norms or questionable projections by companies in embryonic industries. For example, a company projecting 40% growth rates and 50% gross profit margins in an industry characterized by 15% growth and 35% gross margins would be questioned by an investor. Avoid being overly optimistic in developing financial projections. Keep your financial forecasts limited to the time frame of your Launch Plan. Investors often like to see projections that include a set of scenarios showing the best case, the worst case, and the most likely case. This enhances the believability of the entire Launch Plan.

Keep in mind that your financial projections set the standard by which your Launch Plan will be judged. Do you want to spend the rest of your years explaining to investors why the numbers you promised have not been met? Many smart entrepreneurs take the approach of using conservative projections. Then, if these conservative numbers are actually exceeded, they can use this "pleasant surprise of success" as an opportunity to go to the same investors for additional financing when it's needed. This kind of strategic thinking is important when structuring your Financing Sequence Plan (see Step 5). Investors will first react to your offering on the basis of their emotions. Then they will use the logic and soundness of your Evidence Points and numbers to justify their emotional response.[1]

Write It Right. Style, grammar, design, color, texture, weight, and size are all important considerations. Follow these guidelines:

- *Plain English, please.* Find someone skilled in the English language to proofread your business plan. Avoid industry jargon unless you are dealing with investment sources who are thoroughly knowledgeable about your industry.
- *Neat is neat.* Use the best word processing and computer graphics technology you can find. Use only white paper for the text. Use attractive looking type styles, headings, margins, etc. If you don't feel

confident about your knowledge or judgement in this area, consider hiring a graphic designer to design and format your business plan.[2]

- *Avoid prepackaged business plans.* Don't use sterile and standardized business plan packages that many consultants try to sell to companies. This kind of plan can be a "red flag" to investors, warning them that perhaps the leadership team hasn't really done its homework.[3]

- *Pictures say a thousand words.* Use photographs, charts, and graphs carefully and creatively. Use color, if you can afford it.

- *Avoid a loud thud.* Avoid making the business plan a "bible" that takes weeks to read. "More with less," should be the rule, even though it is much harder to write "less rather than more" well.[4]

- *Focus on the customer.* It's easy to get carried away when describing your company's core competencies and products/services. Although it's important to describe them, your prospective investors will be more interested in how you plan to do your marketing. Since most investors are not deeply involved in technology, you will do well to avoid excessively detailed and lengthy descriptions of your product or service. But every investor understands what satisfied customers do—they buy and continue to buy, and they spread the good news. So concentrate on your marketing plans: explain who makes up the market, how many of them there are, and how you're going to reach and keep them. These things are the key to a successful enterprise, regardless of how dazzling (or dull) your product or service is—and investors know this.

- *Avoid fluff.* Investors have seen enough "Barnum & Bailey" type plans driven by hype. If you're a stage 1 or 2 company, or a stage 4 company with a new product line, don't say you'll be in the market in thirty days, if you won't. Never say you have no competitors—there's always someone lurking in the bushes. You had better find them, because your investors probably will.

- *Neutralize "No."* Anticipate and remove or undermine any reason someone can say "no" to your business plan. Investors can't argue with your proven *facts*, but they can, and will, argue with your questionable assertions or opinions. Conclusions based on sound logic, a solid Launch Plan, and many Evidence Points can't be argued with. This is why your Launch Plan and Growth Plan are so important.

THE COVER PAGE

Here is the place to remember the quotation from Brook Byers of Kleiner, Perkins, Caufield and Byers that was quoted earlier in this book: "Open with a bold, sweeping, almost controversial opening statement." The cover page should therefore have a one or two sentence summary of your Paradigm Vision.

THE EXECUTIVE SUMMARY

Investors usually read the executive summary portion of the business plan first.[5] Although it's read first, it's prepared last. Your entire business plan has to be finalized before you can write a powerful executive summary which should be kept to one to three pages in length. Here are some important points to keep in mind:

Overcome the 10-10 Obstacle. Investors and money raisers read only 10% of the business plans submitted to them. (This isn't because they don't have the time, but because 90% of the plans are submitted incorrectly.) If they do pick up a business plan to read, they will give it at most ten minutes to gain their interest. If that all-important interest isn't generated, then it's "sayonara" to the plan.

Lights, Camera, Action. Think of your executive summary as a 3-minute commercial to sell your company.[6] How important is this company to you? How passionate are you about the value it's adding to your customers? Can you describe the essence of these things in a forceful and attention-getting way? The executive summary should be able to pass the "Elevator Story" test: Can you get an investor excited in the time it takes to ride twenty stories in an elevator?[7]

Use Word Power. Choose your words carefully. Make them as powerful as you can in order to sell your dream. But avoid fluffy superlatives and padding.

The Litmus Test. Ask yourself the following questions about every sentence in your executive summary:

> "Who cares?"
> "So what?"
> "Who says?"
> "What's missing?"[8]

By doing this, you'll discover the things that need to be changed to make your executive summary a winner.

Contents of the Executive Summary. Your executive summary should *summarize* the most important points about each of the Chaordic Web Elements covered in Discipline 1 of Step 1 as well as the Evidence Points you're using. Make sure that the following is included:

■ *A financial glimpse.* Use tables to present the highlights of past, current, and Launch Plan financial information.

■ *The funding requirements and use of proceeds.* Use tables, if you can, to summarize this.

■ *Your investment and strategic strategies.* What is the projected return and strategic benefits?

GUIDELINES FOR PREPARING FINANCIAL FORECASTS

Investors want to know how well the company will do in the immediate future. A company waiting around for numbers to add up will be flatfooted in the race to the future. So it's not surprising that a solid financial forecast for the Launch Plan is a prerequisite to winning the attention of investors. J. Morton Davis and Evelyn Geller of D.H. Blain & Co., Inc. provide this observation:

> Numbers and projections, of course, are essential; they reflect the businessperson's aspirations, and if the goals are not ambitious, we will not be interested. We want someone who dreams about being listed on the New York Stock Exchange, about building a major company, about making a fortune. If, however, the entrepreneur projects revenues of $1,935,000.42 in the first year and say he or she hopes to do $27,946,124.88 in the fifth, we know he or she just ran the number through a computer without thinking. If he or she is right about $27 million five years out, which is a gross number, that alone will be a miracle. The details he or she adds are so irrelevant, so insignificant, so impossibly inaccurate as long-term projections, that they are simply stupid.[9]

A complete discussion of preparing financial statements is beyond the scope of this book. However, here are some practical tips:

Include a Summary Table. Develop a one page summary in table form.

Coordinate With Your CPA. Your CPA can provide tremendous support. There are a host of things that your CPA can do to help you develop your financial projections. With the avalanche of investor lawsuits that fell on legal and accounting firms in the mid-1980s to early 1990s (predominately from the real estate development and securities fields), many CPAs will not "sign off" on your financial projections; that is, they will not take responsibility for them. However, CPAs will help you prepare them and advise you on your strategies and footnote assumptions. (Also, by engaging your CPA early on in an Investor Financing™, you gain access to a potential money raiser or advocate messenger—see Step 6.)

Use a Single Format. Use only one format to develop your best, worst, and most likely scenarios. Make sure that your formats meet the accepted accounting principles.

Use Industry Standards. The assumptions and ratios underlying your projections should be based on industry standards and accepted accounting principles. These standards are published by: Dun & Bradstreet, Three Sylvan Way, Parsippany, New Jersey 07054. Phone: (201) 605-6000.

Month to Month, Then Quarterly. The first-year projections should be on a month to month basis. The second-year projections should be shown on either a monthly or quarterly basis. Any forecast beyond two years should be on a quarterly basis.

THE APPENDICES

Your appendices should include schedules, reports, studies, product specifications, and anything else that is too long (or too boring) to include in the body of the business plan. Here is a list of some of the items that are usually placed in the appendices:

- Photographs of company products
- Market surveys
- Flow charts of research and development, production, and marketing
- Price lists and catalogs
- Sample advertisements, press releases, and anything else that's appropriate
- Historical financial statements
- Fixed-asset acquisition schedule
- Past tax returns
- References
- System flow charts and job descriptions
- Miscellaneous Evidence Points (see Step 1)

CONCLUSION

The writing of your business plan tests the completeness of your Step 1 work. Your business plan is, in effect, an Intellectual Capital report, since most of the Evidence Points from Step 1 deal with either Human Capital or Structural Capital issues. The work you do in Step 3 should expose the things in your Phenomenal Message (Step 1) that are missing or in need of shoring up, in order to attract investors and strategic associates. The next step, "Identifying Strategic Associates," will help you overcome these weak spots.

IDENTIFYING STRATEGIC ASSOCIATIONS

Step 1

Step 2

Step 3

STEP 4

Step 5

Step 6

Step 7

Step 8

Step 9

Step 10

The trick is to find . . . a corporate partner who will give to a small company a boost instead of a bite.

—BOTKIN & MATTHEWS

The fourth step in accessing capital is to analyze the opportunities of strategic associations. Strategic associations can be very useful, not only for funding through strategic/stakeholder investors and money raisers, but also for gaining assistance in market development, management, sales, knowledge acquisition, and operations. In short, Step 4 is about Chaordic Web building.

It is rare for a company to get off the ground alone, or for one individual to put together an Investor Financing™. Rugged individualism doesn't cut it these days. The successful start-up entrepreneur with a hot new idea rarely works alone. Even if your only agenda is to access capital, the entrepreneur will get it faster through the leverage power of strategic associations. Leading the company through the launch phase, and then growth phase, requires coalitions. Investors are very sensitive to the importance of strategic associations. Most investors are successful business people themselves. Many owe their success to the wise use of strategic associations. It's a success formula they are familiar with.

Mark Stevens, writing in the December 1992 Dun & Bradstreet Reports, presents an accurate survey of the current use of strategic associations:

> In recent years, a number of factors have combined to make it more difficult than ever to launch and build a small company.
>
> Technology—once subject to gradual change measured over decades—now moves at blinding speed, re-inventing itself in a matter of years.
>
> More then ever before, big companies are competing with small entrepreneurs for niche markets, they used to thumb their collective nose at.
>
> Although this may prompt pessimistic, hidebound entrepreneurs to complain about the changing order of things, their more aggressive

and visionary peers will recognize that problems are often opportunities in disguise.

One of these opportunities is strategic partnering, whereby small companies are joining with other businesses that complement their strengths, shoring up weaknesses and working together. Although the idea of customers and suppliers working together has been gaining ground in recent years, strategic partnering goes beyond that, encompassing the full scope of business activities.[1]

The evidence of the trend toward using strategic associations is compelling. For example, according to *Venture Economics*, in a study which tracked 5,000 alliances, the decade of the 1980s saw a tenfold increase in the use of strategic associations.[2] In a 1989 survey by DataQuest and Arthur Young (now Ernst & Young) 73% of a group of 700 electronic industry CEOs of start-up and growth companies reported forming strategic associations. In 1990 this increased to 81%, and in 1991 it was 90%.[3]

Other industries in the United States do not show such enthusiasm, however. A 1988 Booz-Allen & Hamilton study showed only 17% of American executives gave strategic associations a high approval rating. This same study reported 74% of Japanese executives favored strategic associations.

L. Scott Flaig, partner in Ernst & Young, writing in *Electronic Business*, called strategic association development "the trend toward 'virtual enterprises' as opposed to 'vertical enterprises.' Today, these alliances are actually reshaping the basic nature and structure of the business enterprise and are challenging our old models of success."[4] Robert Lynch, author of *Business Alliances Guide* states it well: "Alliances are *neither internal nor external* to the corporation; rather, they are part of the 'extended' corporation, and as such can be neither commanded nor controlled in the traditional sense. They operate within a different set of rules and frameworks, and we must be aware of this uniqueness if alliances are to be understood and then operated successfully."[5]

The message from these studies is that the fast-paced, information-heavy, electronics industry appears to be keeping pace with the Knowledge/Creation Economy, while other industries are not. Pay attention—the future is today.

DIFFERENT FLAVORS

When opportunity knocks, you need to know which door to open. The wrong kind of strategic association can spell disaster. People are throwing around terms like "partnering alliances" and "joint ventures." Each has different legal contractual arrangements and each is treated differently under the law. Your investors may approve of one and not another. You will discover which they prefer during "Step 8: Testing the Market and List Assemblage."

"Strategic association" is simply a term describing the close relationship between two enterprises. How close you want to make it determines the kind of strategic association that you'll try to structure. There are three kinds of strategic associations:

- Strategic relationships
- Strategic alliances
- Strategic joint ventures

Any one of these three associations can involve a cash investment by one party in the other. This cash investment is known as a strategic business investment. (In step 2, the sources of investor capital were profiled: including the various strategic corporate investors, and the four other sources of investor capital—venture capitalists, Visionary Capitalists, business angels, and adventure stockholders.) The following definitions should prove helpful:

Strategic Relationships. This is the basic business relationship you enter into all the time. This kind of association can be as simple as a verbal or written contract with a vendor, a consultant, or a member of your Board of Directors. The logic behind outsourcing non-core-competency activities, in order to achieve the extended and flat organization model warranted by the Knowledge/Creation Economy, dictates that all vendor relationships be evaluated for their long-term strategic value. Businesses shouldn't just hire vendors anymore. Instead they should form strategic relationships. Sometimes the relationship is so strategic that the vendor actually invests in the vendee's enterprise (a strategic corporate investment—as discussed earlier in Step 2). Conrad Hilton, founder of the Hilton Hotel chain, saved his hotel empire during the great depression by guaranteeing ten vendors lifetime contracts if they would each invest $4,000 so that he could make the lease payment on the last hotel property he still owned.

Strategic Alliances. These are contractual agreements between two or more parties to pool resources for a specific short-term project. The parties involved maintain separate corporate identities. One party may make a strategic corporate investment in the other.

Strategic Joint Ventures. These are long-term associations involving the formation of entirely new entities and organizations. A joint venture is a real marriage of resources—people, money, technology, and customers. Because of this, controls are tighter. One party may make a strategic corporate investment in the other.

VARIETY OF SUPPORT

Are you as quick to spot your weaknesses as investors? How are you going to satisfy an investor who doubts your core competency strength?

The aim of Step 4 is for you to discover as many strategic association opportunities as possible. A good starting place is to inventory your needs. It is wise to look for multiple enhancements that your key strategic associations can bring. A recommended procedure is to use the Chaordic Web Elements from Step 1 and work through them with your team of advisors. Illustration 4-1 is a good form to use for this work. Any internal activities that are not "best in the world," or close to it, should be seriously evaluated to see if they can be improved by one or more strategic associations. In addition, external conditions and market development challenges may dictate the need for strategic association support.

IMPORTANT CONSIDERATIONS

The following items should be reviewed before launching a strategic association. It is especially critical to go through this analysis for any strategic alliance or strategic joint venture that may be considered. Ignoring any of these considerations will reduce the likelihood of a successful venture.

Do You Have a Real Need? The review of your Chaordic Web Elements is serious business. Both Launch Plan and Growth Plan considerations are important.

Be Certain That the Other Party's Need Is High. Relationships work when mutual need and desire are high. The goal of sharing dreams and having a co-destiny relationship with a strategic association partner begins with a mutuality of needs.

See the End Before You Begin. Remember, people, places, and things change. Information/knowledge systems change, and shareholders change. It's wise to anticipate the eventual end of a strategic association. What if things don't work out so well? Or conversely, what's going to happen if the alliance or joint venture is more successful than anticipated? Good planning and frank negotiating at the outset sets the stage correctly for the final curtain call.

Be Sure to Have Good Documentation. Good negotiations, good lawyers, and good attitude are the prerequisites for solid contract documentation. The contract specifies such issues as payments, who owns what, and what reparations will be made if someone violates the agreement. If difficult or tense situations arise that prove difficult to resolve while working out the details, then perhaps it's a sign that the deal is not meant to be.

ILLUSTRATION 4-1:
ENHANCEMENTS NEEDED

Chaordic Web Elements	Launch Plan	Growth Plan	Who can enhance in next				Passive, strategic, or stakeholder
			1 yr.	5 yrs.	10 yrs.	20 yrs.	
1. Paradigm Vision							
2. Principals							
3. Promises of Discipline 2							
4. Path							
5. Positioning							
6. Products/Services							
7. Partners							
8. Processes							
9. Profits/Ownership							
10. Projections/Liquidity							

In most successful strategic alliances and joint ventures, the partners work out the contract with the lawyers, then put it on the shelf and do whatever they need to do to get the goals accomplished. The contract is rarely important for getting the job done, because in the initial stage of the relationship, you don't really know what the job is going to be. However, if things go wrong, the contract becomes vital. You must protect yourself—and you must get it in writing.

Make Sure That the Top Leadership Teams Talk to Each Other. It is important that senior management in both companies have access to one another. Leadership is essential. Top brass must have a meeting of the minds. It's a mistake for top management to make the deal and then not make the deal work over time.

"Cultures" Should Be Compatible. It is not enough that the alliance or joint venture should work out on paper. Don't let the thrill and anticipation of the opportunity cloud the reality of two mismatched "cultures." Personalities, attitudes, and work ethics, to name a few, should be looked at to test the compatibility of the two companies.

Protect Core Competency. For alliances and joint ventures to work over time, each party must continue to dominate its own core competency to such an extent that the other party will not, or cannot, bypass its partner in the marketplace.[6]

Strive for a Win/Win Situation. The operations, risks, and rewards must be allocated fairly. Let the other guy win and you'll win. Everyone in the relationship must be willing to be flexible, creative, and ready to address new risks whenever they occur.[7]

Coordinate Information Systems. Both parties need to create and maintain compatible information/knowledge systems, and provide updating with an agreed upon protocol.

Don't Put All Your Eggs in One Basket. Management should not "bet the farm" on one strategic alliance or joint venture. This applies to the enterprise itself, as well as to a project or market expansion effort.

Don't Give Less Than You Get. It is important to consider the needs of your partner. People who are good at creating joint ventures and alliances work very hard to structure a relationship in which they give as much as they get. Every strategic alliance needs partners who are going to do more than they are told, more than what the contract requires.[8]

Don't Lose Focus. Strategic relationships, alliances, and joint ventures do best with specific objectives, timetables, lines of responsibility, and measurable results.

STRATEGIC ASSOCIATION LEADERSHIP TEAMS

As stated earlier, investors back a company primarily because of the people involved. Perhaps your leadership team is a "group of one" with no prospects of a full-time team until your enterprise (or a special project) is at the market development stage. What you call your leadership team can be a group of separate project teams. Wouldn't it be great if you could start a business, and without spending any money, have a powerful team of experts? This is the art of resourcefulness. Remember, your greatest achievements will always be in all the energy you stir in other people.

Here are the strategic association leadership teams that you can consider utilizing:

- The Inner-Circle Team
- The Board of Advisors Team
- The Board of Directors Team
- The Funding Team

Emerging companies need all of these teams for Investor Financing™ success. Most of these teams are structured as strategic relationships, not as strategic alliances or joint ventures.

THE INNER-CIRCLE TEAM

The creation of an Inner-Circle Team is an excellent way for the entrepreneur to:

1. Secure stakeholder and strategic investors.
2. Get advisory help.
3. Build Evidence Points for the Launch Plan.
4. Get assistance in working the Investor Financing™ steps.
5. Avoid loneliness.
6. Develop an advocate for the Capital Relations™ program (Step 6).

Here are the procedures to follow:

Prepare a List of Close Friends Whom You Trust. You want friends who love and respect you, and want you to succeed. Since you may be asking for their help on a gratis basis, these inner-circle members have to be special people. Consider key vendors and customers as well.

Be Clear with Them About Your Expectations. It is your responsibility to communicate what your expectations are. Be clear about the task, the time, and the compensations, if any. The Inner-Circle Team will probably not need to meet as a group. You can meet with them individually for their advice and support. Lean on them, but don't knock them over with a thousand questions. Save your biggest questions for them, and avoid troubling them with minor concerns.

Don't ask your inner-circle members to invest in your idea. They know you need investors, and they'll respect you if you refrain from asking them to invest. Instead, concentrate on intensifying trust, respect, and mutual admiration. If you work the Investor Financing™ steps well, the inner-circle members will ask to become investors (assuming that they're financially able)—after all, they helped put the enterprise together.

Ask Permission to Use Their Names. Since you'll be communicating with many people while you're working the Investor Financing™ steps, it's a good idea if you can use the names of your inner-circle members to enhance your credibility. If you can, get their permission to list their names as members of your Board of Advisors, or as consultants.

Plan for Continuity. As mentioned above, some of the inner-circle members may be candidates for one or more of the other teams that you will be organizing. Naturally, moving from the informal inner-circle to one of the other formally organized teams will require extensive discussions, as well as the signing of the same agreements, if any, that are required of the other members of those teams.

Don't Rush the Process. Make sure that you don't rush the completion of the Investor Financing™ steps. Of course, this is easier said than done, but you should make the effort to concentrate on quality while working the Investor Financing™ Steps, rather than speed.

THE BOARD OF ADVISORS TEAM

High-growth companies rely on outsourcing techniques to leverage their resources. For a company needing investor capital, the Board of Advisors takes on an even more important role.[9] Two things are going on: first, there is the need for expert advice in order to start or stay in business. And second, there is the "credibility factor" and "advocate factor" (Step 6) that the right Board of Advisors brings to the financing process. Your Advisory Board members may be valuable resources to help design your Paradigm Vision.

Here are the procedures to follow:

Determine the Enhancement Help That You Need. Using your analysis of the enhancements needed in your Chaordic Web (Illustration 4-1), you can determine what help is needed for the company. Select the people and firms you need who can bring a "best in the world" performance and add to your Evidence Points.

Be Clear with Them About Your Expectations. Since most Boards of Advisors are acting in a consulting role, your enterprise may need to formalize your association with them through employment contracts. This is the purest form of a strategic relationship. The contract should be specific on their service obligations and the duration of their service. Avoid, if you can, a strategic alliance, since a higher risk of misunderstanding and early termination exists. The last thing you need when accessing investor capital is a lawsuit with a member of your Board of Advisors. Keep in mind that disputes and lawsuits breed high negative drama. Investors want their companies to stay away from negative drama.

Plan for Continuity. Some of your Board of Advisors members may be candidates for your Board of Directors.

Don't Rush the Process. Just as you shouldn't rush to create your Inner-Circle Team, you also shouldn't rush the creation of your Board of Advisors. Strive to find qualified members.

Illustration 4-2 presents a worksheet to use during Step 4.

THE BOARD OF DIRECTORS TEAM

The Board of Directors is another team that you'll eventually rely on during the funding process. For an early-stage company, it's a good idea to wait until Step 8 testing is completed before selecting the Board of Directors. You may find out that your investor sources have different expectations about the Board of Directors than you do.

When the time does come to form the board, you will follow the same steps that were outlined above for forming your Board of Advisors. Board members may have the kind of perspectives necessary to help the leadership team design its Paradigm Vision points of view.

THE FUNDING TEAM

This team is comprised of the key individuals or firms that you will rely on the most during the Investor Financing™ process. It is a team of specialists, many of whom may already be on your other teams. These specialists will be comprised of both "thinkers" and "doers." As a rule, the kind of strategic association that you'll use is the strategic relationship—not an alliance or joint venture. These individuals or firms comprise the following primary players:

- Corporate finance advisor or coach
- Attorney
- Certified public accountant (CPA)
- Inner-Circle Team members

In addition to the primary players, the following secondary players should be considered:

- Business planning consultants
- Capital Relations™ consultants (P.R. firms)

Illustration 4-2:
Advisory Support Team Enhancements

Names	Contri-butions	Why not needed	Strategic or stakeholder	Will they invest?	Finders possibilities
Inner Circle					
Board of Advisors					
Board of Directors					

Funding team:

Corp. fin. advisor					
Attorney					
CPA					
Bus. Plan consultant					
Collateral sales aids					
P.R. firm					
Capital mkt. research					
Valuation consultant					

- Graphic design consultants
- Market research specialists
- Valuation consultants

THE CORPORATE FINANCE ADVISOR OR COACH—THE FACILITATOR FOR "DOING THE RIGHT THING"

The job of the corporate finance advisor (CFA) is to ensure that the right things are done. It is up to the leadership team and its other advisors to do the right things in the right way. Your corporate finance advisor is the person or firm that you rely on for quarterbacking the Investor Financing™ steps. He or she may not actually execute your offering campaign (see Step 10), but your CFA helps facilitate the right decisions and may work on special projects. For example, your CFA may help with the business plan, collateral sales literature, Capital Relations™ program, research projects, preparation of investor lists, etc.

Good corporate finance advisors should be well positioned in the investment banking community and have a track record of actual fundings to his or her credit. Since Investor Financings™ depends on various investor markets, your CFA should be experienced in retail securities sales, wholesale securities sales, strategic corporate investments, institutional placements, and both public and private placements. In this age of specialization, you may also find a CFA who specializes in your specific industry or the investor market that is perfect for your financing.

If you know your investor source (Step 2) in advance of selecting your corporate finance advisor, it would be helpful to search for a CFA who specializes in that particular investor market. If your financing is suitable for traditional investment banking, then the investment banker you reach agreement with may wear the CFA hat on your deal (Step 2).

Every entrepreneur has to make the decision whether or not to engage professional help. One purpose of the Investor Financing™ steps is to give you the necessary tools to execute all ten steps by yourself, if you have to. Some new enterprises are launched with only one visionary carrying the torch—but this is the exception to the rule.

CONSIDERATIONS IN HIRING A CORPORATE FINANCE ADVISOR:

1. Look for an individual or firm with personal entrepreneurial experience with their own businesses.
2. If possible, you want a CFA who is experienced in raising investor capital for their own projects and companies.
3. Does the CFA have a track record of happy clients?

4. You want to pay your CFA a fee that is part retainer and part "success fee." You also want costs that are structured to fit your budget and needs. Hourly fees will range between $75 and $300 per hour. Flat-fee project pricing is sometimes used. Warrants on stock is a common form of compensation.

5. You want the CFA to demonstrate to you that he or she can:

a. Guide your company through the Investor Financing™ steps.

b. Coordinate everything with the other Funding Team members and management.

c. Give advice with strong, but carefully thought out, reasoning.

d. Develop and implement many of the projects.

e. Be a strong advocate messenger (Step 6).

f. Find strategic associations for you.

g. Provide funding services through good relationships with the investment banking community, the broker/dealer community, the stock brokerage community, the venture capital community, the due diligence community, the business angel market, the strategic corporate investment community, and the government research grant market.

WHAT TO WATCH OUT FOR:

- Individuals or firms who have never owned or operated their own business.
- A CFA who won't work the Investor Financing™ steps.
- A CFA who has no track record with funding.
- Individuals or firms who promise too much.

THE ATTORNEY—THE COMPLIANCE KEEPER

Having an experienced corporate finance attorney on your Funding Team is important. There will be many key decisions that must be made while working these ten steps, and some of them will need the expertise of an attorney.

Even though not every Investor Financing™ will require a Prospectus or Private Placement Memorandum, your attorney will nevertheless be needed.

Your attorney may also be a potential investor and/or advocate (Step 6)—be sure you ask him or her.

If your financing *does* require offering documents, remember that as a matter of law, attorneys do *not* have to be retained to prepare them except if a tax or securities opinion is part of the offering. However, using a good lawyer may accomplish the following:

- Provide credibility.
- Provide competence for the processing and preparation of required documents.
- Free up the leadership team's time to do what they are supposed to do—find investors.
- Coordinate with the CPA and the investment bankers.
- Provide you another investor or advocate messenger (Step 6).

Lawyers will be required for the preparation of offering documents by the traditional investment banking community, the broker/dealer community, and the venture capitalists. Lawyers are also almost always necessary for the registration or qualification of public offerings with state and federal security regulators.

CONSIDERATIONS IN HIRING YOUR ATTORNEY:

1. Fees:
   a. You want affordability.
   b. You want a firm that will work on part retainer and part "success fee."
   c. You want a fee that can be paid in installments.
2. Can the firm act fast? (For example, they should take no more that 15 to 21 days to prepare an offering document.)
3. Do they have a track record of happy clients?
4. You want lawyers who have good connections with the investment banking community, the broker/dealer community, the venture capitalists, the stock brokerage community, and the institutional markets.
5. You want lawyers who believe in the Investor Financing™ steps.
6. Do they have an "influence network" composed of the type of business angels or adventure stockholders who you may be targeting (Step 2)? If so, will they make you a part of it?

WHAT TO WATCH OUT FOR:

- Lawyers who say "I've got investors." (You have to check this out.)
- Lawyers who say "I know investment bankers." (You have to check this out as well.)
- Small fees and small firms with no track record.

THE CPA—THE CONTROLLER

Your accountant, or accounting firm, plays a major role in the success of your financing. He or she will be required to compile accurate financial information that your potential investors will examine carefully.

If your company compiles all of its own financial history, your accountant may be required by the investors or the money raisers to review or audit your information.

Although we have, up to now, referred to your accountant as a CPA, there is no legal requirement that your accountant be one. However, a good CPA can accomplish the following for your financing efforts:

- Provide credibility.
- Supply competence for the processing and preparation of required documents.
- Free up management's time to do what they are supposed to do—find investors.
- Provide another investor or advocate messenger (Step 6).

CPAs will be required by the traditional investment banking community, the broker/dealer community, and the venture capitalist. CPAs will also be required to review or audit financial statements on public offering with state and federal securities regulators.

Your accountant may also be a potential investor or advocate—be sure you ask him or her. And if you use an accounting firm, ask all of the other members as well.

CONSIDERATIONS IN HIRING YOUR CPA:

1. You want affordability.
2. You want a firm that will be flexible with your payment plans.
3. Do they have a track record of clients accessing investor capital?
4. You want a CPA who has good connections with the investment banking community and other investor markets.
5. Can the CPA coordinate with your other Funding Team members?
6. You want a CPA who has sophisticated, but user-friendly, financial forecasting software programs.
7. Do they have an "influence network" composed of the types of business angels or adventure stockholders whom you may be targeting (Step 2)? If so, will they make you a part of it?

What to Watch Out for:

- Accountants who say "I've got investors." (You have to check this out.)
- Accountants who say "I know investment bankers." (You have to check this out as well.)
- Firms with no track record of assisting companies through the process of accessing investor capital.

Secondary Members of Your Funding Team

There are other individuals and firms that can provide assistance and advocate messenger strength during the Investor Financing™ process. A review of these potential strategic relationships will illustrate their possible importance to your company.

Business Planning Consultants. In every city there are specialists who make a living helping companies develop their business plans. Most of these specialists are also in the business consulting field. A business planning consultant may even be a good corporate finance advisor. Your decision to employ one of these consultants must be made carefully. One school of thought says, "If you can't write it, you don't know it." From this it follows that the leadership team needs to write their own business plan. This is especially important for the early-stage company, because the leadership team will be closely scrutinized by potential investors: Does the leadership team know the way? Do they know how to get there? Do they know what obstacles lie ahead, and how to deal with them?

This does not mean that you shouldn't get help preparing your business plan. On the contrary, the proper way to develop a successful financing is for the leadership team to throw themselves into the Investor Financing™ steps, and to employ as many consultants as possible on the Funding Team. If the leadership team needs editorial assistance with the business plan, then a business plan consultant can be helpful. Later-stage companies that have a leadership team that is working full time on the day-to-day problems of the company "need" a business planning consultant.

Companies whose fundings are suitable for top quality investment bankers may find that the money raiser will take on the role of business and finance consultant, often rewriting any business or financial plans that the company may have prepared.

Finding a business plan consultant that specializes in the same industry as the company will obviously present a unique resource opportunity for the company and another advocate messenger candidate (Step 6).

Capital Relations™ Consultants. You may know these advisors by another name—public relations firms. The Investor Financing™ steps involve the creation and use of a Capital Relations™ program (see Steps 6 and 7), and the implementing of this program can often involve a public relations firm. This firm can be another advocate messenger candidate.

Graphic Design Consultants. Often an Investor Financing™ will involve an Offering Campaign that requires collateral sales tools (Step 6). Common ones include brochures, photographs, audio cassettes, video cassettes, and overhead transparencies.

The appropriateness of your sales aids depends on many variables. Which communication tools to select will become clear as you follow the ten steps (they are discussed in depth in Step 6). A consultant can help you in the preparation of the tools you need. These consultants are also advocate messenger candidates.

Market Research Specialists. These specialists can be very helpful if management does not have the time, skill, or resources to perform all of the research projects required in the preparation of the business plan. Unlike the writing of the business plan, this is an area where outside consultants are almost always advisable. These specialists are also advocate messenger candidates.

Valuation Consultants. Often a specialist in business or stock valuations is brought in to help management.

Valuations of current assets, as well as valuation of the "success formula" is a critical process. However, the accountant, corporate finance advisor, and leadership team of a company can usually determine "future-value impact" valuations for financing purposes. They can also become advocate messengers.

CONCLUSION

The central message of Step 4 is leverage. Not the kind of leverage associated with financing, but rather the leverage gained through strategic associations with other companies and professionals who can enhance your business strategies.

If your Inner-Circle Team, or your Funding Team, recommends that the Chaordic Web Elements of "Step 1: Designing the Phenomenal Message" have not yet been adequately addressed, then Step 4 is the place to turn your weaknesses into strengths. Whether it's shoring up a weakness discovered in Step 1 or enhancing an existing corporate strength, other people and firms should be sought for their strategic help.

Carefully selected strategic associates may also lead to their direct investment in your company, or at least in their participation as advocate messengers in your Capital Relations™ program (Step 6).

The name of the game is to gain momentum while working these steps. Investors are impressed by quality people and firms who do business with your company.

When you're satisfied that all the Chaordic Web Elements and Disciplines of Step 1 have been satisfactorily addressed in regard to their need for strategic associations, then you're ready to move on to Step 5.

STRUCTURING
THE
FINANCING

Step 1

Step 2

Step 3

Step 4

STEP 5

Step 6

Step 7

Step 8

Step 9

Step 10

Financial strategy is the essence of the entrepreneur's game.

— J. B. FUQUA

J. B. Fuqua's quote above may be a bit dramatic, but the point he is driving home is important. Your company needs both long-term and short-term financing strategies. Simply having a need for capital and finding a quick solution is not the kind of financing strategy Fuqua is talking about. The structure of any particular financing round should be related to the Launch and Growth Plan strategies of the company. In addition, the financial condition strategies of your company must be coordinated and aligned with these short- and long-term financing strategies.

Financing obtained incorrectly can do more harm than good.[1] Since Investor Financing™ is tough, the temptation is to accept the first investors that come along and to meet their deal structure needs. Entrepreneurs that don't carry out the Investor Financing™ steps (or some sort of logical sequence of financing steps) can find themselves with no choice but to accept these early investors, and their financing structures, which may not be right for the company. The Investor Financing™ steps are designed to produce the opposite result. They are designed to get the immediate job of accessing capital done as quickly as possible, and to provide a momentum for the right kind of future financings for the company. Treating financing strategy as a plan to solve your occasional short-term financing needs is not the aim of these ten steps.

A company whose financing strategy is built only on short-term projects raises warning red flags for many investors.[2] Most investors in early-stage companies are conditioned to companies falling short of projections, requiring going back to the investors for more capital.

Your financing strategy includes decisions, plans, and documents about the following:

1. Short- and long-term financing plans (the Financing Sequence Plan).
2. Current funding requirements (the Funding Requirements Sheet).
3. Current financing instrument (the Term Sheet).

THE FINANCING SEQUENCE PLAN

Your Financing Sequence Plan is your two-fold strategy for the next five to ten years: 1) to obtain the capital that will be needed to make your company grow, and 2) to determine the approximate number of times it will be needed. What you do today should be connected to your future financing plans. This sequencing is a blueprint that investors need when they evaluate your company. They want to know how you're going to finance your company into the $1 million (or $100 million) company your business plan proposes. Is it going to be financed strictly from its own profits (the ideal Launch Plan), or is it going to need additional money, at selected times, to fuel new growth? A great many business plans are discarded by investors simply because the leadership team hasn't taken the time to work out, and disclose in the business plan, the company's Financing Sequence Plan. Your Financing Sequence Plan is a litmus test for many savvy investors. Don't think of your financing strategies only in the context of short-range projects. Today's financing plans are interconnected with the bigger picture that includes the future. Remember, investors are big picture players.

THE BENEFITS OF A FINANCING SEQUENCE PLAN

Developing your Financing Sequence Plan provides the following additional benefits over and above meeting your investors' needs:

Reality Check. You've heard the cliché, "Whatever capital you think you're going to need, you need to double it." There is some truth to this, but it needs an important qualification. This qualification can spell the difference between a successful or unsuccessful funding. The phrase should read, "Whatever capital you think you're going to need, you may need to double it, *but more importantly you may need to extend the time you're going to use this capital.*"

Too often entrepreneurs think they need to develop their companies immediately—overnight, as it were. Their reasons come from a host of personal agendas and from the belief that investors only invest in fast track enterprises. However, personal agendas are usually bad reasons for any business decisions and some businesses need to move along on a "not so fast" pace. Wrong motives for developing a company quickly can lead to all sorts of potentially bad decisions and plans.

Instead of doubling the amount of capital that needs to be raised initially, consider extending the timeline for developing the business. For example, instead of immediately raising $700,000 in a common stock offering, raise only $300,000 in a preferred stock or direct participation offering. Use the funds very carefully, develop the business methodically (i.e., with a realistic

Launch Plan), and then raise $400,000 in a second round of financing two years later if it's needed.

Sometimes valid business reasons exist to develop your company quickly. These are market development reasons, such as a company's unique product/service, or the unusually high market demand or market size, or the threat of competitor moves, which dictate that the right approach is to get as much capital as quickly as possible.

Company Ownership Is Guarded More Carefully. The Financing Sequence Plan can steer the leadership team into non-stock structures that may be quicker and easier solutions to current cash needs. By holding onto the ownership equity, you allow for the possibility of easier future financings.

An Analysis Is Made of Whether or Not You Should Become a Public Company. The look at the future, which the Financing Sequence Plan provides, allows you the opportunity to analyze the pros and cons of becoming a public company someday. The analysis may determine that "going public" with your company may have to happen sooner rather than later.

Liquidity and Exit Tracks Open Up. By thoroughly doing this planning, the leadership team is able to develop the extremely important liquidity and exit tracks that were discussed in Step 1.

Simpler Financial Plans Are Developed. Investors like simple, straightforward structures. The fancy, exotic, and complicated deals are usually not for them.

The Sources, Approaches, Tactics, and Tools Narrow Down. The Financing Sequence Plan allows you to see much more clearly who the right investor sources will be, and what approaches, tactics, and tools to use for developing the right Capital Relations™ plan for the current offering. This clarity makes it easier to develop the enthusiasm and focus that are needed to access investor capital.

SHOULD YOUR COMPANY GO PUBLIC?

Business Builders on a strong growth track need to analyze the ramifications of being a public company. This book cannot provide a complete discussion of all the registration, compliance, and strategic issues involved in "going public." The leadership team must be knowledgeable about all the state and federal rules involved in "going public." Good securities counsel is a must.

ADVANTAGES OF BEING A PUBLIC COMPANY

May Have No Choice. The Financing Sequence Plan and the current Funding Requirements Sheet may dictate that "going public" now is a necessity and not a choice. Your Capital Relations™ plan may also require that your company be a public company.

Prestige. Through public ownership, your company may gain needed prestige.[3]

Acquisitions. Your company may be able to acquire other companies, using stock instead of cash.

Credibility. Your company may be in a better position to attract better employees, vendors, bankers, and investment bankers.[4]

Easier Future Financings. A public offering will usually improve net worth, enabling the company to borrow capital on more favorable terms. Once a public market is created, and if the stock performs well in the continuing after-market, substantial additional equity capital can be raised from the public and also privately from institutional investors on favorable terms. The company can offer investors a security with liquidity and an ascertainable market value. Thus, the leadership team's future financing alternatives are increased following an initial public offering.

The Leadership Team's Egos and Liquidity Improves. By establishing a public market for the stock of a company, the owners usually achieve a psychological sense of financial success and self-fulfillment, as well as a high degree of liquidity for their own investment.

Requirements for a NASDAQ Listing. Illustrations 5-1 and 5-2 summarize the requirements for a NASDAQ listing.

DISADVANTAGES OF BEING A PUBLIC COMPANY

Public Information. Once "public," certain information must be disclosed. The leadership team may be reluctant to make public certain information such as salaries. The leadership team of a privately held business often fear that disclosure of such information as sales, profits, competitive position, mode of operation, and material contracts would place them at a severe competitive disadvantage, although there are rarely the significant adverse consequences that are sometimes envisioned.[5]

Fiduciary Duties. By being public, the leadership team loses some flexibility. There are practical, if not legal, limitations on salaries and fringe benefits, relatives on the payroll, and many other operating procedures. Opportunities which might have been personally available to the leadership team may have to be turned over to the company.

Administrative Costs. There are many administrative problems for a publicly owned company. Routine legal and accounting fees can increase materially. Recurring expenses include the preparation and distribution of proxy material and annual reports to shareholders; the preparation and filing with SEC of reports under the Securities Exchange Act of 1934 (the "'34 Act"); and the expenditure of fees for a transfer agent, registrar, and public

ILLUSTRATION 5-1:
SUMMARY OF FINANCIAL REQUIREMENTS FOR INITIAL LISTING
ON THE NASDAQ NATIONAL MARKET

	Alternative 1	Alternative 2
Registration under Section 12(g) of the Securities Exchange Act of 1934 or equivalent	Yes	Yes
Net Tangible Assets[1]	$4 million	$12 million
Net Income (in latest fiscal year or 2 of last 3 fiscal years)	$400,000	N/A
Pretax Income (in latest fiscal year or 2 of last 3 fiscal years)	$750,000	N/A
Public Float (Shares)[2]	$500,000	$1 million
Operating History	N/A	3 years
Market Value of Float	$3 million	$15 million
Minimum Bid	$5	$3
Shareholders		
—if between 0.5 and 1 million shares publicly held	800	400
—if more than 1 million shares publicly held	400	400
—if more than 0.5 million shares held and average daily volume in excess of 2,000 shares	400	400
Number of Market Makers	2	2

[1] Net Tangible Assets are total assets (excluding goodwill) minus total liabilities.
[2] Public float is defined as shares that are not "held directly or indirectly by any officer or director of the issuer or by any person who is the beneficial owner of more than 10 percent of the total shares outstanding . . . "

ILLUSTRATION 5-2:
SUMMARY OF FINANCIAL REQUIREMENTS FOR INITIAL LISTING
ON THE NASDAQ SMALL-CAP MARKET

Total Assets	$4 million
Total Stockholders Equity	$2 million
Registration under Section 12(g) of the Securities Exchange Act of 1934 or equivalent[1]	Yes
Public Float (Shares)[2]	100,000
Market Value of Public Float	$1 million
Shareholders	300
Minimum Bid Price	$3
Number of Market Makers	2

[1] A temporary, automatic exemption exists for initial public offerings.

[2] Public float is defined as shares that are not "held directly or indirectly by any officer or director of the issuer or by any person who is the beneficial owner of more than 10 percent of the total shares outstanding . . ."

© September 1992, National Association of Securities Dealers, Inc. (NASD). Nasdaq and Nasdaq National Market are registered service marks of the NASD, Inc. The Nasdaq Stock Market and Nasdaq Small-Cap Market are service marks of the NASD, Inc.

relations consultant. There is also a cost in terms of executive time devoted to shareholder relations and public disclosures.

Conflicts of Interest. The leadership team and owners of a privately held business are often in high tax brackets, and prefer that the company pay either no dividends or low dividends, whereas shareholders and money raisers of a public company prefer high pay-outs of dividends.

HOW TO DEVELOP YOUR FINANCING SEQUENCE PLAN

Take these steps to develop your plan, making sure not to omit any of them:

Step A. Determine where you are now. Determine where your company is on its growth track. Are you working on your Launch Plan? Maybe you're past the launch phase, perhaps at stage 5 (profitable).

Step B. Build a scenario. Determine how much capital and how much time it will take for the company to complete its Launch Plan (profitable, and ready for expansion). Developing this scenario will require time and the complete attention of the leadership team. You can't just throw together a bunch of hypothetical assumptions. Your corporate finance advisor can be very helpful here. So is information derived from industry data, and "success models" from competitors and other companies in similar fields.

Step C. Develop a projection. Construct a timeline showing the various points at which you will need to engage in a round of financing. Also indicate the most likely funding instrument(s) that will be used at each stage.

For each round of financing it is important that you include an Offering Campaign Plan summary that will include investor sources along with approaches you plan to use (Step 2). Keep in mind the possibility of using more traditional financing alternatives as the company grows.

Step D. Review your plan and simplify it. You and your corporate finance advisor should look at Step C above and ask yourselves if the projection can be simplified. If so, do it.

Step E. Determine the mini-max amounts of your current funding needs. Calculate the minimum and maximum amounts of capital that you need for the immediate offering. (This will be explained later in the section titled, "Current Funding Requirements.")

Step F. Choose the current funding instruments. You are now ready to narrow down your current funding instrument choices to just a few. (There is a complete discussion of funding instruments later in this chapter.)

Step G. Match current funding instruments with an Offering Campaign. Be sure the current funding instrument that you have chosen is matched with a feasible Offering Campaign Plan. (See Step 7 for details on how to develop your Offering Campaign Plan.)

Step H. Reevaluate your liquidity track. This is an important step. Ask yourself, "Which investors will want this?"

Now, take a moment and look over what you've done so far. Does everything look "do-able"? Test every item in the plan by asking, "Will it work?" If not, review your work and fix the problems.

Illustration 5-3 shows a hypothetical start-up company's Financing Sequence Plan.

CURRENT FUNDING REQUIREMENTS

Preparing the Financing Sequence Plan has put you in a position to know your approximate current capital needs. Now it's time to take a sharp pencil and work out the details of your "mini-max planning." The objective is to find the least amount of capital your company can get by with and still move along on a strong course. When you're implementing your Offering Campaign Plan at Step 10, it will be very important to have the flexibility to "break impound" of the offering and use funds as they come in. You never know for sure how long your Offering Campaign is going to take or if you'll reach your goal of maximum capitalization.

Illustration 5-4 shows an example of an actual company's mini-max and use of proceeds planning. This company was a start-up venture, launching a new cosmetic line of products through infomercial marketing. This company used a Participation Note Offering as its funding instrument and raised its money through adventure stockholders and money raisers. (See later discussion of this kind of funding instrument.)

CURRENT FINANCING INSTRUMENTS

This section will provide a survey of the available financing instruments that can be structured. The definition of a *financing instrument* is: "The structure, agreements, and documents used to create the securities the company offers to investors to raise its capital." The challenge is to determine which financing instruments should be used to appropriately capture the attention and trust of the investor sources while meeting the financial-condition strategies of the company. The tangible result of your analysis will be the development of your Term Sheet, which you'll use throughout Steps 7 and 8. A Term Sheet is a one or two page summary of the financing instrument and the terms of the current offering.

ILLUSTRATION 5-3:
HYPOTHETICAL FINANCING SEQUENCE PLAN

STEP A:	*Company stage:*	Stage 2 — Development stage
STEP B:	*Funding scenario:*	$300,000 now for Launch Plan $500,000 in 24 months $1,000,000 in 48 months $5,000,000 in 72 months
STEP C:	*Projection:*	*Source:*
	Now: $300,000 through common stock sale of 25% of company	Visionary Capitalists and business angels for Launch Plan
	In 24 months: $500,000 through 3-year (or less) private offering debentures and warrants	Adventure stockholders, Visionary Capitalists, and boutique broker/dealers
	In 48 months: $1,000,000 through private offering stock sale of 20% of company. Proceeds to pay off debenture and also for expansion	Adventure stockholders Boutique broker/dealers + boutique stock brokers
	In 72 months: $5,000,000 through IPO stock sale of company	Adventure stockholders Boutique broker/dealers + boutique and regional stock brokers
STEP D:	*Is the above simple?*	Yes
STEP E:	*Mini-max amounts:*	$150,000 – $300,000
STEP F:	*Funding instruments:*	Straight stock sale to 3 to 8 business angels or Visionary Capitalists
STEP G:	*Match funding instruments with Offering Campaign Plan:*	Stock sale and use of PERT chart and Offering Campaign Plan
STEP H:	*Reevaluate liquidity:*	Liquidity in later rounds and expectation of IPO or sale of business

ILLUSTRATION 5-4:
FUNDING REQUIREMENTS SHEET

	Minimum proceeds (150 units)		Maximum proceeds (1000 units)	
	Amount	Percent	Amount	Percent
Gross offering proceeds	$150,000	100.00	$1,000,000	100.00
Offering/organizational expense				
Legal	10,000	6.67	10,000	1.00
Accounting	2,000	1.33	2,000	0.20
Due diligence	5,000	3.33	5,000	0.50
Printing	1,000	0.67	1,000	0.10
Sales literature	2,000	1.33	2,000	0.20
Selling commissions	12,000	8.00	80,000	8.00
	32,000	21.33	100,000	10.00
Amount available for investment	$118,000	78.67	$900,000	90.00
Inventory at cost	0	0.00	100,000	10.00
Secured notes for inventory (at cost)	100,000	66.67	600,000	60.00
Television commercial production	0	0.00	50,000	5.00
Test market media purchase	0	0.00	30,000	3.00
Deposits for telemarketing operations	0	0.00	10,000	1.00
G & A expenses	15,000	10.00	15,000	1.50
Proceeds invested	115,000	76.67	805,000	80.50
Working capital reserves	3,000	2.00	95,000	9.50
Total offering	$150,000	100.00	$1,000,000	100.00

SMORGASBORD

The Library of Investment Banking lists twenty-eight different ways to classify a security (or the financing instrument—these terms are used interchangeably here).[6] Not only are there twenty-eight different ways to classify a security, these twenty-eight classifications can be mixed and matched to create an almost unlimited number of financing instrument possibilities. Illustration 5-5 shows the hierarchy of the generically described securities most commonly used at the various stages of a company's growth track. This illustration also analyzes which securities are most appropriate at the various stages of a company's growth track. Illustration 5-6 lists the most commonly used financing instruments.

Illustration 5-5:
Growth Track Hierarchy of Finance Instruments

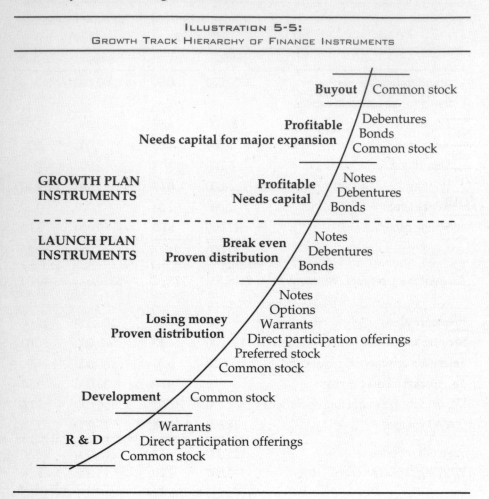

PUBLIC OFFERING INSTRUMENTS

The discussion here is not about whether your company should be a public or a private company, either now or in the future. That analysis was undertaken earlier.

In choosing the current financing instrument, you need to look hard at the question of, "should the offering be structured as a public or private offering?" Keep in mind that a public offering of securities does not necessarily mean your company is "going public." This is very important to understand. Many early-stage companies can increase their chances of accessing investor capital if they analyze fully and carefully the benefits and logistics of using a Staying-

ILLUSTRATION 5-6:
FINANCE INSTRUMENT LIST

	R & D/ Concept	R & D/ Seed	Product Development	Market Development	Losing money/ Proven distribution	Breaking even/ Proven distribution	Profitable/ Needs capital	Profitable/Needs expansion capital	Buyout
INSTRUMENT:									
Public offering	3	3	3	2	2	2	1	1	1
Private offering	1	1	1	1	1	2	2	2	2
EQUITY:									
Primary common	1	1	1	1	1	2	2	2	2
Secondary common	3	3	2	2	2	2	2	2	2
Preferred	1	1	1	1	1	1	2	2	3
Cumulative preferred	1	1	1	1	1	1	2	2	3
Participating preferred	1	1	1	1	1	1	2	2	3
Redeemable preferred	1	1	1	1	1	1	2	2	3
Convertible preferred	1	1	1	1	1	1	2	2	3
Exchangeable preferred	1	1	1	1	1	1	2	2	3
Adjustable rate preferred	1	1	1	1	1	1	2	2	3
Preferred with warrants	1	1	1	1	1	1	2	2	3
DEBT:									
Bonds	3	3	3	3	2	2	1	1	3
Cash flow participating bonds	3	3	3	3	2	2	1	1	3
Pay in kind bonds	3	3	3	3	2	2	1	1	3
Split coupon bonds	3	3	3	3	2	2	1	1	3
Zero-coupon bonds	3	3	3	2	2	2	1	1	3
Redeemable bonds	3	3	3	2	2	2	1	1	3
Bonds with warrants	3	3	3	2	2	2	1	1	3
Debentures	3	3	3	2	2	2	1	1	3
Convertible debentures	3	3	3	2	2	2	1	1	3

Key: 1 = Most often used   2 = Can be used   3 = Rarely used   *Continued*

ILLUSTRATION 5-6: (CONTINUED)
FINANCE INSTRUMENT LIST

	R & D/ Concept	R & D/ Seed	Product Development	Market Development	Losing money/ Proven distribution	Breaking even/ Proven distribution	Profitable/ Needs capital	Profitable/Needs expansion capital	Buyout
DEBT (Continued):									
Notes	2	2	2	2	1	1	1	1	3
Increasing rate notes	2	2	2	2	1	1	1	1	3
Convertible notes	2	2	2	2	1	1	1	1	3
Extended notes	2	2	2	2	1	1	1	1	3
Participating notes	2	2	2	2	1	1	1	1	3
Adjustable notes	2	2	2	2	1	1	1	1	3
Index notes	2	2	2	2	1	1	1	1	3
Notes with warrants	2	2	2	2	1	1	1	1	3
WARRANTS:									
Equity purchase warrants	2	2	2	2	2	2	2	2	3
Exchangeable equity purc.warr.	2	2	2	2	2	2	2	2	3
OPTIONS:									
Put options	3	3	3	2	1	2	2	2	3
Call options	3	3	3	2	1	2	2	2	3
DIRECT PARTICIPATION OFFERINGS:									
Royalty participation certifics.	1	1	1	1	1	2	2	2	3
Captive finance entity	1	1	1	1	1	2	2	2	3
Self-liquidating entity	1	1	1	1	1	2	2	2	3
SPECIAL FEATURES:									
Split funding	1	1	1	1	1	2	2	2	3
Investor note financing	1	1	1	1	1	2	2	2	3
Assessments	1	1	1	1	1	2	2	2	3
Zero-coupon purchase	1	1	1	1	1	2	2	2	3

Key: 1 = Most often used   2 = Can be used   3 = Rarely used

Private Public Offering™, instead of structuring a private offering for their current financing instrument.

Let's look at an example. XYZ, Inc. decides to do a round of investor financing. It decides to structure a preferred stock issue, and targets adventure stockholders as the investor source and boutique stock brokerage firms as money raisers. The company discovers that the best tactic to implement its Capital Relations™ program is to use seminars, ads, and telemarketing to reach potential investors, and to bring in two sales people to execute the Capital Relations™ program. They further decide to have a small minimum investment of $5,000.

The company's legal counsel correctly recommends that the preferred stock offering be a public offering because of securities compliance issues. This does not necessarily mean that the company is "going public." XYZ's public offering is simply an offering that is registered either with the state in which the investors live, or with both the SEC and the appropriate state securities regulators. XYZ, Inc. goes through this public offering procedure with the appropriate government agencies in order to secure a permit to sell the securities to the public-at-large. This allows the company to obtain maximum exposure of its offering in order to secure as many investors as it needs to reach the capitalization levels spelled out in the offering.

Almost any financing instrument that can be structured for a private offering can also be used in a public offering. However, not all private offering funding instruments make attractive securities for trading if the company also wants to "go public" by creating a market for its securities through a listing on a stock exchange.

BENEFITS OF USING A PUBLIC OFFERING INSTRUMENT
Here is a list of the most common benefits of using a public offering finance instrument to fund your current needs. (A complete "how to" discussion on public offerings would take an entire book itself.)

1. *More exposure.* The unlimited publicity through ads, seminars, direct mail, radio, TV, the Internet, and other media gives you wide exposure, not only for your offering, but also for your products and services.
2. *Unlimited number of investors.* Most permits issued by the securities regulators not only allow an unlimited number of investors, but also an unlimited number of offerees (people who you solicit to be investors).

3. *Instant credibility*. There is a mystique of strength and credibility generated when a company sells its securities pursuant to a public offering.

4. *Money raisers appreciate it*. They have a much easier time doing due diligence on your offering when it is a public offering. Their sales representatives have an easier time selling a deal that is public, because it can be offered to individuals as well as businesses.

5. *Employees like it*. Because your offering is public, you can provide your employees with more attractive securities as part of their benefits package. (Most publicly registered securities are less restrictive than privately offered ones.)

6. *Small investments are possible*. This is one of the primary motivations behind public offerings. Typically, private offerings require much larger investments by the investors.

7. *The leadership team ego strokes*. Your leadership team's egos are stroked when you go to the market with a public offering—just like the bigger corporations. So long as there are legitimate business reasons for a public offering, an ego stroke for the leadership team is good once in a while.

8. *Expansion of investor base*. It does not happen very often, but some courageous companies have attempted to "go public" with their very first offering. These companies are subsequently able to place all of their future offerings with the same group of investors privately. Since their investor base has been established through the broad marketing base provided by their first public offering, later rounds of financing have a large source of investors.

9. *Fast paced liquidity track*. In keeping with the trend to provide "trading markets" for small companies, a public offering may put the company in a position to quickly meet the NASDAQ small markets registration requirements. The rule of thumb is, that a company whose stock is qualified on an exchange, and whose stock has a market, will sell at a price 30% higher than it would if the offering were private and there were no market.

10. *May be only way to get deal done*. The public offering structure may be your key to fund any of these scenarios you may find yourself in:

- "Our deal is too small for investment bankers."
- "Our deal is too large for business angels."
- "The leadership team does not know enough adventure stockholders personally."
- "The boutique broker/dealer wants our deal to be a public offering."

11. *Regulators and regulations are getting easier.* The recent SEC, NASD, and state securities commissioners are making it easier all the time to do small public offerings.

DISADVANTAGES OF USING A PUBLIC OFFERING INSTRUMENT

Not everything about public offerings is positive. As with most things in life, there are some downside problems to consider. The following concerns may have solutions if you seek the careful advice of your attorney and corporate finance advisor.

1. *Diluted ownership.* This almost goes without saying. Anytime you raise cash and sell stock, existing shareholders' ownership may be diluted.
2. *Shareholder involvement.* The leadership team will have a more difficult time molding the thinking of a larger shareholder constituency.
3. *Increased reporting burden.* The SEC, and most states, have reporting requirements if a company crosses the "going public" line and has too many shareholders (500 shareholders), or if the size of the company's assets exceed a certain size (three to four million dollars). If a stock exchange listing is obtained, there are additional reporting requirements.
4. *Possible difficulties in later financing rounds.* A stage 1 to 5 company, that has used a public offering for an early round of financing and has over 200 shareholders, may not be a desirable stage 6 company to the investment banking community because there are so many minority shareholders to deal with.

PRIVATE OFFERINGS

No one knows exactly, but the best guess is that well over 80% of all early-stage Investor Financing™ (stages 1–4) are done as legitimate private placements that meet the exempt offering regulations of the federal and state securities laws. The other 20% are done as either public offerings or in some form of a "gray area" securities compliance. Later-stage public companies in the last decade have relied on private offerings to access the insurance company and pension fund markets. Estimates are that over $150 billion to $200 billion of capital is placed annually in over 3,000 of these offerings in the institutional markets.[7]

Section 4(2) of the Securities Act of 1933 exempts from registration with the SEC "transactions by an issuer not involving any public offering," but does not provide definitive rules as to what constitutes a private placement.

In early 1982, the SEC adopted Regulation D (Rules 501–506), which does provide specific guidelines. The type of information that must be furnished under Regulation D varies depending on the size of the offering and the nature of the company. The Private Placement Memorandum on a Regulation D offering can be compared with an initial registration statement filed for a public offering. It should contain the same information that a registration statement would provide, with an emphasis on the same issues that would be considered material by the SEC in a Prospectus (as defined in SEC Regulation 5–K). The major difference is that the Private Placement Memorandum is not subject to the SEC review process, and Regulation D does not require disclosure of certain nonmaterial information that is otherwise required in a Prospectus.

Illustration 5-7 profiles the major requirements of the SEC Regulation D private offering rules. Regulation D provisions have been adopted in most states as the framework for their own private offering regulations. Check to be sure that your state has these same regulations before you begin work on your Prospectus.

So Is It a Public or Private Offering Instrument?

In this step you consider all the possibilities of using a public or private offering as your current financing instrument. In Step 8 you go to the market to test your ideas and strategies. You and your attorney make your final decisions in "Step 9: Finalizing the Documents."

EQUITY SECURITIES

There are two types of equity stock that a company can issue: *preferred stock* and *common stock*. Preferred stock gets its name from the fact that holders of these stocks have "preference" over common stockholders with regard to dividends, liquidation, and voting.

If a company must liquidate its assets, it will first pay its debt securities holders, then its preferred stockholders, and lastly its common stockholders. Debt securities and preferred stocks are also known as the *senior securities* of a corporation, due to the prior claim they have over common stock upon liquidation.

General Characteristics

Stockholders' Rights. As part owner of a corporation, each preferred and common stockholder has certain rights and privileges. Generally, these are detailed in the company's bylaws or in its charter. The usual rights are:

ILLUSTRATION 5-7:
REGULATION D OFFERINGS COMPARISON

	Rule 504	Rule 505	Rule 506
Maximum issue	$1,000,000	$5,000,000	Unlimited
Maximum number of offerees and investors	No limit	35 non-accredited purchasers and unlimited accredited purchasers	35 non-accredited purchasers and unlimited accredited purchasers
Secondary market allowed for stockholders	No restrictions	None Restricted resale	None Restricted resale
Qualifications for investors	None	None	Non-accredited investors must be sophisticated
Advertising and general media solicitation	Prohibited	Prohibited	Prohibited
Financial data requirements	Specified by each state in which offered	Statement required	Statement required
Disclosure requirements	Specified by each state in which offered	Requirement varies by state	Requirement varies by state
Restrictions of issuer	No reporting cos. or investment cos.	No reporting cos. or investment cos.	None
1934 Act reporting obligations	Not unless 500 or more shareholders and $3,000,000 or more in total assets	Not unless 5,000 or more shareholders and $3,000,000 or more in total assets	Not unless 500 or more shareholders and $3,000,000 or more in total assets
SEC filings	Form D	Form D	Form D
State filings	Varies by state Minimum, second original of Form D	Varies by state Minimum, second original of Form D	Varies by state Minimum, second original of Form D

Stock certificates. Each stockholder is entitled to one or more stock certificates which constitutes physical evidence of ownership. A certificate shows:

- The name of the issuing corporation.
- The number of shares represented by the certificate.
- The name(s) of the registered owner(s).
- The names of the transfer agent and the registrar.
- The signature of the corporation's officers authorized to sign the certificate.

The *transfer agent* keeps a record of the name of each registered shareholder, the address, and the number of shares owned. When properly endorsed, certificates are presented for transfer. It is the transfer agent's responsibility to see that they are cancelled and that new certificates are issued to the new owner.

Right of transfer and restricted stocks. Transferability refers to the right to transfer ownership of securities by gift or resale. When the original leadership team has acquired shares by reason of providing original capital or services, the right of transfer may be withheld. Such stock is known as *restricted stock*.

Right of inspection. Normally a stockholder has the right to inspect the stockholder list, the minutes of stockholders' meetings, and the corporate books and records.

COMMON STOCK CHARACTERISTICS

Common stock does not pay a specified dividend. There is no minimum or maximum amount of the dividend. For bookkeeping purposes, common stock is assigned a par value. This is the dollar amount used for a company's financial statements. The par value is usually arbitrarily established at the time the shares are issued.

Common stockholders have specific rights, in addition to those shared with preferred stockholders:

Preemptive Rights. Common stockholders have a preemptive right to buy additional shares whenever the company issues any new stock in order to maintain their proportionate ownership in the company. This is initiated before the new issue is offered (publicly or privately) to non-stockholders.

Rights are offered to shareholders in what is called a *rights offering*. The shares are normally priced below the current market price. This price is known as the *subscription price*.

Rights are freely transferable. They may be exercised by the shareholder or sold to another party.

Voting Rights. Common stockholders have voting rights. Each holder of voting stock of a corporation has the right to attend meetings and vote on important matters, such as who will be elected to the board of directors. Most stockholders vote by proxy. The corporation is responsible for the solicitation of proxies.

There are two general types of voting used by a corporation as detailed below:

- *Statutory voting.* Each shareholder is allowed one vote, for each share of stock owned, for each director. For example, if a shareholder owns 200 shares and there are six directorships to be voted on, the investor may cast 200 votes for each directorship. The investor would have a total of 1200 votes.
- *Cumulative voting.* The shareholder is permitted to multiply the number of shares by the number of directorships being voted on, and vote the shares as the individual wishes, including casting all the votes for one director.

PREFERRED STOCK TYPES AND CHARACTERISTICS

There are several types of preferred stock. The distinction between them lies in the method used to calculate the dividends and the amount of the dividend payment. In addition, there are specific privileges related to each type.

Cumulative Preferred. This stock carries a cumulative dividend provision that prohibits dividends being paid to common shareholders if preferred stock dividends are in arrears. Most preferred stocks are cumulative.

Participating Preferred. Owners of participating preferred stock receive a stated dividend and additional specified dividends if common stock dividends exceed a certain amount. Participating preferred stock may also be cumulative and convertible.

Redeemable Preferred. When preferred stock is redeemable (or callable), corporations have the right to call or buy back their preferred stock at a specified price.

Convertible Preferred. This stock may be exchanged for a designated number of common shares. Convertible preferred is generally callable.

When convertible preferred stock is issued, a *conversion price* is determined. The *conversion ratio* is also determined at this time. This determines how many shares of common stock will be converted for each share of preferred stock. The conversion ratio can be determined by dividing the par value of the preferred stock by the conversion price, as shown in the following example:

A $50 share of preferred stock has a conversion price of $25. The conversion ratio is therefore 2:1 ($50 par value divided by $25). For every share of preferred stock, the investor would receive two shares of common stock.

Exchangeable Preferred. A fixed-rate security that is exchangeable into a debt security of the company at the election of the company.

Adjustable Rate Preferred. These securities, known as "ARPS," have dividends that are reset quarterly at a predetermined reset spread, based on the highest point of a time period average of benchmark rates.

Preferred with Warrants. Preferred securities with warrant rights.

DEBT SECURITIES

Traditional debt securities represent a promise by the company to pay back the amount borrowed. These debt securities are classified as bonds, debentures, or notes.

BOND TYPES AND CHARACTERISTICS

A corporate bond is a long-term promissory note. The essential features are relatively simple. The company promises to pay a specified percentage of par value on designated dates (known as coupon payments) and to repay par or face value (principal) of the bond at maturity. Failure to pay either the principal or interest when due constitutes legal default, and court proceedings can be instituted to enforce the contract. Bondholders, as creditors, have a prior legal claim over common and preferred stockholders as to both income and assets of the corporation for the principal and interest due them, and may have a prior claim over other creditors if liens or mortgages are involved. Bond issues are normally the financing instrument of large public companies, the federal government, and municipalities. Investor Financing™ for emerging businesses are normally not done through bond instruments.

Bonds with Kickers. These are bonds with additional benefits. Examples of these benefits can be redeemable features, pay in kind features, split coupon features, warrants, royalties, and profit or cash flow participation.

Zero-coupon Bonds. This debt instrument structures the service and repayment of interest and principal on a deferred basis. These bonds are essentially stripped of their interest coupons and sold at steep discounts to face value. Zeros match a company's current financial condition with its ability to service debt obligations.

DEBENTURE CHARACTERISTICS

Debentures are like bonds except that debentures are not secured. Investors generally get a higher rate of interest, and they have a claim against the company the same as any general creditor.

NOTES

Sometimes it is best to borrow money from investors through the use of notes rather than structure equity funding instruments or the more formal debt instruments such as bonds or debentures. This decision must be made carefully.

The legal community is almost in unanimous agreement that the creative use of notes, as financing instruments, does *not* circumvent the need for compliance with securities laws. The kind of disclosure documents that you use (see Steps 7 and 9) should be carefully handled by legal counsel.

If you limit the offering of your notes to strategic corporate investors or less than nine sophisticated business angels who have a pre-existing social or business relationship with you, then a business plan and the note agreements will probably be sufficient disclosure.

However, if the notes are being offered broadly to adventure stockholders and/or through money raisers, then you'll need a Private Placement Memorandum, an Offering Circular, or a Prospectus, in addition to your business plan.

NOTE TYPES AND CHARACTERISTICS

Standard Notes. With this kind of note, you can structure the interest rate payment schedule, due date, and security (if any) that best fits the situation. There is no rule of thumb to follow. "Step 8: Testing the Market and List Assemblage" will tell you what you should and should not offer investors to close your fundings.

Your company can issue separate notes to each investor, or it can issue one note, in which case each investor is a co-owner of the note. In most situations, separate notes should be issued.

Participating and Interest Rate Adjustable Notes. These notes call for specific, or adjustable, or indexed interest rates, pay rates, due date, and security (if any), plus a participation in venture or company profits for a specified or indeterminate period of time. These kinds of notes are very popular with investors.

WARRANTS AND OPTIONS

WARRANTS

These instruments represent a privilege to buy securities at a specified price known as the subscription price. Warrants are usually long-term instruments lasting several years. Some warrants are perpetual. Holders of warrants are not usually eligible to receive dividends.

Warrants are usually *detachable*. This means that they can be bought or sold separately from the security they were issued with.

If the market price of the stock is greater than the subscription price of the warrant, it will have an intrinsic value, which may be found by comparing the subscription price to the market price of the stock, as shown in the following example:

> A warrant has a subscription price of $40 and the stock is selling at $20. The intrinsic value is zero since the subscription price is above the market price of the stock. However, if the stock's value rose to $44, the intrinsic value would be $4. (The total value of the warrant would probably be somewhat higher, reflecting the possibility that the market price may go higher yet in the time left before the warrant expires.)

OPTIONS

These instruments represent the right to buy or sell a particular stock, at a specified price, for a stipulated period of time. They are classified according to type, class, and series:

Type. Option contracts are either a call or a put. A call option gives the holder the right to buy shares of the underlying stock, from the writer of the option, at a fixed price. If the holder exercises this right, the writer is obligated to deliver the stock. A put option gives the holder the right to sell shares of the underlying stock at a fixed price. If the holder exercises this right, the writer is obligated to buy the stock.

Class. All option contracts of the same type, covering the same underlying stock are in the same class. For example, all calls on XYZ, Inc. are the same class. All puts on the same company are another class.

Series. All option contracts of the same class, having the same expiration date and exercise price are part of the same series.

DIRECT PARTICIPATION OFFERINGS (DPO'S)

As a result of the increasing popularity of accessing investor capital, the marketplace has become increasingly creative in the development of financing instruments. One such example is the direct participation offering. The basic concept of a DPO is to give the investor a "small piece of a special deal." This usually takes the form of a "small piece" of the revenue stream of a particular business unit or venture. Wall Street uses the term "direct investment" to describe an investment in assets as opposed to corporations.

A DPO can be an excellent funding instrument: the company has access to investor capital without a legal obligation to pay it back, or to give up any equity in the company. By properly structuring a DPO, it is possible to add capital to the company's balance sheet, thereby increasing the company's net worth without adding to its liabilities. A correctly structured DPO shows up on your financial statements only as a footnote showing a contingent liability.

DIRECT PARTICIPATION OFFERINGS:

TYPES AND CHARACTERISTICS

There are several different DPOs that you can use:

1. Royalty participations
2. Captive finance entities
3. Self-liquidating entities

Royalty Participations. This is the most popular DPO. It simply carves out a percentage of gross revenues from a particular venture or product line. Companies that are in manufacturing, wholesale, or retail are in an excellent position to issue DPOs.

This form of DPO is often called *royalty participation certificates (RPCs)*. They can be acquired by your investors for cash, or as the inducement to make a loan or provide a guarantee. RPCs can be used to pay for services or goods and materials. RPCs can be either secured or unsecured, and they can be guaranteed by third parties. They can have a minimum or maximum annual payment, and can be valid for an infinite period or a fixed time. You can structure an RPC to scale up or down and/or terminate upon reaching a certain level.

Royalty participation certificates can be converted into some other security and can be assignable. With RPCs, the ownership of your company is retained by the owners unless you decide to create a conversion feature that allows the sale of the revenue stream equity, or you attach stock warrants to your agreement. The payments to your investors are not required until you start making sales.

Captive Finance Entities. This approach is a great opportunity for a company that has hard-to-finance receivables, purchase orders, or inventory. The structuring is done by forming a separate entity (a partnership, corporation, or trust) that will make loans to your company.

The loan terms are made on whatever basis is necessary to make it work for the investor as well as the company. The loan can be secured by your accounts receivable, pre-receivables, and/or note receivables. It can be a revolving fund or in the form of standard or participating notes.

Self-liquidating Entities. This technique is most appropriate for leveraged buy-outs, acquiring a business, or opening a branch at a new location. The approach is to syndicate an entity (partnership, corporation, or trust) that acquires an existing business or the assets of a business. The new entity provides for its investors to be cashed-out when certain returns are met. Once the expected returns and the return of the capital takes place, the entity liquidates.

The entity can also enter into a joint venture with your company. The joint venture is then entitled to receive revenues, and when certain returns are paid out to investors, both the entity and the joint venture are liquidated.

Another use of the self-liquidating entity is to arrange the sale or leaseback of equipment to the company. (This can also be done with a captive finance entity.) In this situation, the entity purchases either new equipment, or buys the equipment the original company already has, and leases it back to the company. The benefit is that it frees up the company's cash. The lease payments can accrue or ratchet-up over time.

SPECIAL FEATURES OF FUNDING INSTRUMENTS

You also need to know about some special features of financing instruments. These special features, when added to the basic financing instrument you've developed, can help the funding process.

SPLIT FUNDING

It's usually easier to get someone to invest $5,000 than $15,000. A lot of business angels, and adventure stockholder investors, appreciate having the option of investing in increments over several years. Often, an investor will decline making an investment solely because the minimum investment called for in the offering is more than he or she feels comfortable making. As a rule, investors are an egocentric lot, and they may be unwilling to admit that the minimum investment is too much for them. Instead they'll tell you anything but the truth. If investors don't give you truthful feedback, your marketing efforts are sabotaged. Knowing the truth allows you to adjust your plans and structures. Otherwise, you're wasting time, money, and effort. So it makes sense to avoid situations which might cause investors to be less than truthful with you. One way to do this is to offer a low minimum investment by using split funding.

How It Works. To begin with, take another look at your current funding requirements, and see if the requirements can be reworked so that the flow of capital into your company needed to develop your business plan, can be spread out over two or three years. If you can do this, then you and your lawyer should develop your offering so that the total investment is split into two or three installments. For example, if you need a total of $40,000 from an investor, then structure your offering so that it asks for $15,000 now, $15,000 in 12 months, and $10,000 in 24 months.

If the analysis of your funding requirements shows that you need all of your investment capital up front, then try structuring your offering using the next special feature—investor note financing.

INVESTOR NOTE FINANCING

This technique involves using leverage to secure your investor capital. Even in a pure equity offering, there is the possibility of using borrowed money to facilitate your financing.

How It Works. There are essentially two ways to use this technique. One strategy is to have your investors put up a portion of their investment in cash; then they go to their bank and borrow the balance of the note.

The other strategy is for *you* to arrange the investor note financing with a bank (or other lender). This way your investors are spared the hassle of arranging their own loans, and they do not have to reduce their available credit at their own bank. You will have to work with your bank to develop the credit criteria that the bank will require for each investor. You, of course, will also complete all of the loan application procedures for your investors.

There is a variation of the second technique in which your investors put up part of the cash and then sign a note in favor of the company (or a nominee). Your job then becomes to find another investor (or investment pool) to whom you can sell the notes. (One possible source would be your own captive finance entity discussed above.) The investor's note will have to be discounted at least 20% of face value, so you will have to set the amount of your initial offering large enough to allow for this discount and still leave your company with the funds it needs.

ASSESSMENTS

This feature gives the leadership team the right to ask the investors for additional investments in the future. Assessments can be mandatory with forfeiture, or else they can have the leadership team buy-back rights attached to help insure performance. Assessments can also be optional, at the discretion of the investors. If optional assessments are used, the leadership team may want to sweeten the deal for those investors who do come through with the optional assessments, by providing that the additional share price is discounted.

Most new companies are organized with the capital stock structure spelled out in their articles and bylaws as "non-assessable shares." This happens from blindly following the traditional wording in these documents and not because of any legal requirements. If you are planning to use assessments, make sure that your company documents are drafted to allow you this option.

ZERO-COUPONS

This feature is structured so that your investors purchase two classes of securities from you. The proceeds of one class are not used by the company for operating capital. Instead, they are used to purchase highly rated zero-coupon bonds that have been issued by another company. The pay-off of the zero-coupon bond equals the total investment made by the investors.

How It Works. Let's say that $500,000 is brought in by a round of financing. $350,000 of this is used by the company for operating capital. The other $150,000 is invested in zero-coupon bonds that mature in twenty years with a value of $500,000. A great benefit of this feature is the sales pitch you can use with your investors: "You can't lose!"

YOUR TERM SHEET

After carefully developing your Financing Sequence Plan and current Funding Requirements Sheet, and reviewing your finance instrument possibilities, you are ready to prepare your Term Sheet. This is explained in detail in Step 7.

IS THERE AN IDEAL STRUCTURE?

There is no ideal structure because every Investor Financing™ involves so many different variables and considerations. However the following financing structure and strategy comes closest to the ideal for Visionary Business Builders and Traditional Business Builders:

1. Plan to raise enough capital now to get your company past the launch phase. In a perfect world, investors would hope that the company can pay-as-it-goes into the growth phase. This prevents the early investors from being crammed down later on by subsequent investors.
2. Make sure the initial investors and money raisers are "stakeholders" or "strategic investors," and give them an equity position (preferred, non-voting stock) with perhaps a warrant attached.

3. If you need more capital, provide passive investors with a debt instrument.

4. Try not to promise the equity investors an early exit. But if you must, then provide a strategy and promise of liquidity. You can achieve this by structuring in your Financing Sequence Plan a future round of common stock for 300 shareholders for less than 50% of the company. This will then qualify the company for a NASDAQ listing (providing all other NASDAQ requirements have been met). The leadership team and initial stakeholder investors keep more than 50% of the common stock.

CONCLUSION

Step 5 is important because it develops the game plan for financing your company over the next five to ten years—your Financing Sequence Plan. Investors want to see this path because they want to know when they get liquid or when they can get out with a profit.

The structure of the Investor Financing™ you need today is related to your future plans. Measuring your current financial needs against the kind of Offering Campaign that you can successfully execute (see Steps 7 and 10), allows you to determine the following: your current financing requirements, the kind of financing instruments that you should use, and whether or not you should use a public offering or a private placement. In fact, Step 5's analysis may dictate that, with your current financing, it's time to "go public."

Lastly, you need to examine the possibility of using one or more of the special features of your funding instruments to sweeten the offer to your investors. Always stay tuned-in to channel WIFM (What's in It For Me?).

CREATING THE
CAPITAL
RELATIONS™ PLAN

Step 1

Step 2

Step 3

Step 4

Step 5

STEP 6

Step 7

Step 8

Step 9

Step 10

Money follows excitement.

—M. MITCHELL WALDROP

Step 2 gave you a solid look into the sources of investor capital and their basic criteria for making investments in companies. Step 2 also explained the two approaches to use with the sources, including the money raisers who can help find the investors. It would be wonderful if raising investor capital was as simple as writing the business plan to meet the needs of your selected sources and have your financing done. Each year thousands of companies try this, and thousands fail to get funded. If two companies are equal in every way, but one raises its capital and the other doesn't, the difference will almost always be found in the way these two companies hit the road to sell their deal to their investor sources.

Step 6 is a survey of the principles and practices of Capital Relations™ planning. Without a solid grasp of this step there is only an outside chance of a successful funding. There are a few companies that find it relatively easy to get financing. These are either emerging companies with a hot product/service idea or existing growth enterprises with a long track record of profits. But such companies are the rare exception, rather than the rule. The principles and practices outlined in this step form many of the important strategies that will be incorporated into your Offering Campaign (Steps 7 and 10).

CAPITAL RELATIONS™ IS NOT A "PUSH"

The business of accessing investor capital has almost nothing in common with the exaggerated "stock jockey—smile and dial" image portrayed in movies such as *Wall Street*. In fact, most of the commonly practiced "push" selling strategies usually associated with selling financial products have nothing to do with a successful investor capital Offering Campaign. There is a lot of noisy information being pushed on us all. Your campaign to find investors should not be a part of this noisy information glut. People are not hearing the sound bites of pushy selling strategies anymore.

CAPITAL RELATIONS™ IS A "PULL"

Pushing your needs on people is a *disconnecting* process. The aim of Capital Relations™ planning is to be pulled into relationships through *connecting* processes. You will learn in this step that the key to success in accessing any of the four sources of investor capital is to execute an Offering Campaign based on relationship building, versus short-term selling strategies. When your financing is approached in this way, it will seem as though you and your investors are "pulled" into a relationship together.

Many entrepreneurs with a knack and flare for positioning their products and creating customer markets lose all perspective when it comes to their Investor Financing™. Most companies don't think twice about the need for promotion or the need to have advertising budgets to sell their products/services. They hire P.R. firms and show a degree of patience in getting their customers to accept their products/services. They work hard for their first key strategic customers. They understand the new relationship-oriented purchasing behavior of today's customers. They work hard to define and create market segments. It's not a problem for the management of these companies to develop customer relationships based on co-designing and co-destiny practices. All of this is accepted operating procedure today.

These same skills and attitudes must also be used to develop a successful Capital Relations™ program. Investors and money raisers looking at emerging and growth companies are attracted to the future financial investment value and/or the strategic investment value these companies represent to them. They can't try out their investment first, and then make an investment decision. The future holds a heavy dose of fear, uncertainty, and doubt (FUD) for everyone. This FUD is kept under control if you have a personal relationship with your investors/money raisers. A personal relationship helps you determine what it's going to take on your part to give them the assurances they need to feel confident that they are making a good decision to go into the future with you. Your challenge is to address their FUD accurately, quickly, and cost-effectively—in other words you have to make friends fast if you want to raise money fast.

It is difficult to know someone without having, to some degree, a personal relationship with that person. Most sophisticated investors and money raisers who have lost money on a deal wish they had known the leadership team better. In hindsight they believe there was a "seed of failure" buried somewhere in the personality, attitude, or values of the leadership team. If they had only discovered it sooner, the disastrous investment could have been avoided.

In a nutshell, your Capital Relations™ program is based on two components that allow you to experience being "pulled" through the process. The first is the *knowledge component*, which includes all the information/knowledge-rich databases already available or yet to be created by you. The second is the *experience component*, which involves all the one-on-one personal contact and dialogue necessary for you to complete a funding.

RANKING RELATIONSHIP QUALITY

The highest-quality relationship is the kind that has your potential investors or money raisers in a dialogue-centered contact with the leadership team, coupled with a high degree of knowledge on their part about the product/service and industry. In other words, they know you (which is more than knowing *about* you) and they know what you do. The lowest-quality relationship occurs when the potential investor or money raiser has no prior knowledge about the product/service or industry and does not know about the company or its leadership team—definitely a no relationship situation. Illustration 6-1 shows the six levels of relationship quality, called the Familiarity Index.

ILLUSTRATION 6-1:
FAMILIARITY INDEX

Level	Definition
1	No knowledge of product/industry, and no *knowledge about* the company and its people.
2	No knowledge of product/industry, but has *knowledge about* the company and its people.
3	No knowledge of product/industry, but has a *personal relationship* with the company and its people.
4	Knows product/industry, but has no *knowledge about* the company and its people.
5	Knows product/industry, and *knows about* the company and its people.
6	Knows product/industry, and has a *personal relationship* with the company and its people.

Familiarity Index and Corporate Growth Track. Determining the kind of Capital Relations™ plan you need becomes easier when you factor in the Familiarity Index Rating with the corporate growth track stage your company is in. Illustration 6-2 shows which investor sources and approaches are possible, given the company's Familiarity Index Rating and corporate growth track stage. For example, if your company is at stage 2—market development—and you have decided that adventure stockholders are your ideal

ILLUSTRATION 6-2:
INVESTOR SOURCES AND APPROACHES BASED ON FAMILIARITY INDEX RATING AND CORPORATE GROWTH TRACK STAGE

Corporate Growth Track Stage	Familiarity Index Rating					
	1 Doesn't know prod./industry or co./people	**2** Doesn't know prod./industry, but knows about co./people	**3** Doesn't know prod./industry, but personally knows co./people	**4** Knows prod./industry, but doesn't know about co./people	**5** Knows prod./industry, & knows about co./people	**6** Knows prod./industry, & personally knows co./people
7 IPO/Sale	AS-Dir/Mr	AS-Dir/Mr VCP-Dir/Mr	VCP-Dir/Mr AS-Dir/Mr	AS-Dir/Mr	AS-Dir/Mr VCP-Dir/Mr	AS-Dir/Mr
6 Profitable/ major exp.	AS-Dir	AS-Dir/Mr VC-Dir SCI-Dir VCP-Dir/Mr	AS-Dir/Mr VC-Dir/Mr SCI-Dir/Mr VCP-Dir/Mr	AS-Dir/Mr	AS-Dir/Mr VC-Dir/Mr SCI-Dir/Mr VCP-Dir/Mr	AS-Dir/Mr VC-Dir/Mr SCI-Dir/Mr VCP-Dir/Mr
5 Profitable/ needs cap.	AS-Dir	AS-Dir/Mr VC-Dir SCI-Dir VCP-Dir/Mr	AS-Dir/Mr VC-Dir/Mr SCI-Dir/Mr VCP-Dir/Mr	AS-Dir	AS-Dir/Mr VC-Dir/Mr SCI-Dir/Mr VCP-Dir/Mr	AS-Dir/Mr VC-Dir/Mr SCI-Dir/Mr VCP-Dir/Mr
4 Breakeven/ prov. dist.		VCP-Dir/Mr AS-Dir/Mr	AS-Dir/Mr VC-Dir/Mr SCI-Dir VCP-Dir/Mr		AS-Dir/Mr VC-Dir/Mr SCI-Dir/Mr VCP-Dir/Mr	AS-Dir/Mr VC-Dir/Mr SCI-Dir/Mr VCP-Dir/Mr
3 Losing/ prov. dist.		VCP-Dir SCI-Dir	AS-Dir/Mr VC-Dir/Mr VCP-Dir/Mr SCI-Dir BA-Dir		SCI BA-Dir VC-Dir/Mr AS-Dir/Mr VCP-Dir/Mr	SCI-Dir/Mr BA-Dir VC-Dir/Mr AS-Dir/Mr VCP-Dir/Mr
Mkt. devl.		VCP-Dir SCI-Dir	VCP-Dir/Mr BA-Dir SCI-Dir AS-Dir/Mr		SCI-Dir/Mr BA-Dir VC-Dir/Mr AS-Dir/Mr VCP-Dir/Mr	SCI-Dir/Mr BA-Dir VC-Dir/Mr AS-Dir/Mr VCP-Dir/Mr
2 Prod. devl.			VCP-Dir/Mr BA-Dir		SCI-Dir/Mr BA-Dir AS-Dir VC-Dir/Mr VCP-Dir/Mr	SCI-Dir/Mr BA-Dir AS-Dir VC-Dir/Mr VCP-Dir/Mr
Seed			VCP-Dir/Mr BA-Dir		SCI-Dir/Mr BA-Dir VC-Dir/Mr VCP-Dir/Mr	SCI-Dir/Mr BA-Dir VC-Dir/Mr VCP-Dir/Mr
1 Concept			BA-Dir VCP-Dir			BA-Dir VCP-Dir/Mr

*Key:

Sources:
AS = Adventure stockholders
BA = Business angels
SCI = Strategic corporate investors
VC = Venture capitalists
VCP = Visionary Capitalists

Approaches:
Dir = Direct placement
Mr = Money raisers

source, then you will have to make sure that your Capital Relations™ plan moves all investor and money raiser leads and prospects into a Familiarity Index Rating of at least 3, and better yet 5 or 6. This is called moving your leads through the "relationship ladder."

CREATING YOUR OWN INVESTOR/MONEY RAISER MARKET

The power of today's database marketing and information/knowledge systems and resources allows your company the opportunity to develop an investor/money raiser profile and a Familiarity Index Rating for each lead investor/money raiser list you assemble. This is the knowledge component of your Capital Relations™ program.

You can have at your fingertips the quantitative and qualitative rating data on every person or firm you select to be on your lead lists. Couple this knowledge-based power at your fingertips with the need to base your Capital Relations™ plan on a one-on-one dialogue-basis with the investor/money raisers (the experience component of your Capital Relations™ program), and quickly the old marketing paradigms give way.[1] You have the information/knowledge systems today to develop your Offering Campaign so that you are in control of who your company chooses to get into some kind of relationship with.

Who Makes Up Your Investor/Money Raiser Market? Your investor/money raiser market is made up of enough leads from the sources you believe have the right investors/money raisers to allow your company to implement its Capital Relations™ plan successfully. There are two factors to be determined. The first is to determine which investor/money raiser profile a person or firm must fit in order to be included in your investor/money raiser market. The second factor is to determine how many investors/money raisers you'll need to fund your offering—this is the size of your investor/money raiser market. These factors will determine the people and firms on whom you're going to need to spend time and money using your Capital Relations™ program.

INVESTOR/MONEY RAISER PROFILE DEFINITIONS

Actual Investor Profile. The description of the characteristics of the kind of investor that *will* invest in your company during the Offering Campaign. This critical profile is ultimately determined during "Step 8: Testing the Market and List Assemblage." The Actual Investor Profile may be a person or firm that fits any one of the Familiarity Index Ratings. You may find that there are several Actual Investor Profiles that fit your Offering Campaign.

Actual Money Raiser Profile. The description of the characteristics of the kind of money raiser that *will* raise investor capital for your company during the Offering Campaign. This profile is ultimately determined during "Step 8: Testing the Market and List Assemblage." The Actual Money Raiser Profile may be a person or firm that fits any one of the Familiarity Index Ratings. You may find that there are several Actual Money Raiser Profiles that fit your Offering Campaign.

Lead. Someone (or some firm) whom you have good reason to believe fits the Actual Investor Profile or Actual Money Raiser Profile.

Prospect Investor/Money Raiser. Someone who fits the Actual Investor/Money Raiser Profile, but presently *does not know* about the company or *does not personally know* the people in the company.

Candidate Investor/Money Raiser. Someone who fits the Actual Investor/Money Raiser Profile and *knows about* the company.

Super Candidate Investor/Money Raiser. Someone (or some firm) who fits the Actual Investor/Money Raiser Profile and *personally knows* the company and its people.

Actual Investor. Someone who has invested in the company.

HOW BIG IS THE LIST?

Here is the formula for determining how many names of investors or money raisers need to be compiled to constitute a workable investor/money raiser market:

---

25 leads will produce an average of 5 prospects.

5 prospects will produce an average of 5 candidates.

(Remember a prospect becomes a candidate once the prospect *knows about* your company. It does not take much effort for you to inform a prospect about your company.)

5 candidates will produce an average of 4 super candidates.

4 super candidates will produce an average of 2 actual investors.

In venture capital and strategic corporate investor financings you may only need one investor. In such a case less than twenty-five leads are needed. However, from these two sources the Actual Investor Profile may be so narrowly defined (based on "Step 8: Testing the Market and List Assemblage") that there won't be twenty-five venture capitalists or strategic corporate investor leads. For instance, there may be only eight leads, which equal less than two prospects, which in turn, means you have only two prospects to convert into actual investors. It is the actual real-life workings of this arithmetic that explains why venture capital and strategic corporate investor financings can be so tough.

Let's take another example, this time using adventure stockholders. If your company needs to raise $600,000, and you structured the minimum investment per investor to be $8,000, then you will need 900 leads. The leads will be converted into 180 prospects, who will then be converted into 180 candidates. Finally, the candidates will be converted into 150 super-candidates, who will yield the required 75 actual investors.

Keep Your Pipeline Full

Every entrepreneur and company has a certain number of people that qualify as investor/money raiser leads, prospects, candidates, or super-candidates. You need to constantly update your internal information systems to include the profile data on your investor market. Illustration 6-4 is a sample form called the "Investor/Money Raiser Database List." It is the management of this database list that helps determine the quality and efficiency of your Capital Relations™ program and Offering Campaign.

CREATING YOUR COMMUNICATIONS

Take a closer look at Illustration 6-2. Notice that early-stage companies have to have some kind of relationship going on with the investor/money raiser. These capital relationships are based on knowledge about the company and its people, or it is based on knowing personally the company and its people. The illustration also shows the importance of your investor/money raisers having a familiarity with your product and industry as well. Since relationships don't normally happen by accident, your company has to create these relationships with its potential investor market (that it also creates). The success of this creation process depends upon how well your company communicates.

To create the kind of communications that produce the desired quality of relationship, with the desired quantity of investors/money raisers, requires *messages*, *messengers*, and *media*.

Messages

Since a Capital Relations™ program involves creating your own investor/money raiser market, you have the opportunity to also create the reaction the market has about you. In other words, you can control what the market thinks and feels about you.[2] A Capital Relations™ program involves a sequence of one-on-one contacts with the investors/money raisers before they are asked to invest. These sequential contacts (the relationship ladder) are used to move along the message you want to control. (Step 10 includes an actual Offering Campaign Plan describing the sequence of events for a hypothetical company.)

The starting place of effective communication is to have the right message. The right message is: "This phenomenal company is accessing capital." All the work done in "Step 1: Designing the Phenomenal Message" was the starting place. During "Step 8: Testing the Market and List Assemblage," you will find out if your investors/money raisers believe if you're phenomenal or not. Those who become your actual investors will be those who feel drawn to your efforts because of all the Evidence Points of your business plan that excited their imaginations and calmed their doubts. Also during Step 8, you will find out why they believe your message. And you will discover if there is anything about your company and its people that they don't believe in, and what it will take to change their minds and feelings. This credibility is established through the workings of *inference*, *reference*, and *results*.[3]

Inference. This is established when someone else who is credible does business with the company or invests in the company. It is also established by something happening or being in place that was predicted to happen by the business plan. When this happens, investors tend to assume that other things that are predicted in the business plan will also work out well. This is why the Launch Plan is so important.

Reference. What someone else says is more important than what you say. The best references come by word-of-mouth. Obviously, the more credible the referring party is, the more powerful the effect of the reference will be.

Results. Success in the customer markets reinforces itself. Your track record speaks louder than words. Promises kept are valuable. Investors are always impressed with results. This is another reason why the Launch Plan is so important.

The Evidence Points profiled in Step 1 are, in essence, the strategies of inference, reference, and results used to mold the message to fit the needs of your investors/money raisers. Business plans and Capital Relations™ programs that ooze the right Evidence Points get the capital. When Bonnie Raitt sings her popular song, "Let's Giv'em Something to Talk About," it should be taken as a reminder to the leadership team of the importance of Step 1.

MESSENGERS

People judge companies by the quality of the people representing the company. Who delivers the message of credibility is important. These messengers are the ones entrusted with the responsibility of participating in the Capital Relations™ program: a one-on-one dialogue with your investor/money raiser market. The messengers are people—not computers, software, advertising, or direct mail.

A dialogue is a two-way talk/listen program between two people. Although some products/services may be sold through one-way monologue marketing systems (built on traditional prospecting and selling principles), investor capital is accessed through experiential communications between human beings.

A Capital Relations™ program uses information/knowledge systems to provide the company the ability to acquire and organize information on its potential investor/money raiser markets. In turn, this provides the company's messengers with the up-to-the-minute needs and wants of its investor/money raiser market so that the message can be tuned to the individual investor. But, remember, the message is carried by humans—not computers.

There are four categories of messengers that need to be developed. These are the customer infrastructure messengers, advocate messengers, capital infrastructure messengers, and the leadership team itself. Here are the definitions of these terms:

Customer Market Infrastructure Messengers. These are the key influence makers in your industry and sub-markets. This is the important 10% of the market that the other 90% follow. When they talk, other people listen and buy. When they support a product/service, others support it as well. Your job is to control what they think and say about your company and its people. Keep in mind, however, the possibility that your industry infrastructure may not even understand what you're trying to do. Do not be discouraged. It may even be a sign that you're really on the right track.

Advocate Messengers. Another important messenger of your message are those individuals or firms that know enough about your company to be interested in helping the company find its investors—these are the advocate messengers.[4]

Capital Market Infrastructure Messengers. In the investor markets (see Step 2), there are people and firms who have an influence on other people and firms in the market. When they talk, other people listen, invest, and raise money. Your job is to control what they think and say about your company and its people.

The Leadership Team. Key leadership team members need to be ready to "press the flesh" with the potential investors/money raisers, as well as with the other messengers.

DEVELOPING THE CUSTOMER MARKET INFRASTRUCTURE MESSENGERS

In the section on the "Positioning" Chaordic Web Element in Step 1, customer market infrastructure development was discussed. It is emphasized again here because the other messengers of your message may be strongly influenced by the customer market infrastructure. Your advocate messengers and capital market infrastructure messengers have to turn to somebody for corroboration and verification that what you're saying about your company is credible. You will note in Illustration 6-6 that the customer market infrastructure messengers are listed first on the time line. They weren't placed there by accident. The media or communication tactics and tools that you choose to use during your Capital Relations™ program will determine how well you carry your message, and what people are saying about the message to all the other messengers and people that make up your investor/money raiser market.

DEVELOPING THE ADVOCATE MESSENGER PROGRAM

One vital ingredient any company has available in developing a successful Capital Relations™ formula is to leverage its constituency. The power of leveraging your constituency, when done properly, results in your company being "pulled" through this process. Your constituency presents the best source of people and firms who have a "stake" in your success.

So often the theoretical formulas and strategies that are necessary when accessing investor capital seem impossible for the leadership team to execute alone. However, once the simplicity and power of developing an advocate messenger program is understood, the challenges that once seemed insurmountable now seem possible.

Here are the stages of developing your advocate messenger program:

> Stage 1: Determine the number of advocate messengers you need.
> Stage 2: Identify potential advocate messengers from your circle of influence.
> Stage 3: Win support from your advocate messengers.
> Stage 4: Lead and manage the advocate messengers during your Offering Campaign.

Stage 1: Determine the Number of Advocate Messengers You Need. Make sure you understand the definitions previously given in the section, "Creating Your Own Investor Market." Determining how many people/firms you need to help carry your message to your investor/money raiser market starts with understanding that every advocate messenger may be able to have an existing personal relationship with five prospect investors or money raisers. Let's look at two examples:

Example one: business angel financing. If your company has determined that business angels are your ideal source for investors, and that you need eight of them, then the following arithmetic applies:

8	Business angels are needed to fund the offering
16	Super-candidates are needed
20	Candidates are needed
20	Prospects are needed, therefore,
4	Advocate messengers are needed

Example two: adventure stockholder financing. Maybe you've determined that your financing is best suited for adventure stockholders. Perhaps your financing requires $600,000. You've also decided that each investor needs to invest a minimum of $8,000. Here's how the math plays out:

75	Adventure stockholders are needed to fund the offering
150	Super-candidates are needed
180	Candidates are needed
180	Prospects are needed
36	Advocate messengers are needed

This arithmetic is based on extensive experience gained from working the Investor Financing™ steps over the years. For example, your company may have some advocate messengers who have more or less than five prospects. Many of your advocate messengers, especially if they are not educated by you ahead of time, may believe they have relationships with prospects, when in reality, their prospects really fit the "lead" definition explained earlier.

ILLUSTRATION 6-3:
THE CIRCLES OF INFLUENCE

Stage 2: Identify Potential Advocate Messengers From Your Circle of Influence. There are nine basic influence areas of your business from which you'll find your advocate messengers. These areas are referred to as the "circles of influence" and are shown in Illustration 6-3. Not only does your company have its own circle of influence, but the persons or firms targeted as advocate messengers will each have their own circles of influence. It is from each advocate messenger's circle of influence that the prospects for your offering emerge.

Let's do an exercise to demonstrate the power of an advocate messenger program.(see page 246)

Stage 3: Win Support From Your Advocate Messengers. Each person or firm you have identified as an advocate messenger will require a customized plan of action to win their support in carrying your message to the prospects in their own circle of influence. Each advocate messenger will have a different relationship with your company, which means you'll need to have meaningful one-on-one dialogue to determine exactly how to finally win the support of your advocate messenger. "Step 8: Testing the Market and List Assemblage" is when you determine these important points. Here's a list of "win support" items that you might find helpful:

1. Hire the advocate messenger as an employee or consultant.
2. Invite the advocate messenger to be on the board of advisors or board of directors.
3. Agree to pay a "finder's fee," if any of their prospects invest.
4. Provide warrants or stock options to advocate messengers based on their performance (i.e., the number of their prospects who invest, and the amount invested by their prospects).
5. If the advocate messenger is a vendor, then promise more business.
6. If the advocate messenger is a customer, then promise better service.

Stage 4: Lead and Manage the Advocate Messengers During Your Offering Campaign. You have to take responsibility for leading and managing the advocate messengers during the Offering Campaign. Your internal information/knowledge systems have to accommodate the needs of your one-on-one, dialogue-based Capital Relations™ program. Each advocate messenger will have a different profile, as will each of the advocate messenger's prospects.

To make a good beginning on leading and managing your advocate messengers during your Offering Campaign, start with gathering, searching, analyzing, and compiling the data you need. Illustration 6-4 is an example of a form for your Investor/Money Raiser Database List.

1. How many people/companies can you list from the Enhancement Chart (Illustration 4–1) that have a "stake" in your business and who therefore may be possible advocate messengers? Be sure to include people/firms in both your Launch Plan and Growth Plan: _____

2. Add the number of people/companies from the Advisory Support Team Enhancement Chart (Illustration 4–2) that have a "stake" in your business: +_____

   Total advocate messengers: _____

3. Multiply the total advocates by nine (since every advocate has nine circles of influence):   x 9

   Total circles available: _____

4. Multiply the total circles available by five (since it's probable that each advocate has five possible leads from each of their circles of influence):   x 5

   Total who could be leads/prospects: _____

5. Calculate the expected number of actual investors:

   a. Multiply the total number of people/companies who could be leads by .2 (since only 20% of the initial number typically become leads):   x .2

      _____

   b. Multiply the total number of possible leads by .2 (since only 20% of the initial leads typically become prospects):   x .2

      _____

   c. To determine the number of candidates, simply duplicate the number of prospects (since all prospects can be made to "know about" your company):   _____

   d. Now multiply the number of candidates by .8 (since 80% of your candidates can become super-candidates by getting to know the leadership team):   x .8

      _____

   e. Finally, multiply the number of super-candidates by .5 to determine the number of actual investors (since typically 50% of the super-candidates become actual investors):   x .5

      _____

Leading and managing your advocate messengers requires you to fine-tune your final Offering Campaign. "Step 8: Testing the Market and List Assemblage" will help you determine how long your Offering Campaign will likely take to move all the investor/money raiser leads to prospects, all the prospects to candidates, all the candidates to super-candidates, and all the super-candidates to actual investors/money raisers. Step 8 will also allow you to find out which communication tactics and tools support everything you're doing in order to have a successful Capital Relations™ program. Determining all of this is, of course, one of the objectives of the Investor Financing™ steps. Each step builds on the previous step. Answers and strategies will evolve by following these steps until a final Offering Campaign is launched during Step 10.

Illustration 6-6 profiles those people who are possible advocate messengers.

DEVELOPING THE CAPITAL MARKET INFRASTRUCTURE MESSENGERS

Additional messengers for your message, vis-a-vis word-of-mouth tactics, are the various people or firms that comprise your company's capital market infrastructure. These are the key people who stand between you and your investor/money raiser market. It was explained in "Step 1: Designing the Phenomenal Message" that the ultimate aim is to create entirely new customer markets and own a relationship with the entire market. Likewise, when accessing capital, you create your investor/money raiser market and own a lasting relationship with it as well. Whether it's establishing credibility with customers or capital, influence makers (the infrastructure) play a major role.

Many of your potential advocate messengers will base their decision of support on the strength of what members of both the customer and capital market infrastructure say about your company. Often it is impossible to gain any strong capital market infrastructure messenger support without first having a strong customer market infrastructure messenger support. There is always a degree of communication and information passing back and forth between these two groups of infrastructure messengers. Your advocate messengers become more enthusiastic and confident as they hear or observe positive things about your company from both groups of infrastructure messengers. Like the development of the customer market infrastructure messenger, the aim is to find those 10% of the people who influence the investing and money raising decisions of the other 90%.

ILLUSTRATION 6-4:
INVESTOR/MONEY RAISER DATABASE LIST

Name[1]	List status[2]	Money raiser responsible[3]	Broker/ dealer[4]	Career category[5]	3rd party influence[6]	Industry[7]	Familiarity index rating[8]

1. The name of the investor or money raiser.
2. The person/firm is an advocate messenger, infrastructure member, lead, prospect, candidate, super-candidate, actual investor, or money raiser.
3. The money raiser responsible is the person/firm who introduced the investor to the company.
4. The broker/dealer is the firm the money raiser is licensed with.
5. The career of the person: business owner, executive, self employed professional, sales and marketing professional, etc.
6. Who this person is influenced by (CPA, attorney, consultant, infrastructure member, etc.).
7. The industry this person is in.
8. The Familiarity Index Rating of this person (1–6).

Here are the stages for developing your capital market infrastructure messengers:

Stage 1: Develop a good Advocate Messenger Program Plan.

Stage 2: Develop a good Financing Sequence Plan (Step 5).

Stage 3: Identify the influence makers in each capital market infrastructure that you're interested in.

Stage 4: Lead and manage a good infrastructure Capital Relations™ program.

Stage 1: Develop a Good Advocate Messenger Program Plan. By developing a good plan for utilizing advocate messengers, you'll have some idea who in the capital markets may influence your advocate messengers. The reverse is also true. Because of their business or social standing, some of your targeted advocate messengers may be in a position to influence other members of the capital market, such as other advocate messengers, money raisers, investors, and other infrastructure messengers.

Stage 2: Develop a Good Financing Sequence Plan. "Step 5: Structuring the Financing" explained how to do this. Essentially your Financing Sequence Plan is the five- to ten-year plan for the company's future financing needs.

As you learned in Steps 1 and 2, investors are interested in knowing how they are going to be financed-out and/or provided with liquidity for their investment. The plan you develop to show this is called your Financing Sequence Plan. When you develop this plan, you'll put into sharp focus what future investors and money raisers you'll need to be successful with these later financing rounds. These future sources of capital can have a strong influence on your immediate investor/money raiser market for your current offering. By showing that you have already begun a relationship with your future financing sources, you give investors and money raisers a strong sense of credibility about your promise to either cash them out through later financings, or to find additional financing sources to fuel the growth of the company.

Stage 3: Identify the Influence Makers in Each Capital Market Infrastructure That You're Interested In. The current and future capital market sources will most likely have their own infrastructure of influence makers. Your job, with the help of your Funding Team (Step 4), is to identify these separate infrastructures, find out who the players are, and plan how you are going to communicate with them. The goal is to initiate and manage a strong word-of-mouth campaign. Word-of-mouth campaigns create or change the attitudes and opinions of the people in the targeted infrastructure groups. You will need to study and understand the system of each group.

ILLUSTRATION 6-5:
NASD CAPITAL MARKET INFRASTRUCTURE

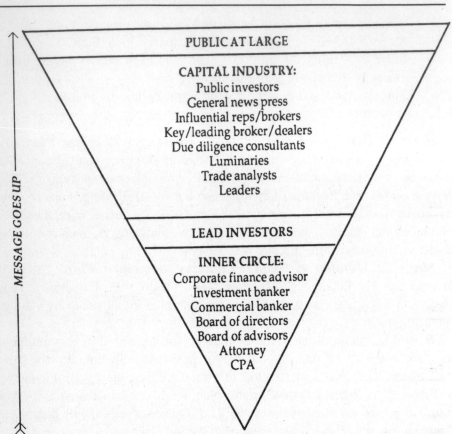

MESSAGE GOES UP

PUBLIC AT LARGE

CAPITAL INDUSTRY:
Public investors
General news press
Influential reps/brokers
Key/leading broker/dealers
Due diligence consultants
Luminaries
Trade analysts
Leaders

LEAD INVESTORS

INNER CIRCLE:
Corporate finance advisor
Investment banker
Commercial banker
Board of directors
Board of advisors
Attorney
CPA

For example, Illustration 6-5 presents a list of categories in the NASD community where you will find the people who will push or pull your message up through to the capital sources and money raisers you've targeted. (Not all of these categories exist in each capital source's infrastructure.)

Illustration 6-6 profiles the kinds of capital market infrastructure messengers that are possible.

Stage 4: Lead and Manage a Good Infrastructure Capital Relations™ Program. The communication tactics and tools offer you a wide choice of strategies to design and implement the kind of information (monologue) and communication (dialogue) you need to have for a successful word-of-mouth campaign.

ILLUSTRATION 6-6:
CAPITAL RELATIONS™ WORD-OF-MOUTH MESSENGERS

	Customer market infrastructure messengers	Advocate messengers	Capital market infrastructure messengers
TIME →			
Public	Customers General press	Customers Key adven. stkhlds.	General press Key adven. stkhlds.
Industry	Consultants Luminaries Financial analysts Trade press Financial press	Consultants Luminaries	Due diligence consults. Consultants Luminaries Financial analysts Trade analysts Trade press Financial press
Customers	Innovators Key accounts Lead users Beta users Alpha users	Late adapters Early adapters Innovators Key accounts Lead users Beta users Alpha users	Key accounts Lead users Beta users
Friends		Social friends Business friends New friends Old friends	
Vendors/ suppliers		Future suppliers Key suppliers Future vendors Key vendors	
Investors/ money raisers		Future money raisers Strat. corp. investors All existing investors Lead investors	Future money raisers Strat. corp. investors Lead reps Lead broker/dealer Lead investors
Employees		Staff Key staff with stock	CFO
Strategic alliances & joint ventures	Production alliances Selling chain alliances	First mgmt. team Production alliances Selling chain alliances	First mgmt. team Lead money raiser
Inner circle	Attorney CPA Corp. finance adv. Commercial banker Bd. of advisors Bd. of directors	Attorney CPA Corp. finance adv. Commercial banker Bd. of advisors Bd. of directors	Attorney CPA Corp. finance adv. Commercial banker Board of advisors Bd. of directors

MESSAGE GOES UP ↑

DEVELOPING THE LEADERSHIP TEAM'S COMMUNICATION SKILLS

The fourth messenger is the leadership team itself. It has been said before that the leadership team must take responsibility for allocating a healthy portion of their time for personal contact with the investor/money raiser market. Even if your offering has money raisers lined up to do all the investor solicitation and closings, the leadership team will still be expected to participate in many meetings and presentations. Money raisers always depend on the leadership team for personal presentations. The leadership team needs to be prepared to develop all the tools needed for the offering and to carry out most of the tactics. If the leadership team lacks highly qualified members to prepare the necessary tools and carry out the required tactics, then the leadership team will have to rely on the corporate finance advisor and a host of vendors for help.

MEDIA

In order to implement your Capital Relations™ program, it is not enough to have a unique message and the right messengers. Both the message and the messengers need media. This media provides the two-way dialogue communication program with the forms and forums to implement the entire Capital Relations™ program. The right message and messengers provide the context of success. The media provides all the content of day-to-day plans and activities that move the Offering Campaign along. In order to differentiate all the possible action steps your company can take, media is categorized in the following way:

Communication Tactics. These are strategies of action that help you find, or get in contact with, investors and money raiser leads. They can also be used to help turn leads into prospects, prospects into candidates, and candidates into super-candidates. Eventually these tactics can help you turn super-candidates into actual investors.

Communication Tools. These are the tangible things that you use to implement the various tactics.

The old saying, "There's more than one way to skin a cat," couldn't be truer than when it comes to the tactics and tools available to implement the approaches you've chosen for accessing the sources of investor capital. There are more tactics and tools then you'll be able to use during a single Offering Campaign. There are many factors to consider when deciding which tactics and tools are right for your Capital Relations™ program: the personality of your leadership team, the kind of industry you're in, the kind of financing instruments that you're using (Step 5), the amount of capital you need to raise, and who the messengers are.

Your corporate finance advisor's job is to help you analyze all of these factors and select the right tactics and tools. It is also very important to keep in mind that your final selection should not be made until you complete Step 9. The Investor Financing™ steps work from a broad base of tactics and tools, and then gradually narrow the focus until a tight, efficient, successful Offering Campaign emerges in Step 10.

As you'll learn, some tactics and tools will only be used for a specific investor source or money raiser. Others will be appropriate when casting your net for as many leads and prospects as possible.

These tactics and tools are not just clever ideas. You'll see that, in many cases, they grow out of the very manner of your "being," that is to say, your lifestyle. You'll discover that many of the tactics and tools will involve permanent or part-time lifestyle choices that you either have made or will make. What you do with your personal and business time can have a great influence on the success or failure of accessing investor capital.

Don't be discouraged if some of the tactics and tools are beyond your capabilities and resources. Every entrepreneur will find several that he or she will be able to use.

Most of the tactics and tools have nothing to do with asking an investor for a check. Instead, they help to position you and your company so that you are able to get the attention, and build the trust, of your potential investors/money raisers through a two-way dialogue with the company's messengers. Asking for the check only comes after you have completed an aggressive and efficient Offering Campaign using the tactics and tools to move potential investors/money raisers all the way to super-candidate status.

THE MAJOR COMMUNICATION TACTICS

1. The One-on-One Meeting Tactic. This is the most obvious tactic, but it is often overlooked. The first rule of the Universe is: *Ask.* If you're going to get your offering funded, then at some point you're going to have to ask people to invest. All of the work involved in carrying out the Investor Financing™ steps will never mean anything unless you go out and ask for the check from an investor or ask a money raiser to do it for you. Boldness, pride, and self-worth are the essential personal qualities necessary to insure that you will arrange enough personal one-on-one meetings with investors and/or money raisers, so that eventually, when a lead is converted to a super-candidate, you'll be able to "ask for the check."

2. The Expert Tactic. Since people love to invest with experts, this strategy is important. It is worth working hard to position yourself, your leadership team, and your company as experts in your field.

If you're not an expert, then hire people who are for the leadership team. Once you have the expertise, use your public relations firm, your imagination, and your energy to get the word out about your expertise. Compile newsclippings, articles, and testimonials. If you and your company develop the reputation of an expert, then you have a good start on capturing the trust of your investor sources and money raisers.

3. The "Convoy Surfacer" Tactic. With this strategy, you target your time and marketing efforts to place yourself in the middle of particular groups of affluent people (affinity groups) who might become investors or money raisers once you get to know them.[5] A simple, if expensive, approach would be to move into an affluent neighborhood, where you can become acquainted with your well-to-do neighbors.

Another example would be as follows: suppose that you have identified a group of affluent people (let's say it's the Porsche Club of Atlanta) whom you don't know, and more importantly, they don't know you. Find out where these people meet (that is, the organizations and groups they belong to), and what they read (trade journals, newspapers, etc.). Now, surface at their meetings so you can meet them. Also, arrange to publish articles in the trade journals and newspapers they read. Before long, you'll have their names, their attention, and their trust. There are many "convoys" you can find, work, and play in.

4. The Civic Leader Tactic. This tactic is akin to convoy surfacing. Become involved in charities, politics, civic organizations, and other groups. This can be an important method for gathering information and starting relationships with prospective business angels, adventure stockholders, and money raisers. The key is to make sure that you involve yourself in your official capacity as a representative of your company whenever possible.

Agree to act on the steering committee. Volunteer to be chairman of the fundraising committee, the membership committee, or the ticket sales committee. If the group is prestigious enough, you'll have the opportunity to set up appointments with important people who you otherwise never would have met.

5. The Charity Volunteer Tactic. An excellent tactic to meet the affluent is to volunteer to head up activities of charities and fundraisers. When you call on the powerful and affluent, in the official capacity of a representative of the charity, you'll be able to talk or meet with people you might never have had the opportunity to meet otherwise.

6. The Industry Leader Tactic. This is a combination of being an expert and a convoy surfacer. Get involved in key industry committees on a level that puts you in contact with other business owners (many of whom may be eager to find new opportunities). These owners may be impressed enough to make a major investment in your company, especially if they see the strategic alliance as beneficial to their own business.

7. The Business Leader Tactic. Spending time, money, and talent supporting the business community can lead to valuable contacts.

8. The Social Butterfly Tactic. Have fun and make contacts at the same time. Spending time and money attending all the parties and other high society events can be great for meeting investors and money raisers.

9. The Country Club Tactic. Join, and be active in, country clubs, yacht clubs, garden clubs, etc. These are all great places to meet potential investors and money raisers.

10. The Public Seminars/Forums Tactic. Presenting a public seminar or forum is an excellent way to meet adventure stockholders and perhaps a few business angels and money raisers. Your securities attorney should be consulted when planning public seminars. As a rule, you cannot solicit investors for your company at public seminars unless the offering is publicly registered with the SEC and/or appropriate state securities commissioner. You *can* use public seminars to present topics other than investment opportunities. The trick is to find topics and speakers that are relevant to your company's product/service, its industry, and its mission. Some possible subjects are the current economic situation, popular "cause" topics, topics of appeal to new business owners, or a demonstration of your product/service. As you can see, there are many possible topics; the trick is to select one that will appeal to your targeted prospective investors or money raisers.

Here are some ideas to help increase attendance: Invite well-known guest speakers to make all or part of the presentation. A related possibility is to hold a forum, which you chair, with a number of prominent guest participants.[6] Hold the seminar or forum in an unusual and interesting location. Charging admission may help legitimize the event. Use a prize drawing. Publicize the event well. It may be necessary to use telemarketing and direct mail, and other advertising techniques to insure a strong attendance.[7]

Consider giving the seminar as a joint venture with a law firm, a CPA firm, a vendor, or even a prospective investor. This not only reduces your cost for the seminar, but it gives you an opportunity to get to know the co-sponsors.

11. The Private Sales Seminar Tactic. This is a tactic to convert candidate or super-candidate adventure stockholder investors into actual investors. Again, consult with your securities attorney for securities compliance. Make sure those invited to attend meet the "accredited investor" standards or "prior relationship" standards imposed by the federal and state securities laws. Your attorney will probably be able to give his blessing to the seminar, even if your offering is a private placement. Your private seminar should be coordinated with your money raisers, so that they can invite their candidate and super-candidate investors. You can use direct mail tactics and telemarketing tactics, as well as an assortment of other tools that are discussed later in this section to insure strong attendance.

12. The Private Workshop Tactic. If you have a unique skill or talent, you can share it in an educational format. This tactic can be very powerful if you can develop a workshop that can be modified to appeal to different affinity groups among the business angels, adventure stockholders, and money raisers. This focus and segmentation increases satisfaction for the workshop attendees, and thereby increases your chances of developing new candidate investors.

13. The "Bait and Switch" Tactic. The basic concept is to first get involved with lead and prospect investors or money raisers on a one-on-one basis, and then, after the contacts are established, approach them as potential investor sources or money raisers. For example, suppose you hire ten financial planners from XYZ Broker/Dealer, Inc. to counsel you on how to best structure your company's current offering (using a technique known as a *focus group* that is explained in "Step 8: Testing the Market and List Assemblage"). Their hourly consulting fee is the "bait." The meeting establishes a relationship with them, and after you've paid them, you can "switch" your tactics and approach them as potential money raisers.

14. The Strategic Association Tactic. The idea here is to develop the fine art of arranging business relationships with individuals and firms so that they can help "pull" you through your funding. In Step 4, we analyzed how you can enhance your company's position through the use of strategic associations. These associations can bring a number of enhancements to your company in the areas of advice and guidance, management, business performance, and financing. To this list you can add the possibility of your associate becoming an investor source or an advocate messenger. When considering entering into a strategic association, ask yourself this double-barreled question: "Will this person or company be able to invest in my company someday, and/or can they find investors for me?"

15. The Watching "Money in Motion" Tactic. You can, in a short period of time, identify a lot of potential investors by simply reading the newspapers and business press, keeping an eye out for people selling businesses, real estate, or other sizable assets. Probate notices and records can also lead you to people who have "fallen into" cash. Lottery and prize winners are candidates as well.

16. The Wholesaler Tactic. Developing a working relationship with one or more wholesalers is a solid strategy—especially if your financing is well suited for broker/dealer or stock brokerage firms.[8] You can hire a wholesaler either full or part time. If your budget doesn't allow you to hire a wholesaler, then perhaps you can develop a relationship with the wholesaler as a friend. Then you can approach him or her with an offer to pay them a finder's fee for any introductions to reps, broker/dealers, or stock brokerage firms who might sign a selling agreement with you.[9]

17. The Sales Force Tactic. This tactic consists of building up a sales force to sell your offering directly to investors. The number of sales people you hire depends on many factors. Hiring many salespeople results in what is negatively called, a "boiler room." If you decide to hire salespersons, make sure that you comply with the securities laws. Consult with your attorney. It's a lot easier to find and motivate salespeople if your offering is a public offering rather than a private placement.

18. The Telemarketing Tactic. Consider using telemarketing to supplement your Offering Campaign. If you use this tactic, your offering as a rule, should qualify as a public offering to comply with securities law. Consult your attorney. You may use telemarketing to complement many of the other tactics. Direct mail, seminars, and market research are all tactics that can be supported by telemarketing. Telemarketing should be focused on complementing those tactics that get people to attend meetings or to confirm that materials were received.

19. The Family Tapper Tactic. Having an affluent and generous family willing to invest in your company, or at least interested in investing, is a wonderful gift to be blessed with.

20. The Advertiser Tactic. This approach consists of placing advertisements to attract potential investors *if* your offering is qualified as a public offering to comply with the securities laws. Again, consult with your attorney to ensure compliance. As a rule, advertising for a generic seminar is not a securities law problem. But you can't advertise for a seminar where you plan to sell a private placement to nonaccredited investors. You may use advertising to support many of the other tactics. It's a good idea to make sure that any advertising includes a direct-response coupon.

21. The Vendor Tactic. Never overlook your vendors as potential investors. The bigger the vendor is, the better, since a larger company is more likely to have funds from a pension plan to invest. If the vendor does have pension funds available, study the *approaches* to pension funds investments discussed later. Study the material again on strategic corporate investors.

22. The Referral Tactic. Your Offering Campaign (Step 10) will necessarily include many presentations and meetings with potential investors and money raisers. It should become automatic for you to ask everyone you contact for a referral to someone else. Ask for a referral even if they have already said no to investing in your offering.

23. The Infomercial Tactic. The development of infomercial marketing for selling financial products is now in its infancy. Federal and state securities regulators are wrestling with the dilemma posed by the inability of companies to predetermine the suitability of the audience prior to airing an infomercial. However, the new communication superhighways being developed, along with the technological developments in segmenting viewer audiences, could bring about revolutionary changes in securities marketing. Certainly infomercials could be crafted to provide a way to generate lead lists by taking advantage of a "bait and switch" tactic, and selling your company's products/services in the infomercial, and then using the resulting customer list as a lead list for your Capital Relations™ program. Your securities counsel needs to be involved in any infomercial strategic planning.

24. The Focus Group Tactic. In Step 8, you'll learn about using focus groups as an aid to selling your offering. This is a powerful tactic in Investor Financing™. Everything you want from a tactic is provided by focus group work. The power of this tactic cannot be over emphasized.[10]

25. The Guest Speaker Tactic. This solid tactic can substantiate your role as an expert in your industry. Use it only if you feel comfortable as a speaker. If public speaking frightens you, consider enrolling in a public speaking class or join your local Toastmasters.

Make sure that you secure the attendees' names and addresses if you can. They belong on your mailing list.

In most cities, there are firms that publish directories of meetings and groups. (Your local business journal can provide their names and addresses.) The organizations listed in these directories are always looking for speakers with interesting topics. The best strategy is to build a speech around some of the value-added work that your company does.

26. The "Use a Mentor" Tactic. This is a tested and proven tactic. If you have not developed a strong mentor relationship with someone you love and trust, start now. If your mentor is satisfied with the relationship, he or she may even be a potential investor, money raiser, or advocate messenger. One way to work with mentors is to seek their advice early on during the concept and seed level of your product/service development. Since a lot of their ideas will probably have been implemented, they're likely to want to make an investment or at least become an advocate messenger.

27. The "Be A Mentor" Tactic. If you have special skills, talents, or knowledge that you are willing to share, then you can make a contribution to people by serving as their mentor for some important aspect of their life.

Survey your current candidate investor list (the Investor/Money Raiser Database List) to see if there is anyone you could develop a mentor relationship with.

28. *The Consultant Tactic.* This is a great tactic. If you use paid consultants, they feel a conscious (or unconscious) obligation to your company. You may be able to obtain leads from them for potential investors or money raisers.

One way to afford more consultants is to analyze your staff to see if there is someone whom you could let go, and then replace with consultants. (This is a classic outsourcing strategy.)

For example, suppose you have a $45,000 a year marketing director whose job it is to develop and create marketing programs. If you eliminate the job, you could hire five or six top consultants for $5,000 each to create your marketing programs, and you could gain their loyalty through long-term contracts.

If you do this, you will be able to find a group of loyal strategic associates for your company. These associates, being top people in their field, should be well-connected, and they will now be motivated to expand your circle of potential investors by being advocate messengers.

29. *The Publicist Tactic.* The idea here is to take one or more of your candidate investors and do what you can to help that person and his or her business gain publicity and endorsements.[11] Every successful business person enjoys, and can utilize, all of the public relations that they can get. As an example, perhaps your business and industry contacts are such that important suppliers or customers of yours can leverage off your own public relation contacts. By generating this added value, you intensify your relationship with the candidate investor, and increase the possibility of bringing them into your circle of influence.

30. *The Buyer's Buyer Tactic.* Review your database list and determine who could use your offer of friendship services as their purchasing agent. Through this tactic your prospective or candidate investor gets help in purchasing. Perhaps you have skills or contacts with certain vendors or in certain industries that your potential investors could leverage off of. This is another tactic to intensify your relationship with potential investors.

31. *The "Cause" Tactic.* Many people and companies (especially business angels) have "causes" and "missions" that need support. If you find the "causes" that are important to your future investors, you can offer to do something to support the cause they're fighting for.[12]

32. *The Enhancer Tactic.* This is a tactic that asks you to go beyond the normal call of duty. Find where your prospective and candidate investors need help beyond that which your company's product/service offers.[13] Areas to look for are revenue enhancing areas, cost saving items, new customer enhancements, etc. A simple approach is to ask the people on your database list to send you their business cards so that you can send some people to them who can provide some help.

33. The Social Network Tactic. In every city, there are formal and informal social and business network groups. Your Chamber of Commerce can help you find them. Not all of these groups will be useful, but it's worth checking them out to see if you can find any with a membership that contains potential investors or money raisers.

34. The Strategic Networker Tactic. A strategic networker is someone who goes beyond just joining and participating in social/business networks. The strategic networker is serious and focused. Strategic networking consists of influencing the people who influence the patronage behavior of other affluent people. To become a strategic networker, you need to find affinity groups with future investors and money raisers. Then you need to determine who are the influence makers in the groups. Then you do whatever is necessary to win the loyalty and support of the influence makers, so that you can get endorsements and referrals from them.[14] Many studies have revealed a strong relationship between the level of an affluent person's wealth and that person's use of opinion leaders in selecting investments, as well as other services and products. Dr. Thomas Stanley, the head of Affluent Market Institute, and author of three popular works on marketing to the affluent, offers these conclusions:

1. Most affluent people are members of one or more affinity groups. These groups include trade associations, professional societies, alumni groups, etc.
2. The quality of referrals and endorsements runs higher within groups than between groups. Intra-group word of mouth recommendations travel quickly.
3. The affluent market in the U.S. is growing seven times faster than the household population.
4. Strategic networkers get endorsements and receive referrals to affluent people for reasons beyond the value of their products/services.

The strategic networker can use the following tactics with influence markers in their selected affinity groups: the buyer's buyer tactic, the "use a mentor" tactic, the enhancer tactic, and the publicist tactic.

35. The Securities License Tactic. Consider obtaining your own securities license and affiliating with a boutique or regional broker/dealer. Ask money raisers for referrals to several brokers/dealers, and interview them prior to your selection. Then, when your company is ready to start its Offering Campaign, you'll have a strong tie with at least one broker/dealer. You should be able to at least secure a limited selling agreement. After the first selling agreement, you'll be amazed how fast the next few selling agreements can be obtained. If you have some production on your license (i.e., generating securities sales), your broker/dealer will be more prone to help you with your company's offerings.

36. The Become a Broker/Dealer Tactic. This is a big step, but it is a viable approach. In the halcyon days of real estate syndication, it was very common for a real estate sponsor company to form their own broker/dealership. Of course, being a broker/dealer is a pure liability unless you can afford a sales force. The approximate cost to establish yourself as a broker/dealer is $5,000. The NASDs paid in capital requirements can range from $5,000 to $250,000, depending on the level of activity contemplated. There is also a lot of annual compliance to be done. Carefully weigh the pros and cons before rushing out and setting yourself up as a broker/dealer.

37. The Incubator Tactic. Find and qualify for your area's business incubation programs. These programs create shared facilities and services that are available for less than market rates. The incubators can lease space to your company and offer the leadership team support and other services, such as secretaries, fax machines, copying and answering machines, etc. Often these incubator facilities are near a university, enabling you to tap into their facilities, computers, libraries, and other technical expertise. In this environment, you may discover business angels or venture capitalists looking for their next home run.

38. The Joint Venture Tactic. One way to close in on an aggressive money raiser is to make his or her participation with you a joint venture. In other words, make it clear that you value the money raiser's participation so much that you're willing to allocate a significant percentage of your stock ownership to the money raiser. Of course, you'll need to make sure that you get all that's coming to you as well. They should get your stock only if they hit performance levels based on the amount raised within a specific time frame. If you are using direct participation offerings (Step 6), or a limited or general partnership, then you will not have to give up ownership in the operating company.

39. The Direct Mail Marketing Tactic. There are many valuable uses for direct mail marketing campaigns apart from product sales. The most common use will be for moving your prospect list to candidate status. Remember, a prospect becomes a candidate once they *know about* your company. Direct mail—if read—can give the prospect information *about* the company. The pressure has been on for several years to bring financial products to the consumer on a low- or no-commission basis. Direct mail can be used to sell your offering. Any such use requires your offering to be registered as a public offering. Always consult with your legal counsel when using this tactic. (Special note: direct mail to cold lead lists *can* be done—that's why it's mentioned here—but the basic strategy of a Capital Relations™ program is not consistent with the use of direct mail for direct sales.) Direct mail can also be used as a "bait and switch" tactic. For example, find a reason to offer affluent people your product/service or some derivative product/service. The mailing list you obtain from this will contain potential investors whom you can approach. If they like your product/service, they may like your company as an investment.

40. The "Look Out Yonder" Tactic. To use this approach, simply direct part, or all, of your Offering Campaign to rural areas that are away from the maddening crowds. Many financial service salespeople have had great success with this tactic. There are more affluent people than you might think living "out yonder."

41. The CFO as a Money Raiser Tactic. This tactic centers on getting as much out of your CFO as possible. Perhaps it's not enough anymore for CFOs to just handle the traditional finance officer's responsibilities. The whole discipline of investor finance needs to be firmly understood by all CFOs of emerging businesses. To date, the CEOs of emerging and growth companies have carried the responsibility for accessing investor capital. It appeared that one of the rites of passage for becoming a CEO was to bring in the capital. The new paradigms of organizational structure would strongly infer that raising investor capital may no longer "be just for the CEO."

42. The Rep Finder Tactic. If you are interested in securing a selling agreement with a broker/dealer or stock brokerage firm, one way of doing it is to get their attention by finding them a new rep. Do you know of any strong financial product sales persons, or any "young lions" looking for a career in financial product sales? If so, then you're in a position to introduce them to the broker/dealer or stock brokerage firm of your choice. Amazing possibilities exist when you satisfy people's biggest needs. Keep in mind that the quality and quantity of the reps of a broker/dealer or a stock brokerage firm are their "life blood," and they always need new ones.

43. The Merger Tactic. Perhaps this should have been listed first. It's a great approach to get things going. Too many entrepreneurs are afraid to consider the possibilities of mergers with other companies. Many investment bankers and business brokers offer merger and acquisitions services. When implementing "Step 4: Identifying Strategic Associations," always consider the possibilities of merging your company with another. If you're a Business Builder and have an attitude that "this is not the last company I'm going to start," you'll be able to creatively explore merger strategies.

44. The "Use Your Customers" Tactic. Why not go to your customers and ask them to invest? Why not ask them for referrals? Why not ask them to be an advocate messenger? The strength of your customer lists, and the quality of your relationships with your customers, will determine the effectiveness of this approach.

45. The Pension Mover Tactic. This tactic appoints a self-directed pension plan administrator to take roll-over funds from your investor's pension plan, if their pension plan will not allow an investment in your offering. This tactic allows you to go where the potential investors are most liquid—their pension plans. Many of your investor's pension plans are managed by larger pension plan administrators who operate in a "limited choice" environment. For example, your investor could roll over $30,000 of his small business/Keogh pension plan, which had been administered by Merrill Lynch, into a self-trusted Keogh plan administered by a local, self-directed pension plan specialty firm.

46. The Information Bulletin Boards Tactic. There are information networks springing up around the country that allow for their members to talk to each other electronically. These members could be a good contact source for investor and money raiser leads and also for advertising. The most popular bulletin boards are found on the Internet, America Online, Microsoft's Internet Explorer, and Prodigy. These services can be contacted at the following numbers:

Internet—There are many direct providers of Internet service. In addition, most major bulletin board services, including America Online, have gateways to the Internet, with varying degrees of access and costs.

America Online	MS Internet Explorer	Prodigy
(800) 827-6364	(800) 485-2048	(800) 776-3449

47. The Adaptive Sequence Tactic. This involves the fine art of incorporating into your Offering Campaign a logical sequence of approaching your investors based on their own investment tendencies. Investors and money raisers are like any other customer. Some are bold, others are timid. You should determine what class your investors/money raisers fall into. They will be either innovators, early adapters, late adapters, or laggards. The late adapters and laggards generally invest in something only after the innovators and early adapters first do their homework and have actually proven that the investment is legitimate.[15]

48. The Sponsorship Tactic. This strategy is used with securities licensed money raisers—especially regional and boutique broker/dealers and stock brokerage firms. With some of these firms it is necessary to have a certain number of reps who want to raise money for your deal. These reps then sponsor your company in their firm. Broker/dealers and stock brokerage firms like to know if your deal will "move" in their firm. Sponsorship helps assure the firms that there is support.

49. The "Give a Rep a Client" Tactic. The quickest way to get sponsorship is to give a rep at a broker/dealer or stock brokerage firm a list of your investors, and let the planner/broker earn a commission off your investor's investment in your offering.

50. The Momentum Builder Tactic. This strategy is listed last among the major tactics for a reason. It relies on the principle of "incremental development." All of the previous tactics can provide tangible results—in time. If you need your tactics to produce investor checks in two weeks, you're probably in for a disappointment. Careful development of your Capital Relations™ plan (Step 6), Offering Campaign Plan (Step 7), and your plans for testing the market (Step 8) should include an analysis of incremental development of the tactics that seem right for your company.

THE MINOR COMMUNICATION TACTICS

51. The Public Information Tactic. Local, state, and national governmental agencies can provide you with a wealth of information on large contributors to political campaigns, copies of deeds to homes, and demographic breakdowns of population by age and income, based on census data.

52. The "Watch for Large Contract Awards" Tactic. Review daily papers for large contracts awarded to private companies. Many of these people and firms may fit the Actual Investor Profile and thus qualify to be on the prospect list. (Don't forget to contact the salesperson in the company who got the contract—he or she is also a potential investor.)

53. The Legal Records Tactic. Legal cases are open to the public. Review recent divorce cases for the details of the settlement. One or both of the parties may be prospective investors.

54. The Advertising Tactic. Make sure that potential investors can find you. Establish a yellow pages listing, and post your needs in as many locations as you can afford. Be sure to clear your advertisements through your legal counsel.

55. The "Make a Video" Tactic. For the "can't miss" candidate and super-candidate investors, send a copy of a video overviewing the investment opportunity. You can ask for the video to be returned, but it's probably better to offer to stop by and pick it up—it's another opportunity for you to present your offering.

56. The "Look for Investors by Age" Tactic. The largest growing segment of the population is also the wealthiest—those 55 and older. (In San Diego county, for example, there are over 150 senior groups that meet every month and they are always looking for interesting speakers.) This segment can be targeted through RV clubs and national retirement organizations.

57. The "Look for Investors by Profession" Tactic. Many professions have associations that will provide lists of members. (Some good professions to consider are real estate agents, engineers, and doctors.)

58. The "Look for Investors by Education" Tactic. Prestigious universities have a wealth of information on their graduates. Alumni associations, and other former-student clubs can also supply the names of potential investors.

59. The "Look at Home Sales" Tactic. Check in the "Home" section of your local paper, or at the city or county Registry Office, to see which homes have recently been sold, and for how much. The seller may be "cash rich" at the moment and looking for investments. It is also a good idea to approach the agent who sold the home, since he or she has just made a large commission on the sale, and may be interested in investing.

60. The "Look at Stock Sales" Tactic. Business periodicals publish weekly or monthly summaries of insider trading and sales of stock by corporate executives through their profit sharing programs.

61. The "Read the Classifieds" Tactic. Many daily papers have a section for investors who are looking for a tax shelter or other investment opportunities. You can also place an ad yourself, with a brief description of your offering. Be sure to clear the ad with your attorney.

62. The "Give a Dinner" Tactic (Version 1). Schedule a series of formal "invitation only" dinner meetings, and present your offering at the dinner.

63. The "Give a Dinner" Tactic (Version 2). Same tactic as above except ask the invited guest to bring a qualified prospective investor.

64. The "Use Government Agencies" Tactic. The Small Business Administration and the U.S. Department of Commerce continually have contact with small business owners, and occasionally provide financing programs for selected businesses.

65. The "Review Business Publications" Tactic. Business publications offer a number of outstanding leads to potential investors including promotions of executives, earnings of public firms with major stockholders, etc.

66. The "Acknowledge Business Owners" Tactic. They already have money—now give them what they don't get all the time—acknowledgment. Send them a congratulations letter, or cut out an article about them and have it framed.

67. The "Look Closely at Your Competition" Tactic. Analyze your competition and find out their initial sources of financing. Chances are, if the original investors did well the first time around, they will be ready to give it another try. It's not easy to get this information. Some state recording laws may require filing of investor lists.

68. The "Look at the Large Penny Stock Investors" Tactic. Penny stocks attract a certain type of adventure stockholder who is willing to take large risks in exchange for large returns. Names of these individuals can be found in OTC penny stock publications.

69. The "Barter and Bootstrapping" Tactics. Through arrangement with vendors, use shares of your company to gain the necessary start-up equipment and raw materials you need to begin the operation. This can also be done with office space, furniture, phones, etc.

70. The "Find the Litigators" Tactic. Take the legal news and find those attorneys who win big contingency cases.

71. The "Look at Trade Magazines" Tactic. There are trade publications in almost any industry you can think of. For example, there is one called *Rock and Dirt* for those in the earth moving equipment industry. These publications often have articles about successful business owners—they can be a great source.

72. The "Be an Interviewer" Tactic. Do a research paper or book, and pick successful people to interview. This is a great way to start a relationship.

73. The "Look Up Old School Friends" Tactic. Take out your old yearbook and find out which of your former classmates are doing well. They could be happy to hear from you.

74. The "Co-sign Loans for Medical School Graduates" Tactic. Contact a soon-to-be rich medical graduate and co-sign his or her first-practice loans—now you'll have an investor for life.

75. The "PTA" Tactic. Look for PTA members in wealthy neighborhoods. Often, PTA organizations have listings of members, which may provide a rich source of names and numbers to contact.

Illustration 6-7 provides a chart that rates the importance of these tactics to investor sources and money raisers. Illustration 6-8 provides a chart of when these tactics are to be used during an Offering Campaign.

ILLUSTRATION 6-7:
IMPORTANCE* OF TACTICS FOR INVESTOR SOURCES AND MONEY RAISERS

MAJOR TACTICS:	Venture capitalists	Strategic corp. invstrs.	Business angels	Adventure stockholders	Visionary Capitalists	Money raisers
1. One-on-one meeting	M	M	M	M	M	M
2. Expert	M	M	M	M	M	M
3. Convoy surfacer	H	H	H	H	H	H
4. Civic leader	I	I	I	H	I	H
5. Charity volunteer	I	H	H	H	H	H
6. Industry leader	H	H	H	H	H	H
7. Business leader	H	H	H	H	H	H
8. Social butterfly	I	I	H	H	H	H
9. Country club	I	I	H	H	H	H
10. Public seminars/forums	I	H	H	H	H	H
11. Private sales seminars	I	I	I	I	I	H
12. Private workshops	I	H	H	H	H	H
13. Bait and switch	I	I	H	H	H	H
14. Strategic association	H	H	H	H	H	H
15. Watching "money in motion"	I	H	H	H	H	H
16. Wholesaler	I	I	I	H	I	H
17. Sales force	I	I	I	I	I	H
18. Telemarketing	I	I	H	H	H	H
19. Family tapper	I	I	H	I	H	I
20. Advertiser	I	I	H	H	H	I
21. Vendor	I	H	I	H	I	I
22. Referral	M	M	M	M	M	M
23. Infomercial	I	I	H	H	H	H
24. Focus groups	I	H	M	M	M	M
25. Guest speaker	I	I	H	H	H	I

*Importance key: M = Mandatory   H = Helpful   I = Irrelevant   Continued

ILLUSTRATION 6-7: (CONTINUED)
IMPORTANCE* OF TACTICS FOR INVESTOR SOURCES AND MONEY RAISERS

MAJOR TACTICS (Continued):	Venture capitalists	Strategic corp. invstrs.	Business angels	Adventure stockholders	Visionary Capitalists	Money raisers
26. Use a mentor	I	I	H	H	H	H
27. Be a mentor	I	I	H	H	H	H
28. Consultant	I	H	H	H	H	H
29. Publicist	I	I	H	H	H	H
30. Buyer's buyer	H	I	H	H	H	H
31. Cause	I	H	H	H	H	H
32. Enhancer	I	I	H	H	H	H
33. Social network	H	H	H	H	H	H
34. Strategic networker	H	H	H	H	H	H
35. Securities license	I	I	I	H	I	H
36. Become a broker/dealer	I	I	I	H	I	H
37. Incubator	H	H	H	H	H	H
38. Joint venture	H	H	H	H	H	H
39. Direct mail	I	I	H	H	H	H
40. Out yonder	I	I	H	H	H	H
41. CFO money raiser	H	H	H	H	H	H
42. Rep finder	I	I	I	H	I	H
43. Merger	H	H	H	I	H	H
44. Use your customers	I	H	H	H	H	H
45. Pension mover	I	I	H	H	H	H
46. Information bulletin boards	I	I	H	H	H	H
47. Adaptive sequence	H	I	H	M	H	M
48. Sponsorship	H	I	I	I	I	M
49. Give a rep a client	I	I	I	I	I	H
50. Momentum builder	H	H	H	H	H	H

*Importance key: M = Mandatory   H = Helpful   I = Irrelevant

Continued

ILLUSTRATION 6-7: (CONTINUED)
IMPORTANCE* OF TACTICS FOR INVESTOR SOURCES AND MONEY RAISERS

MINOR TACTICS:	Venture capitalists	Strategic corp. invstrs.	Business angels	Adventure stockholders	Visionary Capitalists	Money raisers
51. Public information	I	I	H	H	H	I
52. Contract awards	I	H	H	H	H	I
53. Legal records	I	H	H	H	H	I
54. Yellow page ad	I	I	I	H	I	I
55. Video	H	H	H	H	H	H
56. Investors by age	I	I	H	H	H	I
57. Investors by profession	I	H	H	H	H	I
58. Investors by education	I	I	H	H	H	I
59. Homes sales	I	I	H	H	H	I
60. Stock sales	I	I	H	H	H	H
61. Read classifieds	I	I	H	H	H	I
62. Give a dinner (version 1)	I	I	H	H	H	I
63. Give a dinner (version 2)	I	I	H	H	H	I
64. Government agencies	I	H	H	H	H	I
65. Business publications	H	H	H	H	H	I
66. Acknowledge owners	I	I	H	H	H	H
67. Look at competition	H	H	H	H	H	H
68. Penny stock investors	I	I	I	H	I	H
69. Barter and bootsrapping	I	H	H	H	H	I
70. Find the litigators	I	I	H	H	H	I
71. Trade magazines	H	H	H	H	H	H
72. Be an inventor	H	H	H	H	H	H
73. Old school friends	I	I	H	H	H	H
74. Co-sign loans for medical students	I	I	H	H	H	I
75. PTA	I	I	H	H	H	I

*Importance key: M = Mandatory   H = Helpful   I = Irrelevant

ILLUSTRATION 6-8:
COMMUNICATION TACTICS MOST COMMONLY USED BY MESSENGERS DURING OFFERING CAMPAIGNS

To generate leads	To determine if leads are prospects	To move prospects to candidates	To move candidates to super-candidates	To move super-candidates to actual investors
All the tactics will, in some way, help to generate leads. Almost everyone you come in contact with is a lead and should be on your database list.	One-on-one	One-on-one	One-on-one	One-on-one
	Public seminars	Public seminars	Public seminars	—
	Private sales seminars	Private sales seminars	Private sales seminars	Private sales seminars
	Private workshops	Private workshops	Private workshops	Private workshops
	Strategic associations	Strategic associations	Strategic associations	Strategic associations
	Wholesaler	Wholesaler	Wholesaler	Wholesaler
	Sales force	Sales force	Sales force	Sales force
	Telemarketing	Telemarketing	—	—
	Family tapper	Family tapper	Family tapper	Family tapper
	Vendor	Vendor	Vendor	Vendor
	Referral	Referral	Referral	Referral
	Focus group	Focus group	Focus group	Focus group
	Use a mentor	Use a mentor	Use a mentor	Use a mentor
	Be a mentor	Be a mentor	Be a mentor	Be a mentor
	Consultant	Consultant	Consultant	Consultant
	Buyer's buyer	Buyer's buyer	Buyer's buyer	Buyer's buyer
	Cause	Cause	Cause	Cause
	Enhancer	Enhancer	Enhancer	Enhancer
	Strategic networker	Strategic networker	Strategic networker	Strategic networker
	Become a broker/dealer	Become a broker/dealer	Become a broker/dealer	Become a broker/dealer
	Incubator	Incubator	Incubator	Incubator
	Joint venture	Joint venture	Joint venture	Joint venture

ILLUSTRATION 6-8: (CONTINUED)
COMMUNICATION TACTICS MOST COMMONLY USED BY MESSENGERS DURING OFFERING CAMPAIGNS

To generate leads	*To determine if leads are prospects*	*To move prospects to candidates*	*To move candidates to super-candidates*	*To move super-candidates to actual investors*
	Direct mail	Direct mail	—	—
	CFO	CFO	CFO	CFO
	Merger	Merger	Merger	Merger
	Customers	Customers	Customers	Customers
	Pension mover	Pension mover	Pension mover	Pension mover
	Adaptive sequence	Adaptive sequence	Adaptive sequence	Adaptive sequence
	Sponsorship	Sponsorship	Sponsorship	Sponsorship
	Public information	—	—	—
	Legal records	—	—	—
	By age	—	—	—
	By education	—	—	—
	Home sales	—	—	—
	Stock sales	—	—	—
	Classifieds	—	—	—
	Dinner (version 1)	Dinner (version 1)	Dinner (version 1)	Dinner (version 1)
	Dinner (version 2)	Dinner (version 2)	Dinner (version 2)	Dinner (version 2)
	U.S. government	—	—	—
	Business publications	—	—	—
	Acknowledge bus. owner	Acknowledge bus. owner	Acknowledge bus. owner	—
	Find litigators	—	—	—
	Interviewer	Interviewer	Interviewer	Interviewer
	Old school friends	Old school friends	Old school friends	Old school friends

THE COMMUNICATION TOOLS

Here is a list and brief description of the most commonly used tools to help you implement the tactics you'll choose to use during your Offering Campaign (Step 10).

1. Corporate Brochure. This is a good tool to profile the mission, product/service, track record, vision, and management of the company. It can be a stand-alone piece or made to fit inside a presentation folder. Many companies get caught up in their own industry jargon. Investors are not interested in jargon—so use language they understand. If your business plan is comprehensive, then limit the corporate brochure—simply capture the future vision of the company. Photos say a 1,000 words, so be generous with them.

2. Offering Documents. Your Private Placement Memorandum (private offering) or Offering Circular (intra-state public offering) or Prospectus (SEC registered offering) are documents that can be used as sales tools. You can even incorporate part of your corporate brochure into your offering documents, if you use some creativity. Subscription agreements are always part of your offering documents.

3. Offering Fact Sheet. This is a brochure, usually four pages or less, summarizing the terms and benefits of your offering.

4. Presentation Folder. This generic collateral tool is used to hold all the other communication pieces your company may generate. If you can afford it, make sure the corporate identity (through your logomark, logotype, or other graphics) is on the presentation folder.

5. Photo Pages. This is a specially designed, one page, high-gloss sheet with key positioning photos of the leadership team, product specifications, and just about anything else.

6. Special Topic Brochures/Pamphlets. These are collateral pieces that can be developed for special agenda items that you want to highlight. Topics can be the leadership team, customers, industry, track record, future, regulatory environment, endorsements, product specifications, trends, etc.

7. Letters. Aggressive and creative use of correspondence is always advised. Of course, the mailing list you use for the letters must be carefully selected. Thank-you letters, introductory letters, annual letters, and quarterly letters can be planned.[16]

8. Announcements. Careful planning is in order to make sure you don't miss the opportunity to announce something. Announcements keep people interested in your company.

9. Bulletins. Much like letters, bulletins are for posting news and giving updates. Creative design of bulletins is in order.

10. Newsletters. Newsletters containing general-interest articles about the economy and industry issues will significantly enhance your reputation as an expert and help position you as an industry leader. Don't be intimidated by the idea of a newsletter. Think of it as merely a periodic letter to your investor candidates and investors, updating and advising them on significant events and opportunities your company is working on, plus other bits of information that might be of interest.[17]

A common complaint among executives about newsletters is that they don't have the time to produce them on a regular basis. If this is your situation, hire someone to produce it for you. With direction from you, an independent writer can handle the entire process—writing the articles, layout, paste-up, and printing—saving you time and ensuring you a professional and well-designed product. Desktop publishing has additionally made newsletter publication a lot easier and less expensive.

11. Quarterly Reports. Developing regular reports and standardizing their formats and topics is an excellent tool. Using your corporate identity creatively will help assure good results.

12. Annual Reports. Public companies are required to furnish stockholders an annual report. The private company can do the same. Borrow your ideas by examining the type of information and design used by public companies.

13. Audits/Reviews. A voluntary and periodic audit of your financial condition is impressive, if it doesn't cost too much. Of course, public companies are required to be audited once a year. A private company might reduce the cost of an audit by engaging an accounting firm to do a "review report" instead of a full audit.

14. News Articles. The power of news articles about your company is something special. Work with your P.R. firm to create publicity for your company. Try to control your message. Time news articles around an Offering Campaign. You might even be able to do a regular article on your industry for the newspaper.

15. Press Releases. A press release should be short, no more than two to three double-spaced pages. Make it newsworthy. Include interesting and relevant quotations that can be used as callouts or highlights. Don't hesitate to include photographs, graphs, or charts, if appropriate. All of these elements will make the release more interesting to the editor who receives it, and therefore make it more publishable.

16. Article Reprints. If the company receives any press coverage, make sure the article is attractively set up for reprint purposes. Article reprints are good tools to combine with other announcement, bulletin, and newsletter mailings.

17. Television. Although not commonly used, television may be a good tool to directly sell a public offering (but *not* a private offering). Consult with your securities counsel to ensure securities laws compliance. Of course, television can also be a medium to run advertising about your company, or to announce an upcoming investor seminar. Watch closely the accelerated developments in the communications/entertainment industries. The new communication/technological world around the corner may entirely revolutionize how your company will plan an Offering Campaign. Stay tuned.

18. Infomercials. Some companies are trying their own infomercials to sell their offerings. The progress being made by the cable television industry will shortly allow you to target the exact households your infomercials run in.

19. Radio. Like television, radio presents an opportunity for mass coverage. Companies generally do not use radio to present an offering, however, it is possible to make a radio announcement about "public seminars/forums" (see the earlier discussion titled, "The Public Seminars/Forums Tactic"). Before any use of radio is planned, consult with your attorney for securities laws compliance.

20. Audiocassettes. Your imagination can run wild here. You could summarize the terms of the offering documents (private offerings only). This medium could also be used to summarize or explain almost any aspect of your business to investors. Perhaps you could provide an audiocassette that summarizes the entire business plan: "Executive Summary on Tape."

21. Videocassettes. Although more expensive than audiocassettes, this medium can be used more creatively. Many companies that use video, design a program that profiles or positions the company and its products/services. If your company uses video to sell its products/services to customers, the video can become a good tool to use with investors as well.

22. Gifts. The discreet and careful use of gifts can be helpful. Acknowledging the Inner-Circle, Board of Advisors, Board of Directors, and Funding Teams with timely gifts of appreciation can be in order.

23. Mementos. Mementos of all sorts are appropriate: hats, T-shirts, buttons, awards, and prototypes of products in toy form. The symbols and traditions you want or have for the company can be communicated through mementos.

24. Trade Shows. This is listed as a tool because it is the specific action plan you might want to use with such tactics as *expert, convoy surfacing,* and *industry leader.* You can participate on a lot of different levels at trade shows. You can rent booths, be a guest speaker, just participate, or all of the above.

25. Mailing Lists. It goes without saying how important your mailing lists are. The lead list you generate, and how you track and push your leads all the way to super-candidate status, is of vital importance. You will use various lists to accomplish different projects in implementing your Offering Campaign.

26. Answering Machine/Receptionist. Have an answering machine in your office, or have your receptionist leave a message/announcement that contains interesting information about the fact that the company is raising capital to expand. The message might elicit calls from people wanting information about the offering who might not otherwise have been inclined to contact you. If you're using an answering machine, the recording could conclude with something like, "If you'd like additional information, or if you'd like to talk to X, Y, or Z, please leave your name and number after the tone."

27. Phone Calls. Don't forget the power of the telephone. Pick it up and call the targeted people with whom you need to keep a relationship alive.

28. Fax. This tool is an excellent transmitter of communications. Creativity is in order here. Make sure the creativity and frequency of this tool does not cross the line and become a nuisance to the people with whom you communicate.

29. Open Houses. Periodic open houses are valuable marketing tools. These open houses can range from your normal Christmas party to an event launching a new product.

30. Birthday Cards and Postcards. These are old tools which are worth their weight in gold. Everyone, including everybody in your circle of influence, enjoys receiving birthday cards.

31. Lunches/Dinners. This tool can be used in combination with "The Private Seminar/Workshop" tactic.

32. Parties. This tool is often overlooked as an effective way to enhance an Offering Campaign. A party feature, such as a dance, can even be combined with a shareholders' meeting. (Yes, this has actually been done.) Now the shareholders can invite guests, exposing the company to more investors.

33. Shareholders' Meetings. This is a valuable tool. Instead of annual meetings, have quarterly meetings, and special update meetings. Remember the Party tool as well.

34. The Leadership Team's Shareholder Speaking Tour. The oil, gas, real estate, and leasing partnership sponsors are famous for putting key leadership team people on an "existing investors speaking tour." This tool requires the leadership team to go to the city where the investors live, rent a hotel conference room, and give a presentation updating the investors on the company's progress or problems.

ILLUSTRATION 6-9:
IMPORTANCE* OF TOOLS FOR INVESTOR SOURCES AND MONEY RAISERS

TOOLS:	Venture capitalists	Strategic corp. invstrs.	Business angels	Adventure stockholders	Visionary Capitalists	Money raisers
1. Corporate brochure	H	H	H	M	H	M
2. Offering documents	M	M	M	M	M	M
3. Offering fact sheet	M	M	M	M	M	M
4. Presentation folder	H	H	H	M	H	M
5. Photo pages	H	H	H	H	H	H
6. Special topic brochures	H	H	H	H	H	H
7. Letters	M	M	M	M	M	M
8. Announcements	M	M	M	M	M	M
9. Bulletins	H	H	H	H	H	H
10. Newsletters	H	H	H	H	H	H
11. Quarterly reports	H	H	H	H	H	H
12. Annual reports	M	M	M	M	M	M
13. Audits/reviews	M	M	H	H	H	H
14. News articles	H	H	H	H	H	H
15. Press releases	H	H	H	H	H	H
16. Article reprints	H	H	H	H	H	H
17. Television	I	I	H	H	H	H
18. Infomercials	I	I	H	H	H	I
19. Radio	I	I	H	H	H	H
20. Audio-cassettes	I	I	H	H	H	H
21. Video-cassettes	H	H	H	H	H	H
22. Gifts	H	H	H	H	H	H
23. Mementos	I	I	H	H	H	H
24. Trade shows	H	H	H	I	H	H
25. Mailing lists	H	H	H	H	H	H

*Importance key: M = Mandatory H = Helpful I = Irrelevant

26. *Answering machine/ receptionists*	H	H	H	H	H	H
27. *Phone calls*	M	M	M	H	M	M
28. *Fax*	M	M	M	H	M	H
29. *Open houses*	H	H	H	H	H	H
30. *Birthday cards/ postcards*	H	H	H	H	H	H
31. *Lunches/dinners*	M	M	M	H	M	M
32. *Parties*	H	H	H	H	H	H
33. *Shareholders' meetings*	M	M	M	M	M	M
34. *Leadership team speaking tours*	H	H	H	H	H	H
35. *Surveys*	H	H	H	H	H	H

*Importance key: M = Mandatory   H = Helpful   I = Irrelevant

35. Surveys. A good tool to help the leadership team demonstrate their expertise in the industry. You can find many important industry topics/issues for surveys.

Illustration 6-9 provides a chart that rates the importance of these tools to investor sources and money raisers. Illustration 6-10 provides a chart of which tools are most often used at the different stages of the Offering Campaign.

Illustration 6-10:
When Communication Tools are Commonly Used by Messengers During Offering Campaigns

To generate leads	To determine if leads are prospects	To move prospects to candidates	To move candidates to super-candidates	To move super-candidates to actual investors
		Corporate brochure	Corporate brochure	Corporate brochure
			Offering documents	Offering documents
			Offering fact sheet	Offering fact sheet
		Presentation folder	Presentation folder	Presentation folder
		Photo pages	Photo pages	Photo pages
		Special topic brochure	Special topic brochure	Special topic brochure
	Letters	Letters	Letters	Letters
		Announcements	Announcements	Announcements
		Bulletins	Bulletins	Bulletins
		Newsletters	Newsletters	Newsletters
		Quarterly report	Quarterly report	Quarterly report
		Annual report	Annual report	Annual report
		Audits	Audits	Audits
		News releases	News releases	News releases
		Press releases	Press releases	Press releases
		Article reprints	Article reprints	Article reprints
Television				
Infomercials				
Radio				
		Audio-cassettes	Audio-cassettes	Audio-cassettes
		Video-cassettes	Video-cassettes	Video-cassettes
		Gifts	Gifts	Gifts

ILLUSTRATION 6-10: (CONTINUED)
WHEN COMMUNICATION TOOLS ARE COMMONLY USED BY MESSENGERS DURING OFFERING CAMPAIGNS

To generate leads	To determine if leads are prospects	To move prospects to candidates	To move candidates to super-candidates	To move super-candidates to actual investors
—	—	Mementos	Mementos	Mementos
Trade shows	Trade shows	—	—	—
Mailing lists	Mailing lists	Mailing lists	Mailing lists	Mailing lists
Phone calls	Phone calls	Phone calls	Phone calls	Phone calls
Fax	Fax	Fax	Fax	Fax
Open houses	Open houses	Open houses	Open houses	Open houses
—	—	Birthday cards	Birthday cards	Birthday cards
—	Lunches/dinners	Lunches/dinners	Lunches/dinners	Lunches/dinners
—	—	Parties	Parties	Parties
—	—	—	—	Shareholders' meeting
—	—	Speaking tour	Speaking tour	Speaking tour
—	—	Surveys	Surveys	Surveys

CONCLUSION

Step 6 began by explaining that the Capital Relations™ program is a key component of Investor Financing™. The two concepts the Capital Relations™ program revolves around are "knowledges" and "relationships."

The most important knowledge is the Actual Investor and Actual Money Raiser Profiles most appropriate for your current funding requirements. This step also introduced you to the concept of creating your own investor market. Naturally, the starting point is the determination of which investor sources and money raisers are viable for your company (Step 2). The Actual Investor and Actual Money Raiser Profiles are finally established during "Step 8: Testing the Market and List Assemblage." From the Actual Investor Profile you can build your lead lists.

This step explained that your Offering Campaign will consist of messages, messengers, and media that will move your leads (the persons and firms who fit the Actual Investor and Actual Money Raiser Profiles) up the relationship ladder from prospects (who are your leads) to candidates (who are prospects who *know about* you); from candidates to super-candidates (who are candidates who *know you personally*); and finally from super-candidates to actual investors (who are the people or firms who write the checks).

This step also showed you how other people need to believe in your company and then talk about your company to others. It also showed you that winning an investor ultimately hinges on what others say about, or do with, your company. This, in turn, shows the importance of influencing customers and investor market infrastructure sources.

Finally, this step presented you a long list of tactics and tools to use during Investor Financing™. Selecting the tactics and tools that are appropriate usually requires the input of your Funding Team (Step 4). Pay close attention to all the illustrations in this step—there is a lot of insight to be gained from them.

DEVELOPING
THE DISCUSSION
DOCUMENTS

Step 1

Step 2

Step 3

Step 4

Step 5

Step 6

STEP 7

Step 8

Step 9

Step 10

The idea is that you must sell your business idea to another person to get the money . . . so you must think creatively to convince the venture community to invest in your business idea.

—Bruce Blechman

The first six steps presented a survey of all the important considerations that go into the process of getting your company ready to answer the investor's ultimate question: "Why should I invest in you?" Step 7 brings it all together. The data, information, history, ideas, hunches, strategies, and possibilities that you have developed and analyzed in the previous steps will now be incorporated into written documents and plans—the discussion documents. During "Step 8: Testing the Market and List Assemblage," these documents will be presented to a carefully selected group of people and firms that will make up your focus group meetings. These focus group meetings will provide your company with its first investor/money raiser feedback on your plans and financing strategies. Step 8 will help you determine the Actual Investor and Money Raiser Profiles, and prepare the requisite lead lists to use during the Offering Campaign. You will not prepare the final version of the discussion documents until Step 9.

You may be wondering why it's necessary to prepare preliminary documents for discussion purposes. Why not jump right into preparing the final documents and start raising money? The answer is simple. Approximately 75% of the companies trying to access investor capital do not adequately test their presentation documents. As a result, a lot of time, money, and enthusiasm is lost and these are precious resources that are normally in short supply. Steps 7 and 8 are designed to safeguard these resources. The pressure to get funded as soon as possible must be held in check. You will learn in Step 8 that the proper use of focus groups is the surest way to guarantee a quick funding.

The discussion documents are:

- The business plan
- The Term Sheet
- The Funding Requirements Sheet
- The Offering Campaign Plan
- The collateral marketing tools

THE BUSINESS PLAN

Your first draft of the business plan was done during Step 3. You should have received valuable feedback on it from your work during "Step 4: Identifying Strategic Associations." Now during Step 7, you need to update the business plan. One of the key points to remember about your business plan is that it's written for investors and money raisers. This would be a good time to go back and review the advice in Step 3 about how to develop a business plan. Once you've done that, you're ready to work your way through Step 7 in order to improve your business plan.

THE TERM SHEET

This is the first document your attorney should prepare for you when using the Investor Financing™ steps. The Term Sheet is a one or two page summary of the financing structure and terms of your offering. It allows you to go to the investors and money raisers for feedback about your offering's financing structure and terms without using a full blown offering document. You will use the Term Sheet during "Step 8: Testing the Market and List Assemblage." Illustration 7-1 is a sample Term Sheet for a company that is proposing to

---

ILLUSTRATION 7-1:
TERM SHEET EXAMPLE

1. Number of preferred shares: 250,000 – 600,000

2. Price: $1.00 per share

3. Equity split:

     a. Shares:

	Number of shares (Common stock equivalents)	Percentage
Founders/leadership team	900,000	78 – 60%
Holders of preferred stock	250,000 – 600,000	22 – 40%
Total	1,150,000 – 1,500,000	100%

     b. Vesting:

     Leadership team shares shall vest 1/3 for each whole year of continuous employment.

     c. Right of first refusal:

       (1) The company shall have the first right to purchase vested shares.

       (2) Right terminates on closing of underwritten public offering of common stock.

ILLUSTRATION 7-1: (CONTINUED)
TERM SHEET EXAMPLE

4. Terms of preferred stock:

    a. Dividends:

        (1) Cumulative dividends at annual rate of $0.08.

        (2) Priority over common stock.

    b. Liquidation:

        (1) Preference of $1.00 per share plus accrued and unpaid dividends, whether or not earned.

        (2) Reorganization not considered a liquidation.

4. Terms of preferred stock (continued):

    c. Redemption:

        (1) Redemption at the company's option after three years at liquidation preference.

        (2) If any preferred stock is redeemed, all must be redeemed.

    d. Voting:

        (1) In general, vote with common stock with number of votes equal to largest number of shares of common stock into which preferred stock may be converted.

        (2) Majority of preferred stock needs to approve:

            (a) Redemption of preferred stock otherwise than pursuant to redemption provisions;

            (b) Repurchase of common stock (except for buybacks from directors, employees and consultants, not exceeding $25,000 in any 12-month period);

            (c) Declare or pay dividends on or make any distribution on account of common stock;

            (d) Sell or assign substantially all of the company's assets;

            (e) permit subsidiary to sell stock to third person; or

            (f) Increase or decrease authorized preferred stock.

    e. Conversion:

        (1) Convertible into common stock at any time at option of holder.

        (2) Initial conversion price of $1.00 (one-for-one conversion) offering of common stock.

ILLUSTRATION 7-1: (CONTINUED)
TERM SHEET EXAMPLE

---

(3) Automatic conversion on closing of underwritten public offering of common stock.

(4) Anti-dilution protection for stock dividends, other securities dividends, reclassification, exchange, substitution, reorganization, merger, consolidation, and sale of assets.

(5) Average down of conversion price for sale of shares below conversion price.

f. Closing: August 30, 1998.

   (Unless extended for up to one 30-day period.)

---

raise $250,000 to $600,000 of preferred stock through adventure stockholders and money raisers.

THE FUNDING REQUIREMENTS SHEET

In Step 5, you analyzed how much capital your current financing dictated. You also learned the importance of developing both minimum and maximum capitalization figures. The end product of the work in Step 5 is your current Funding Requirements Sheet (see Illustration 5-4).

THE OFFERING CAMPAIGN PLAN

This is the action plan for picking up investor checks at Step 10. This plan is first developed during this step, tested in Step 8, finalized in Step 9, and then implemented in Step 10. The final Offering Campaign Plan is perfected through this cyclical process of getting reactions to your ideas and plans from investors/money raisers and advocate messengers from "the real world," revising the ideas and plans as needed, and then repeating the process again until the campaign is perfected and ready for implementation at Step 10. A complete Offering Campaign Plan includes the following parts which must be reduced to writing as plans, forms, and charts:

1. A Strategy Summary
2. A PERT chart
3. A budget plan

THE STRATEGY SUMMARY

This is a summary of most of the ideas and decisions that have been made during the previous steps of the Investor Financing™ process. This

ILLUSTRATION 7-2:
OFFERING CAMPAIGN PLAN STRATEGY SUMMARY FOR PERSONAL COMPUTER
PUBLISHING ASSOCIATES, INC

1. *Financing Sequence Plan:*

Private offering of preferred stock:	Now
Bank loan or debenture offering:	In 24–36 months
Staying-Private Public Offering™ of common stock, or strategic alliance, or joint venture with a larger company:	In 36–48 months
IPO:	In 7th year

2. *Current funding requirements:*

$350,000
$150,000 minimum
$350,000 maximum

3. *Current financing instrument:*

Private offering
Preferred stock with 10% cumulative (not compounded) dividend; conversion to common; company's option to redeem stock

4. *Sources:*

Choice 1: Strategic corporate investors, Visionary Capitalists, and business angels
Choice 2: Adventure stockholders
Choice 3: Venture capitalists

5. *Approaches:*

Direct Placement Approach for choice 1, 2 ,and 3 sources
Money Raiser Approach for choice 1 (Strat. corp. investors only) and choice 2 sources

6. *Capital Relations™ program:*

Choice 1:	*Alternative Choice 1:*	*Choice 2:*	*Choice 3:*
5 Visionary Capitalists	1 Strat. corp. investor	43 Adventure stockhldrs.	1 Venture capitalist
5 Business angels	2 Super-candidates	86 Super-candidates	2 Super-candidates
10 Super-candidates	3 Candidates	100 Candidates	3 Candidates
20 Candidates	3 Prospects	100 Prospects	3 Prospects
20 Prospects	15 Leads	500 Leads	15 Leads
100 Leads	1 Advocate messeng.	20 Advocates messengs.	1 Advocate messengs.
4 Advocate messengs.	10 Infrast. messengers	30 Infrast. messengers	10 Infrast. messengers
20 Infrast. messengers	16 Major tactics chosen	18 Major tactics chosen	8 Major tactics chosen
16 Major tactics chosen	11 Minor tactics chosen	10 Minor tactics chosen	0 Minor tactics chosen
10 Minor tactics chosen	22 Tools chosen	24 Tools chosen	13 Tools chosen
22 Tools chosen			

compilation of your strategies is important because it serves as your compass during Step 10 when you complete your Offering Campaign. Illustration 7-2 presents a sample Strategy Summary for a fictional late-stage 2 publishing company, in the personal computer industry, called Personal Computer Publishing Associates, Inc.

Below is a list of decisions that must be made in order to complete the Strategy Summary. It is recommended that all members of your Funding Team participate in making these decisions. Try to make them in the order presented, if you can.

Decision 1: The Financing Sequence Plan. In Step 5 you learned about the elements and options that are part of financing sequence planning. Now it's time to decide (if you haven't already done so during Step 5) which of those options are going to be incorporated into your company's financing for the next five to ten years.

Decision 2: The Current Funding Requirements. Step 5 also asked you to determine the amount of investor capital that you're going to need to implement your company's immediate growth and developmental needs, including the mini-max figures (the low- and high-side capital requirements). Now is the time to decide exactly what those numbers are going to be (if you haven't already done so).

Decision 3: Current Financing Instrument. You must decide which financing instrument to use for your offering (see Step 5).

Does it look like a direct participation offering is better suited to your needs than a stock offering? Perhaps a convertible preferred stock structure is best. Or maybe your financial requirements, in view of your Financing Sequence Plan, dictate that a simple promissory note needs to be sold to four business angels.

Your attorney and corporate finance advisor should be consulted when making this decision.

Decision 4: Sources. Step 2 surveyed the investor market and identified the five sources of investor capital: venture capitalists, strategic corporate investors, business angels, adventure stockholders, and Visionary Capitalists. It's time to decide which sources hold the most promise. You should rank your choices in order of priority. If you choose two, or even all four, you must include each of the sources separately in your Strategy Summary and the rest of your Offering Campaign Plan.

Decision 5: Approaches. Next, you must decide which approaches you will use to deal with your potential investors: the Direct Placement Approach or the Money Raiser Approach. (If you're going after strategic corporate investors and/or adventure stockholders, it's quite possible that you might use both approaches.) Follow the principles and suggestions explained in Step 2 very closely as you make your decision.

If you select the Money Raiser Approach, then decide which segments of that market are most likely to be accessible to your company and have an interest in your financing.

Decision 6: Capital Relations™ Program. Next, you develop as many final decisions as you can about the overall Capital Relations™ program. You will need to determine the following:

1. The size of the lead and prospect lists needed for each investor source choice.
2. The number and identity of advocate messengers needed.
3. The number and identity of both your customer and capital market infrastructure messengers.
4. The tactics and tools to use.

THE PERT CHART

You will need to prepare a timeline showing the timing of all the action steps you're including in your Offering Campaign. There is a technique that is well-suited for this, known as PERT (Planning Evaluation Review Technique). The final preparation of your PERT chart is made during Step 9. Illustrations 10-3 to 10-5 show examples of PERT charts.

THE BUDGET

Quite often it takes money to raise money. How much money is it going to take to execute your Offering Campaign Plan? Your corporate finance advisor can help you draw up and itemize a budget.

Make sure that you have the financial resources you need before you start. Depending on the approaches and Capital Relations™ program you selected for your offering, it may be necessary to set aside a little "war chest" to pay for the execution of the Offering Campaign. The final revised PERT chart you develop in Step 9 will give you a clear and complete picture of all the activities that you need to budget for. Example of budgets are shown in Illustrations 10-6 to 10-8.

COLLATERAL MARKETING TOOLS

Are the offering documents enough to present to investors when you're executing your Offering Campaign? No one can tell for sure in advance, but there is a way to find out. The next step, "Step 8: Testing the Market and List Assemblage," will give you a chance to get investor and money raiser feedback. You may find that your capital market is very happy with just the offering documents. However, you may discover that "more" is needed to win the attention of your funding sources. If that's the case, then you must be prepared to make use of collateral marketing tools. In Step 6, there is a list of the marketing tools available to support your Offering Campaign, including your investor relations program.

CONCLUSION

During Step 7, you prepared everything that you plan to present to investors during your Offering Campaign. This material will be tested in "Step 8: Testing the Market and List Assemblage." Steps 7 and 8 are intended to be worked together in order to identify the exact Actual Investor and/or Money Raiser Profiles for your offering. You will probably have to repeat these steps more than once—it's rare for a company to prepare its offering plan and marketing documentation exactly right the first time. The only way to take the guess work out of the Investor Financing™ process is to test it thoroughly.

Even if you're certain your discussion documents, especially your collateral marketing tools, are the way you and your advisors "want them to be," make sure that the vendors and developers of these documents and tools understand that at this point you only want "mock-ups," "rough copy," and "prototypes." Don't print 5,000 brochures or have 1,000 videos made before you thoroughly complete Steps 7 and 8.

TESTING THE
MARKET AND LIST
ASSEMBLAGE

Step 1

Step 2

Step 3

Step 4

Step 5

Step 6

Step 7

STEP 8

Step 9

Step 10

8

What's more crucially at stake are usually a lot of complex, slippery, and difficult intagibles that can make or break success.

—THEODORE LEVITT

Your company wouldn't think of selling a new product or service without including alpha and beta site market testing. The same policy should be followed when accessing investor capital. Don't be tempted to go to the investor markets too soon with your offering documents and business plan. Time and time again, companies seeking investor capital financing feel they've done enough planning, have enough contacts, or have enough knowledge about the entire process to rush to the investor markets. If your company does even 60% of what the first seven steps of the Investor Financing™ steps ask you to do, you may feel that you're overprepared. The urge to get going heightens when the CEO feels that his or her corporate finance advisor, attorney, accountants, board of advisors, and board of directors "have the answers" and they're saying, "go for it."

Unsuccessful Investor Financings™ can usually be traced back to impatient or naïve CEOs who didn't have accurate Actual Investor/Money Raiser Profiles and/or hadn't tested their advocate messengers before they launched their Offering Campaign.

Step 8 is your opportunity to let the investors, money raisers, and advocate messengers tell you themselves how to secure their attention and trust, so that they will invest in and/or support your company. Step 8 takes the guesswork out of the Investor Financing™. You will be able to find out what it is about your company and its offering that grabs or hooks the investors, money raisers, and advocate messengers. These offering hooks[1] can become the basis for much of the strategy for the final Offering Campaign Plan. Illustration 8-1 describes the hooks that most often show up as the central motivating reasons for investors, money raisers, and advocate messengers to want to invest and/or get involved with a company.

DETERMINING INVESTOR/MONEY RAISER PROFILES AND ASSEMBLING LISTS

The aim of Step 8 is twofold: The first aim is to get an accurate idea of the Actual Investor/Money Raiser Profile(s). This process will allow you to know

ILLUSTRATION 8-1:
OFFERING HOOKS

Hook	Investor reaction
Strategic hook	My business benefits by investing.
Greed hook	The "success formula" and Paradigm Vision of this company is going to make me a lot of money.
Found a sleeper hook	I've found a hidden golden nugget, and, boy, am I lucky.
Superstar hook	I love investing with the best in the business.
Credibility hook	I trust.
Know the leadership team personally hook	I know them — and they're good.
Know about the industry hook	I know this deal will work — it's on the cutting edge, and I know the industry.
Leadership team investment hook	The leadership team already has a lot of "sweat" equity and cash invested.
Endorsement hook	If "so and so" is in the deal — count me in.
Niche hook	My business had a niche too.
New industry/market hook	I could be the next Arthur Rock.
Easy exit hook	They are getting me out soon.
Worst case hook	Even the worst case is good.
Offering structure hook	They have my interests above their own.
Investment banker hook	Look — "so and so" is in on the deal and is helping the company. If they're in, I'm in.
Get control hook	We investors can take over easily if the leadership team fails to do the job.

what needs to be changed or added to your offering and sales documents. The following discussion documents, developed in Step 7, along with the selected collateral marketing tools, provide the materials and data that will be tested to determine the profiles:

- The business plan
- The Term Sheet
- The Funding Requirements Sheet
- The Offering Campaign Plan
- The collateral marketing tools

The second aim is to prepare your investor/money raiser list(s).

FOCUS GROUPS

Line Up the Players. Go back and review the Strategy Summary in your Offering Campaign Plan. In it you'll find the investor sources and advocate messengers that you have preliminarily determined will make up the playing field you're about to go out on. You need to select a handful of these people to meet with to talk about your upcoming offering. This meeting is called a *focus group*. You should try to make your selections a true cross-section of the investor sources you plan to raise capital from. One logical place to look for investors and money raisers is from your Investor/Money Raiser Database List. However, if this database is not prepared yet, then you'll need to carefully select people that you believe may be candidate investors or money raisers. Your corporate finance advisor can help you with this.

Once you've selected the people you want for your focus groups, you need to convince them to participate. Here are some suggestions:

"No Kidding—We're Just Testing." When asked to join a focus group, many investors, money raisers, and advocate messengers fear a sales pitch. The integrity of what you're trying to accomplish has to be communicated up front. It helps if the person making the appointment call is not employed by the company. The corporate finance advisor is often the right person for this job.

"Now It's My Turn." Some of the people you will ask to join your focus groups may be involved in strategic associations with your company. In the course of building these strategic associations you will have undoubtedly assisted their companies in some way (otherwise there would have been no motivation for their companies to have formed associations with you). This makes it easy for you to call in some chips, and say something as simple as, "Now it's my turn for a favor; I need to ask you some questions."

"We'll Be Happy to Pay You for Your Time." This technique will not work for everyone. Some money raisers, such as broker/dealers, due diligence consultants, financial planners, and investment bankers, may feel a conflict of

interest in "selling their time." The key word here is "some." There are many securities licensed money raisers who will consult with you for a fee. Business angels and adventure stockholders are also often willing to consult for a fee. The fee you'll have to pay will range from $50 to $250 per hour.

There's a surprising pay-off from this technique—often the people you pay money to (even though they've earned it) feel a sense of responsibility to you for the advice they've given. They're people you can go back to for more help. And the more help you ask for, and the more they give, the faster a relationship develops between you and the investor/money raiser or advocate messenger source. You will be amazed at how many paid focus group members end up investing or becoming an advocate messenger, and/or providing other forms of help. It's a classic case of a legal "bait and switch" tactic.

SOME TIPS ABOUT FOCUS GROUPS

Use Your Corporate Finance Advisor. He or she is the ideal person to set up and conduct your focus groups.

Save the Best for Last. Don't invite your "A" list of investors/money raisers and advocate messengers to attend your focus groups. You may not want them to see your campaign and your presentation of it until you have it perfected.

This Is Not Product Testing. Don't confuse product focus groups with the investor focus groups. Normally you will not use the same consultants who help you conduct your product focus groups to run the investor/money raiser/advocate messenger focus groups.

The CEO Does It. Although the work of setting up and conducting the focus groups can be delegated to others, the CEO should be in attendance at the focus groups.

Have the Business Plan Read Before the Meeting. Since you'll have limited face-to-face time, you might consider sending the business plan to the participants for them to read before coming to the focus groups.

Shut Up and Listen. It's a good idea to let the corporate finance advisor lead the focus group meetings. The right questions need to be asked in the right way. The CEO's job is to listen, watch, and absorb.

Look for What the Participants Don't Say. There's a lot to be learned from what's not said. Body language, tone of voice, pauses, etc., are all part of the information that you want to gather. This kind of information is what Henry Mitzberg of McGill University calls "thick" information. It's the intuitive, gut-feeling that can only be gotten from person-to-person communication. As Mitzberg says, it's "information rich in detail and color, far beyond what can be quantified and aggregated. It must be dug out on site by people intimately involved with the phenomenon they wish to influence."[2]

"Can We Tape This?" Ask permission to tape the proceedings. You can take notes when you review the tape. This frees you to concentrate on the "thick" information during the session. Try to place the microphone and camera inconspicuously to avoid making participants feel self-conscious.

Don't Mix Investors, Money Raisers, and Advocate Messengers. The agenda is different enough for investor sources, money raisers, and advocate messengers that you shouldn't mix these people together. You will need to set up different meetings for each group that you have targeted from the capital market.

Have an Agenda. Come prepared, and be ready to lead a good meeting.[3] Because of the many variables involved, every Offering Campaign is unique. Failure to adequately prepare for a focus group meeting can often do more harm than any good derived from the meeting. Analyze your discussion documents and prepare a prioritized list of points and/or questions you want to cover. Here's a list of possible agenda points and questions, but it's by no means all inclusive:

Profile of focus group participants:

Are you a venture capitalist, business angel, adventure stockholder, or money raiser? What is your age? Financial status? Business position? Experience? Expertise? Familiarity Index Rating?

The Leadership Team:
Is our leadership team impressive? Do we cover all the bases?

Product or service:
Have you seen a product (or service) like this? What is, or isn't, different about it? How could it be better?

Financial condition:
Do you understand our financial condition? Are we strong enough? What could be better?

Term Sheet:
Is our offering structured right? What could be better?

Business plan:
Do you understand our business plan? Is it convincing? What's missing? What's not believable? Are the growth and liquidity tracks believable? Do you understand the financial forecast? Are our Evidence Points strong enough?

Executive summary:
Does our executive summary excite you about our company? If not, why?

Offering hooks:
Which offering hooks are the attention getters? Which ones don't work?

Capital Relations™ plan:
How can we communicate with you to win your attention and trust? How long will it take? What can we do that is vitally important to you? How much about the industry do you need to know?

Tactics:
Will our tactics work in getting you to learn about and/or become involved in a relationship with our company?

Tools:
Do you like our marketing and sales tools? What could be better?

Investment desire:
Are you motivated to invest? If so, why? If not, why not? How much would you be willing to invest? Would you refer this to others? How many?

Launch Plan:
Do we have a good Launch Plan? If not, why?

Paradigm Vision:
Do you see any weaknesses in our Paradigm Vision? How can we strengthen it?

Strategic associations:
Do we need any additional strategic associations? Who? Where? When? Do you think we can get them? If not, why not?

If the focus group is with advocate messengers, then all of the above topics should be included. In addition, the following should also be covered:

Advocate messenger's attitude:
Would you be an advocate messenger?
If not, why not? What will it take for you to say yes?
If yes, how many prospects do you know? How many leads do you have? How can we verify these together?

"Can We Do This Again?" Before the focus group session is over, always ask if they'll be willing to work with you again in another focus group. Try to get an open invitation from them. This can be the key to starting an ongoing relationship.

After the Focus Group

Always follow up with the appropriate correspondence: sometimes a phone call or short thank-you note is sufficient. If you agreed to pay them, do it quickly. Quick payment earns trust. If people met with you gratis, then perhaps a gift of appreciation is in order.

How Many Focus Groups Are Needed?

The answer is, as many focus groups as it takes to get it right. Getting it right means having a clear definition of what the Actual Investor/Money Raiser Profile is. In addition, you need to feel comfortable that you will be able to line up the required number of advocate messengers for your Offering Campaign, and that these advocate messengers have enough prospects in their circles of influence.

Reach for the Highest Outcome. It is entirely possible that Step 8 can result in enough good relationships with prospect investors/money raisers so that 30–50% of your offering is already committed to by the people you met during your focus group meetings. The power of these consultive-type two-way meetings cannot be underestimated. During Step 8, patience and planning can pay big dividends.

HOW TO ASSEMBLE YOUR LISTS

With your Actual Investor/Money Raiser Profiles determined and your advocate messengers screened, you are now in a position to assemble your lead lists. At this time, you may already have many people and firms on your various lead, prospect, candidate, and super-candidate lists. During the preparation of your Strategy Summary in Step 7, you made a preliminary decision about how many leads you will need per investor source to complete your Offering Campaign. Review again Illustration 7-2. You will note that the hypothetical company used in the illustration had determined the exact number of leads that the company needed. (This was covered in Step 7 in the section titled "Offering Campaign Strategy Summary—Decision 6: Capital Relations™ Plan.") Step 8 will clarify and validate the decisions you made during Step 7.

Assembling your lead lists can be as simple as buying *Pratt's Guide to Venture Capital Sources*, purchasing a list of business owners and sales managers in a given industry, or getting a list of names and addresses from your advocate messengers of the people in their circle of influence who the advocate messengers believe fit the Actual Investor/Money Raiser Profile. Your corporate finance advisor can help you with the list research and assemblage. Creativity, commitment, and patience are the ingredients needed here.

CONCLUSION

You need to be honest about your work so far. Have you conducted enough quality focus groups to be able to accurately define your Actual Investor/Money Raiser profiles? Have you assembled a strong lead list with a sufficient number of qualified leads to execute your Offering Campaign? Remember how the math works:

> 25 leads produce 5 prospects
> 5 prospects produce 5 candidates
> 5 candidates produce 4 super-candidates
> 4 super-candidates produce 2 actual investors

Be careful of the "slam dunk" investors and money raisers who are too quick to tell you they want in on your deal. People who do this probably haven't done their homework yet, and when they finally do it, you'll find they have all kinds of excuses for not showing up with their checks. A good rule of thumb is to discount half of those people who indicate they want it. This gives you a more realistic number to plan with.

If your market testing has been thorough, if accurate Actual Investor/Money Raiser Profiles have been determined, and if you have a strong lead list, then you're ready to move to "Step 9: Finalizing the Documents."

Step 1

Step 2

Step 3

Step 4

Step 5

Step 6

Step 7

Step 8

FINALIZING
THE
DOCUMENTS

9

*It is wonderful how much is done in a short space,
provided we set about it properly, and give our
minds wholly to it.*

—WILLIAM HAZLITT

Having thoroughly performed Steps 7 and 8, you are now ready to finalize
your offering documents, Offering Campaign Plan, and collateral marketing
tools. The high anxiety normally associated with an Investor Financing™
should have cooled down to only a small case of the jitters, because you have
taken the guesswork out of the business of raising investor capital. Most
Business Builders who have accessed investor capital will admit they did not
enjoy hiring attorneys, accountants, and all the collateral marketing tool
vendors, while they were still uncertain about the eventual success of the
offering. Testing the market is the only way to remove this uncertainty—even
though there can, of course, be no absolute guarantee that the Offering
Campaign will be successful.

Here is the list of the documents and materials that need to be finalized:

The business plan (to be used with the market)
The offering documents (to be used with the market)

- Investment Memorandum (to be used with venture capitalists, business angels, or strategic corporate investors)
- The Private Placement Memorandum (to be used with business angels
  and adventure stockholders in private offerings)
- Offering Circular (to be used with adventure stockholders in intra-
  state public offerings)
- Prospectus (to be used with adventure stockholders in SEC public
  offerings)

The Offering Campaign Plan (to be used only internally)

- Strategy Summary
- PERT chart
- Budget

The collateral marketing tools (to be used with the market)

FINAL PREPARATION TIPS

Review the information you gleaned from your focus groups. Make sure that all of the suggestions and recommended changes have been squarely faced by the leadership team. It's easy for the leadership team to slip back to its own ideas about how to get the offering done. Double-check the following:

THE BUSINESS PLAN

Is the business plan written from the viewpoint of the actual investors/money raisers detailed in your Actual Investor/Money Raiser Profiles? Are you going to have to write several different versions of the business plan because of the different sources you plan to market to? Are the accounting numbers accurate, the assumptions verifiable, and the claims substantiated? Does the Paradigm Vision leap out and grab attention? Is the writing clear ("more with less")? Have you used plain English? Has the grammar and spelling been double-checked (especially in the revised sections)? Is the layout graphically appealing within the framework of the corporate image? Are the appendices complete?

THE OFFERING DOCUMENTS

As a rule, your attorney should prepare the necessary offering documents. In smaller offerings, under $300,000, the leadership team will often do most of the preparation. However, any tax sections or opinion letters must be prepared by legal counsel. Many state laws make it a crime for a non-lawyer to practice law, so be sure that an attorney does those sections of your offering documents that are required "by law" to be prepared by an attorney. Illustration 9-1 lists the sections that should be included in the offering documents.

The Cost of Offering Documents. The fees for investment memorandum and private placement work, performed by law firms, will range from $2,000 to $20,000. There is no industry standard or published Bar Association policy. Your job is to find the best lawyers available at competitive prices. (See the earlier discussion in "Step 4: Identifying Strategic Associations" in the section titled "The Attorney—The Compliance Keeper.") Efficient and experienced lawyers should complete their work in one to three weeks. Many times, however, the company will not have completed its financial forecasts or other appendix items, thus delaying the final printing of the offering documents.

THE OFFERING CAMPAIGN PLAN

Your Offering Campaign Plan is comprised of the following:

- Strategy Summary
- PERT chart
- Budget plan

ILLUSTRATION 9-1:
OFFERING DOCUMENTS CONTENTS

Item	Investment Memorandum	Private Placement Memorandum	Offering Circular	Prospectus
Cover page	X	X	X	X
Table of contents	*	X	X	X
Summary of offering	*	X	X	X
Summary business description	X	X	X	X
Summary product/service description	X	X	*	*
Summary industry/competitive environment	*	*	*	*
Description of securities	X	X	X	X
Terms of offering	*	X	X	X
Use of proceeds	X	X	X	X
Plan of distribution of the securities	X	X	X	X
Risk factors	*	X	X	X
Leadership team resumés	X	X	X	X
Leadership team compensation	X	X	X	X
Leadership team track record	*	*	*	*
Conflicts of interest	*	X	X	X
Tax considerations	*	X	X	X
Legal matters	*	X	X	X
Glossary	*	X	X	X
Subscription agreements	*	X	X	X
Tax opinions	*	*	*	*
Securities opinions	*	*	*	*
Appendices†	*	*	*	*

* Sometimes used, but it depends on the circumstances.

† The appendices can include financial and marketing forecasts, photographs, reports, surveys, article reprints, maps, charts, specifications, contracts, broker/dealer selling agreements, etc.

In Step 10, a sample Offering Campaign will be presented for a hypothetical company. Reference should be made to that discussion. If you have properly performed Steps 1 through 8, you have done 90% of the work associated with accessing investor capital. Your Offering Campaign Plan incorporates all the ideas and strategies of your investor relations program.

Strategy Summary. Is it complete? Did your corporate finance advisor help you with it? Was every point in the summary tested at Step 8?

PERT Chart. Now that your Offering Campaign Plan is finally decided upon, you should prepare your PERT chart that was discussed in Step 5. This will allow you to organize your action steps in carrying out the Offering Campaign.

Using a PERT chart will give you a visual display of the activities of the Offering Campaign Plan, and will help you do the following:

- Remain focused
- See danger signals quickly
- Balance trade-offs between time and resources
- Identify critical areas requiring special attention
- Improve the budgeting of the time and money that is spent on your offering
- Quickly see the current status of your offering project

A PERT chart can be simple or complex, depending on the number of activities included, and the amount of detail included. It can be prepared manually or by using computer software programs. For a small company, preparing the PERT chart by hand, and displaying it on an erasable "white" board in your office, will work well. In a larger company, the best approach is to select a PERT software package to develop the chart, and then have copies printed out for you and your staff. Illustrations 10-3 to 10-5 show examples of manually prepared PERT charts for the hypothetical company, Personal Computer Publishing Associates, Inc.

Budget. Refer to Step 10 and the model budgets shown there. Did your corporate finance advisor help you? How many of the expenses can be reimbursed to the company from the offering? Have the costs of the Investor Financing™ tools been adjusted from the first time you prepared this budget during Step 7?

The Collateral Marketing Tools

The results of your focus group sessions will make clear which, if any, collateral marketing tools you'll need. Were you careful to discuss all the possibilities with the focus groups? Do you have sufficient funds budgeted to develop the necessary tools? It may be necessary to increase your budget to pay for them. If the necessary funds are not available, then you will have to determine the likelihood of your offering succeeding without the tools.

CONCLUSION

The preparation of the final documents should be an exciting experience because you now know that these documents are exactly what is needed for your Offering Campaign. You know what your investor sources, money raisers, and advocate messengers need, and you're giving it to them. At this point, there is very little guesswork involved.

While your leadership team, attorney, accountant, and vendors are busy preparing the final version of these documents, you should begin the execution of your Offering Campaign—Step 10.

Step 1

Step 2

Step 3

Step 4

Step 5

Step 6

Step 7

Step 8

Step 9

EXECUTING
THE OFFERING
CAMPAIGN

STEP 10

Try? There is no try. There is only do or not do.
—YODA, *THE EMPIRE STRIKES BACK*

Your leadership team deserves a big pat on the back for making it successfully to Step 10. You have now completed 90% of the real work. Enthusiasm should be running high, and the light at the end of this long tunnel should be in view. If your team is tired, your budgets strained, and patience is running low, then perhaps a break is in order to celebrate a job well done and to recharge everyone's batteries. The rest of your staff, who may not have been involved over the past months, may need a complete briefing about the progress of the Investor Financing™ steps that the company has been working on. Tell the troops what the company has accomplished. Everyone connected to your company (including spouses) needs to know how well the company has done thus far in its quest for capital. This whole business of raising capital is a big thing—so make it a big thing with everyone.

NO MORE REHEARSALS

In Step 7, you prepared the best guesstimate you could about the details of your Offering Campaign. Everything was reduced to writing and included the following:

- Your Offering Campaign Plan Strategy Summary
- Your PERT chart
- Your budget

With your Offering Campaign Plan, you performed enough focus groups during Step 8 to be satisfied that you had discovered the Actual Investor Profiles and/or the Actual Money Raiser Profiles from the sources of investor capital that you've found are available for your company and its offering. You also tested the strength of your list of advocate messengers. Through the focus group work you probably made note of many adjustments necessary for the Offering Campaign and its required documents (Step 9). These adjustments were probably in response to four areas of discovery:

1. The final definitions of your Actual Investor Profiles and/or Actual Money Raiser Profiles may have surprised you—perhaps pleasantly, perhaps not. The exact profiles dictated many of the strategies and decisions that went into the Capital Relations™ program of your Offering Campaign. Your current prospect and candidate lists may be smaller than anticipated, which means the effort in qualifying-out the lead lists and moving these investors/money raiser leads up through the various stages of the "relationship ladder" may require more work than you expected. Originally, you may have thought that 75% of your offering was going to be funded through money raisers, only to find that, at best, only 25% of the offering can probably be funded through them. This, in turn, may have had an effect on your decision about using a private offering rather than a public offering.

2. The final investor/money raiser lead lists you assembled during Step 8 may have given you some surprises—either good or bad.

3. The actual number of people from your circle of influence who you approached through the focus groups, and who said, "Yes," to being an advocate messenger, may have surprised you either favorably or unfavorably.

4. The communications tactics and tools that you discovered are necessary to execute your Capital Relations™ program may be quite different than what you had originally planned on.

The number of surprises and the resulting obstacles, if any, will vary greatly. If you marched on through Step 9, your company's principals and advisors must have had strong reason to believe that any obstacles can be overcome. In any event, the final offering documents, prepared during Step 9, were done on the basis of concrete, tested facts and assumptions.

ON WITH THE SHOW
Lights, camera, action—it's time to roll back the curtains and let the show begin. The show, of course, is the execution of your Offering Campaign—the action steps for funding the offering. Everything should be in place, so it's time for the actors to play their parts. No one wins Academy Awards for less than all-out lifetime performances. Are you and the rest of the Funding Team ready for an all-out push to close the offering successfully? Let's look at an example.

A HYPOTHETICAL OFFERING CAMPAIGN
In Step 7, the Offering Campaign Plan Strategy Summary of Personal Computer Publishing Associates, Inc. was described. It's repeated here for

---

ILLUSTRATION 10-1:
OFFERING CAMPAIGN PLAN STRATEGY SUMMARY FOR PERSONAL COMPUTER
PUBLISHING ASSOCIATES, INC

---

1. *Financing Sequence Plan:*

Private offering of preferred stock:	Now
Bank loan or debenture offering:	In 24–36 months
Staying-Private Public Offering™ of common stock, or strategic alliance, or joint venture with a larger company:	In 36–48 months
IPO:	In 7th year

---

2. *Current funding requirements:* $350,000
$150,000 minimum
$350,000 maximum

---

3. *Current financing instrument:* Private offering
Preferred stock with 10% cumulative (not compounded) dividend; conversion to common; company's option to redeem stock

---

4. *Sources:* Choice 1: Strategic corporate investors, Visionary Capitalists, and business angels
Choice 2: Adventure stockholders
Choice 3: Venture capitalists

---

5. *Approaches:* Direct Placement Approach for choice 1, 2 ,and 3 sources
Money Raiser Approach for choice 1 (Strat. copr. investors only) and choice 2 sources

---

6. *Capital Relations™ program:*

Choice 1:	Alternative Choice 1:	Choice 2:	Choice 3:
5 Visionary Capitalists	1 Strat. corp. investor	43 Adventure stockhldrs.	1 Venture capitalist
5 Business angels	2 Super-candidates	86 Super-candidates	2 Super-candidates
10 Super-candidates	3 Candidates	100 Candidates	3 Candidates
20 Candidates	3 Prospects	100 Prospects	3 Prospects
20 Prospects	15 Leads	500 Leads	15 Leads
100 Leads	1 Advocate messeng.	20 Advocates messengs.	1 Advocate messengs.
4 Advocate messengs.	10 Infrast. messengers	30 Infrast. messengers	10 Infrast. messengers
20 Infrast. messengers	16 Major tactics chosen	18 Major tactics chosen	8 Major tactics chosen
16 Major tactics chosen	11 Minor tactics chosen	10 Minor tactics chosen	0 Minor tactics chosen
10 Minor tactics chosen	22 Tools chosen	24 Tools chosen	13 Tools chosen
22 Tools chosen			

---

your convenience in Illustration 10-1. This hypothetical case study is presented not as an example of exactly how you should execute your Offering Campaign, but as an illustration of the planning process involved. Every company's Investor Financing™ program will result in a different set of decisions, plans, tactics, and tools for the Offering Campaign.

STRATEGY SUMMARY OBSERVATIONS

You will note from Illustration 10-1 that the funding requirements of $150,000 to $350,00 are small enough for a private offering. The leadership team of this company discovered during "Step 8: Testing the Market and List Assemblage" that an Actual Investor Profile existed for both strategic corporate investors and business angels. This combination became the leadership team's first choice. You will recall from Step 2 that business angels are accessed, as a rule, through the Direct Placement Approach, rather than through the Money Raiser Approach. However, the Money Raiser Approach is suitable for locating strategic corporate investors and visonary capitalists. Generally, investment bankers or business brokers would be the most likely money raiser source for strategic corporate investors. Should both of these first choice sources prove unsuccessful, then adventure stockholders are the next choice. Hopefully, the leadership team organized enough focus groups during Step 8 to assure themselves that they have an accurate Actual Investor Profile for adventure stockholders, and that they can locate enough advocate messengers to support the Capital Relations™ program that will be necessary for accessing adventure stockholders.

It should be noted here that during Step 8, many management teams, believing that their first funding sources will be sufficient to raise the required capital, do not do the necessary list assemblage for their second investor source choice. When this happens, and the first choice does not fund the offering, it then becomes necessary to revise the PERT chart, and budget, and to do the additional list assemblage required for other funding sources during Step 10.

Enough time must be allotted then to execute an Offering Campaign for each of the chosen investor sources. This is why many companies find that accessing investor capital can take much longer than originally planned. It might appear that the solution to this "time" dilemma is to execute an Offering Campaign where all three investor/money raiser choices are integrated into one campaign. Although this is possible, experience has proven that targeting one investor/money raiser choice at a time, with a focused Offering Campaign, is more successful. The PERT charts in Illustrations 10-3, 10-4, and 10-5 show how this can be done. This hypothetical company, Personal Computer

---

ILLUSTRATION 10-2:
SELECTED TACTICS AND TOOLS FOR HYPOTHETICAL OFFERING CAMPAIGN

Visionary Capitalists, business angles and strategic corporate investor/money raisers	*Adventure stockholders/ money raisers*	*Venture capitalists*
Major tactics	*Major tactics*	*Major tactics*
1. One-on-one	1. One-on-one	1. One-on-one
2. Expert	2. Expert	2. Expert
3. Convoy surfacer	6. Industry leader	6. Industry leader
6. Industry leader	10. Public seminars	7. Business leader
9. County club	11. Private sales seminars	14. Strategic assocs.
12. Private workshops	12. Private workshops	22. Referral
14. Strategic assocs.	15. Money in motion	38. Joint venture
15. Money in motion	16. Wholesaler	41. CFO money raiser
21. Vendor	17. Sales force	
22. Referral	20. Advertiser	
24. Focus group	21. Vendor	
26. Use a mentor	22. Referral	
34. Strategic networker	24. Focus group	
41. CFO money raiser	34. Strategic networker	
44. Customers	39. Direct mail	
45. Pension mover	41. CFO money raiser	
46. Info. bulletin bds.	47. Adaptive sequence	
50. Momentum	48. Sponsorship	
51. Public information	51. Public information	
52. Contract awards	52. Contract awards	
53. Legal records	53. Legal records	
54. Yellow page ads	54. Yellow page ads	
57. Investors by profession	55. Video	
62. Give a dinner	57. Investors by profession	

Visionary Capitalists, business angles and strategic corporate investor/money raisers	Adventure stockholders/ money raisers	Venture capitalists
Major tactics	*Major tactics*	*Major tactics*

65. Business publications	59. Home sales	
66. Acknowledge	60. Stock sales	
70. Find litigators	62. Give a dinner	
71. Trade magazines	68. Penny stock investors	
	70. Find litigators	

Tools	*Tools*	*Tools*
1. Corporate brochure	1. Corporate brochure	1. Corporate brochure
3. Offering fact sheet	2. Offering documents	3. Offering fact sheet
4. Presentation folders	3. Offering fact sheet	4. Presentation folder
6. Special topic brochure	4. Presentation folder	5. Photo pages
7. Letters	5. Photo pages	6. Special topic brochure
8. Announcements	6. Special topic brochure	8. Announcements
9. Bulletins	7. Letters	9. Bulletins
10. Newsletters	8. Announcements	10. Newsletters
11. Quarterly reports	9. Bulletins	11. Quarterly reports
12. Annual reports	10. Newsletters	12. Annual reports
14. News articles	11. Quarterly reports	14. News articles
15. Press releases	12. Annual reports	15. Press releases
16. Article reprints	14. News articles	16. Article reprints
20. Audio cassettes	15. Press releases	29. Open houses
25. Mailing lists	16. Article reprints	30. Lunches/dinners
26. Answering machine	17. Television	35. Surveys
27. Phone calls	20. Audio cassettes	
28. Faxes	21. Video	
29. Open houses	25. Mailing lists	
31. Lunches/dinners	26. Answering machine	
35. Surveys	27. Phone calls	
	28. Faxes	
	29. Open houses	
	30. Lunches/dinners	
	35. Surveys	

Publishing Associates, Inc., has planned a separate Offering Campaign for each of its three chosen sources in the order of its preference for investors.

You also learned in Step 2 that if adventure stockholders have to be used, they will not, as a rule, be part of a financing with business angels or strategic corporate investors. So if adventure stockholders are used, the management team will have to attempt a private offering using a minimum investment of $10,000 ($350,000 divided by 35). If, on the other hand, a Staying-Private Public Offering™ is used, the minimum investment could be brought down to $3,000 or less.

If the necessary funding cannot be raised using adventure stockholders, then the third choice, venture capitalists, can be tried. The leadership team may have left venture capitalists as its last choice because it believed that this source would expect too much ownership for its investment.

"Step 8: Testing the Market and List Assemblage" also revealed the necessary Capital Relations™ tactics and tools that are needed for the investor and money raiser choices of the Offering Campaign. The tactics and tools chosen by Personal Computer Publishing Associates, Inc. are listed in Illustration 10-2. (The numbers correspond to the reference numbers of the tactics and tools described in Step 5.)

THE PERT CHART

As part of the planning for its Offering Campaign, Personal Computer Publishing Associates, Inc. has to prepare three PERT charts—one for each of the three choices of investor capital that it has identified as being suitable for its offering. If it is not possible to successfully fund the offering from the first source of investors, then it will be necessary to conduct an Offering Campaign for the second preferred choice, and if that is not successful, then a third campaign will have to be mounted.

Illustration 10-3 presents a PERT chart for the company's first choice of investors: business angels, visonary capitalists, and strategic corporate investors. Illustration 10-4 is a PERT chart for choice 2: adventure stockholders. And finally Illustration 10-5 is a PERT chart for the third choice: venture capitalists. These PERT charts are examples of what a manually prepared PERT chart looks like. PERT charts prepared on a computer may be formatted somewhat differently.

THE BUDGET

Each Offering Campaign Plan which Personal Computer Publishing Associates, Inc. develops will require its own budget because the costs for the campaigns can vary substantially from each other, depending on the investor source being targeted. In order to arrive at an accurate estimate of costs for each plan, the leadership team must determine the cost of each selected tactic

ILLUSTRATION 10-3:
PERT CHART FOR BUSINESS ANGELS AND STRATEGIC CORPORATE INVESTORS

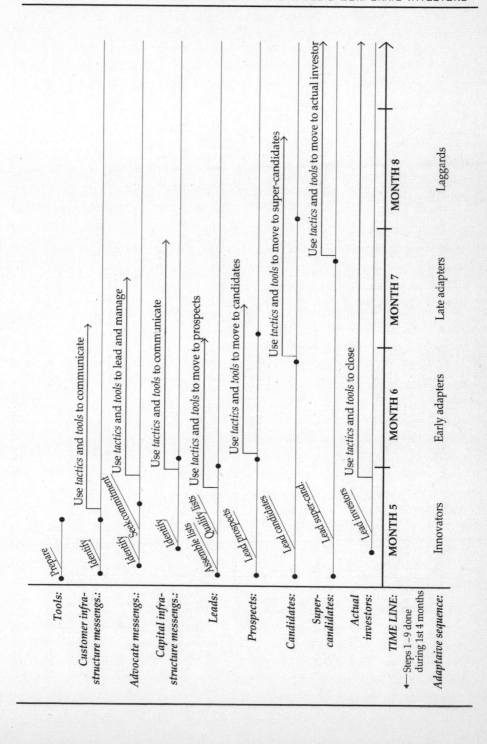

Illustration 10-4:
PERT Chart for Adventure Stockholders

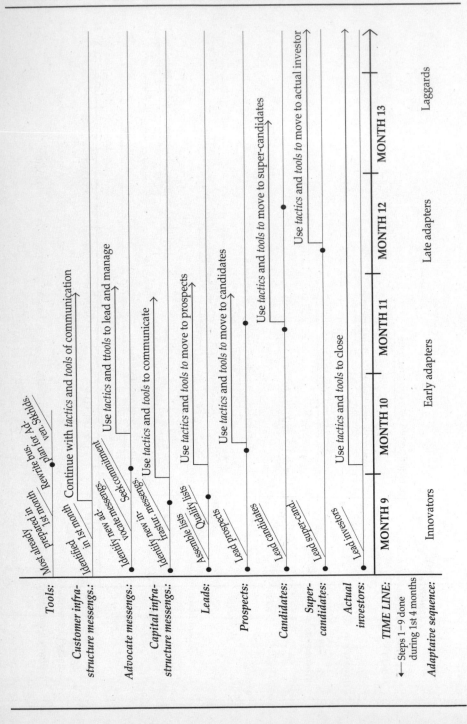

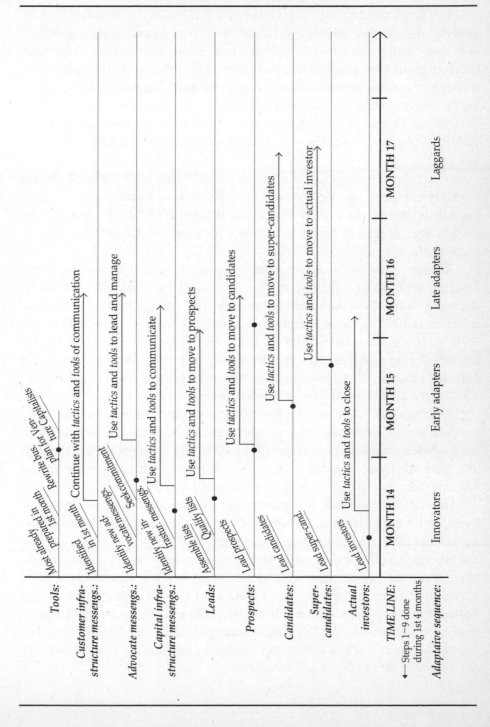

ILLUSTRATION 10-5:
PERT Chart for Venture Capitalists

and tool, keeping in mind that they are frequently used more than once during the campaign.

Most Capital Relations™ plans involve activities that are designed to move leads up through the "relationship ladder" until they become super-candidates and then finally actual investors. Every company embarking on an investor financing will have unique needs and experience different challenges, so it is difficult to provide accurate rules of thumb for budget amounts. There is one exception, however. The securities industry, over the years, has observed enough public and private offerings directed toward adventure stockholders that it is possible to state a rule of thumb for accessing capital from that source.

As a rule, offering costs for an Investor Financing™ targeted toward visonary capitalists, business angels, strategic corporate investors, or venture capitalists should not exceed 3% of the money to be raised. However, if finders' fees need to be paid to reach these investor sources, then the offering costs could increase by 5% to 10%.

Offering costs for a private offering directed toward adventure stock-holders, net of sales commissions, due diligence costs, and wholesale costs, average 3% to 5% of the offering proceeds. The average cost of sales com-missions is 10%, so a total offering cost, net of wholesale costs, would be 13% to 15%. If a professional wholesaler is needed, their costs average about 3% of the offering proceeds. So it is possible that the total offering costs for an Investor Financing™ targeted to adventure stockholders could equal 15% to 19% of the total capitalization of the offering.

Offering costs for a public offering, net of sales commissions, due dili-gence costs, and wholesale costs, normally run 5% to 10% of the offering pro-ceeds. Sales commissions average 7% to 10%, due diligence costs can equal 2%, and wholesale costs can equal 3%, so it's not uncommon for public offering costs to equal 20% to 25% of the total funds raised.

Allocate Carefully. It is important to be aware of which costs are reim-bursable by the offering and which costs are not reimbursable. Many of the tactics and tools can be viewed as ongoing corporate expenditures that should not be charged off to the offering. Many investors and money raisers are sen-sitive about the amount allocated for offering costs. They want minimal costs if possible. Their feelings center on their need to have capital spent on the business and not on the offering. If you're confronted by investors or money raisers on the size of your Offering Campaign budget, just remind them that raising capital is just like every other corporate function, and adequate funds must be allocated to do the job successfully.

ILLUSTRATION 10-6:
OFFERING CAMPAIGN BUDGET FOR BUSINESS ANGELS, VISONARY CAPITALISTS,
AND STRATEGIC CORPORATE INVESTORS

	Offering costs	General corporate costs*
TACTICS:		
1. One-on-one		✓
2. Expert		✓
3. Convoy surfacer		✓
6. Industry leader		✓
9. Country club		✓
12. Private workshops	$2,000	
14. Strategic associations		✓
15. Money in motion		✓
21. Vendor		✓
22. Referral	*Could have finders' fees in offering costs*	✓
24. Focus group	*Could reimburse corp. for cost of focus group ($9,000)*	
26. Use a mentor		✓
34. Strategic networker		✓
41. CFO money raiser		✓
44. Customers		✓
45. Pension mover		✓
46. Info. bulletin bds.		✓
50. Momentum		✓
51. Public information		✓
52. Contract awards		✓
54. Yellow page ads	*Some ads could be structured and costs borne by offering*	✓
57. Investors by profession		✓
62. Give a dinner	$600	
65. Business publications		✓
66. Acknowledgments		✓
70. Find litigators	500	
71. Trade magazines		✓
Tactics Total:	$3,100	

	Offering costs	General corporate costs*
TOOLS:		
1. Corporate brochure	$2,000	
3. Offering fact sheet	200	
4. Presentation folder	300	
5. Photo pages	75	
6. Special topic brochure	150	
7. Letters		✓
8. Announcements	200	
9. Bulletins	100	
10. Newsletters	300	
11. Quarterly reports	100	
12. Annual reports	100	
14. News articles		✓
15. Press releases		✓
16. Article reprints		✓
20. Audio cassettes	200	
25. Mailing lists	500	
26. Answering machine		✓
27. Phone calls		✓
28. Faxes		✓
29. Open houses	600	
31. Lunches/dinners		✓
35. Surveys		✓

* These costs are not reimbursable from the offering.

ILLUSTRATION 10-7:
OFFERING CAMPAIGN BUDGET FOR ADVENTURE STOCKHOLDERS

	Offering costs	General corporate costs*
TACTICS:		
1. One-on-one		✓
2. Expert		✓
6. Industry leader		✓
10. Public seminars	$2,000	
11. Private sales seminars	2,000	
12. Private workshops	2,000	
15. Money in motion		✓
16. Wholesaler	9,000	
17. Sales force	35,000	
20. Advertiser	If public offering could run ads	
21. Vendor		✓
22. Referral		✓
24. Focus group	Could reimburse corp. for costs of focus groups	
34. Strategic networker		✓
39. Direct mail	Could be used in combo with sales force	
41. CFO money raiser		✓
47. Adaptive sequence		✓
48. Sponsorship		✓
51. Public information		✓
52. Contract awards		✓
53. Legal records		✓
54. Yellow page ads	Could run ads	
55. Video	Could be used with sales force	
57. Investors by profession		✓
59. Home sales		✓
60. Stock sales		✓
62. Give a dinner	1,000	
68. Penny stock investors		✓
70. Find litigators		✓
Tactics Total:	$51,000	

TOOLS:

1.	Corporate brochure	$4,000	
2.	Offering documents	4,000	
3.	Offering fact sheet	500	
4.	Presentation folder	600	
5.	Photo pages	200	
6.	Special topic brochure		✓
7.	Letters		✓
8.	Announcements	200	
9.	Bulletins	100	
10.	Newsletters	300	
11.	Quarterly reports	200	
12.	Annual reports	200	
14.	News articles		✓
15.	Press releases		✓
16.	Article reprints		✓
17.	Television		✓
20.	Audio cassettes	500	
21.	Video	3,000	
25.	Mailing lists	500	
26.	Answering machine		✓
27.	Phone calls		✓
28.	Faxes		✓
29.	Open houses	500	
30.	Lunches/dinners	1,500	
35.	Surveys		✓

Tools Total:	$16,300
Grand Total:	$67,300

* These costs are not reimbursable from the offering.

ILLUSTRATION 10-8:
OFFERING CAMPAIGN BUDGET FOR VENTURE CAPITLISTS

	Offering costs	General corporate costs*
TACTICS:		
1. One-on-one		✓
2. Expert		✓
6. Industry leader		✓
7. Business leader		✓
14. Strategic associations		✓
22. Referral	*Finders' fees:* 17,500	
38. Joint venture		✓
41. CFO money raiser		✓
Tactics Total:	$17,500	
TOOLS:		
1. Corporate brochure	$2,000	
3. Offering fact sheet	200	
4. Presentation folder	300	
5. Photo pages	75	
6. Special topic brochure	150	
8. Announcements	200	
9. Bulletins	100	
10. Newsletters	300	
11. Quarterly reports	100	
12. Annual reports	100	
14. News articles		✓
15. Press releases		✓
16. Article reprints		✓
29. Open houses	600	
30. Lunches/dinners		✓
35. Surveys		✓
Tools Total:	$4,125	
Grand Total:	$21,625	

* These costs are not reimbursable from the offering.

Illustrations 10-6, 10-7, and 10-8 show the Offering Campaign budgets developed for Personal Computer Publishing Associates, Inc. You will note that the offering costs for visonary capitalists, business angels, and strategic corporate investors equals approximately 2%. The offering costs for adventure stockholders equals 19% of the money to be raised. And the offering costs for venture capitalists is 6%.

THE OFFERING CAMPAIGN

While executing the action steps shown on your PERT charts, keep in mind the following principles and practices:

Hard Work Got You Here. Don't second guess yourself now. If you did Steps 1 to 9 well, then you will be successful in closing your funding.

Be Ready for Surprises. Don't expect the campaign to go perfectly. You have to expect and be prepared for some of your "slam dunk" investors who told you they were "in the deal" to suddenly have excuses for not investing.

Stay Committed. The one ingredient your leadership team must have is a strong commitment to succeed. This is not the time to give or accept excuses. If some things are not working, then treat these disappointments as learning experiences. Make the necessary adjustments, and then continue to move forward.

Keep Listening. When NASA launches a spacecraft to the moon, it adjusts the trajectory and speed a thousand times as it receives feedback from the spacecraft. Likewise, even though you've completed "Step 8: Testing the Market and List Assemblage," that doesn't mean that you're finished listening to the market. If you find the Offering Campaign is taking some turns in the road, be prepared to compensate.

For example, suppose your market testing had indicated that investors would be happy with a stock offering of 30% of the company, but now that you're into the campaign, you're finding that this is no longer satisfactory to your investor sources. Be prepared to respond with a fall-back strategy by redrawing the offering documents to meet your investors needs. One possibility would be to give them a priority return position. For instance, your leadership team might be able to negotiate a highly favorable "earn-in" formula, so that once certain financial and business benchmarks are achieved, the leadership team earns back more stock. This gives the investors their initial high percentage position, but allows the leadership team to regain a larger share of the business after they've proven their worth.

There are many possible fall-back strategies—the point to remember is that you must be willing to make the financing work. You always need to keep your investor channel tuned to WIFM (What's in It For Me?).

The Momentum Factor. It is important to realize that almost all offerings go through three different stages of momentum:

Stage 1: The Opening. During the first 45 to 90 days, when you first hit the street with your offering, you will hopefully have already used some tactics and tools that have produced a good deal of fanfare and excitement. The first 25% of your offering will probably be funded rather quickly. When this happens, it's a sign that you have performed the Investor Financing™ steps well. But don't be fooled into thinking that the balance of the offering will go as smoothly.

Stage 2: The Middle. The next 50% of the funding usually comes in more slowly than it did during the opening stage. It may seem that you have to "slug it out" for every new investor. Don't be discouraged. Keep an upbeat attitude and be creative with your use of tactics and tools. It may also be necessary to make adjustments in the offering terms during this stage. Most of the changes will probably be pro-investor, so the investors that you've already lined-up will most likely find the changes acceptable. You will find it easier to change an Investor Financing™ for venture capitalists, business angels, visonary capitalists, and strategic corporate investors than it is for adventure stockholders and money raisers.

Stage 3: The Closing. Closing the last 25% of your offering will probably require the creative use of your tactics and tools. Your leadership team (and money raisers—if they're involved) will likely need a shot of adrenaline. Look to your existing investors to help you pick up momentum. Announce to your targeted candidate and super-candidate investors that you expect your funding to be complete by a certain date. The drama and finality of a closing date will often get "fence sitters" and procrastinators stirred into action.

AFTER THE OFFERING CAMPAIGN

Once your funding is complete, take a short vacation, celebrate with the troops, send the author of this book a thank-you note, count your blessings, and get ready to keep your promises.

Now that you have new business associates—your investors and money raisers—you must move from the courtship stage of your relationship with them into a lasting marriage. You cannot afford to be a short hitter. Investors have needs that you must address. You must establish a solid shareholder relations program. This is important, because many of your new investors will just be beginning to get to know your company.

SHAREHOLDER RELATIONS

Your shareholder relations program will involve many of the same principles, tactics, and tools, that you used in your Investor Financing™ planning during

---

ILLUSTRATION 10-9:
CHECKLIST OF SHAREHOLDER RELATIONS TACTICS AND TOOLS

Tactics	Tools
1. One-on-one meetings	1. Corporate brochure (updated)
2. Expert	4. Presentation folder
4. Civic leader	5. Photo pages
6. Industry leader	6. Special topic brochure
7. Business leader	7. Letters
10. Public seminars/forums	8. Announcements
11. Private seminars	9. Bulletins
12. Private workshops	10. Newsletters
14. Strategic association	11. Quarterly reports
25. Guest speaker	12. Annual reports
39. Direct mail	13. Audits/reviews
62. Give a dinner	14. News articles
	15. Press releases
	16. Article reprints
	21. Video
	22. Gifts
	23. Fax
	29. Open houses
	30. Birthday cards
	32. Lunchs/dinners
	33. Surveys

Additional Tactics	Additional Tools
• Annual meetings of shareholders	• Collect call privileges
• Regional shareholder meetings	• Issued-oriented publications on corporate ethics, public responsibility, global business, etc.
	• Updated business plan
	• Anniversary posters
	• Glossaries of industry terminology

Step 6. Illustration 10-9 is a list of selected tactics and tools from Step 6 that can be used in your shareholder relations program. Keep in mind that some of these tactics require constant activity in order to maintain the credibility of the company and its leadership team. The tools listed below are to be used to communicate to your shareholders the things they need to know in order to be fully up-to-date on your company. Use of these tools will also help your shareholders feel they are a part of the corporate "family."

Use Attorney and Corporate Finance Advisor. It's a good idea to plan shareholder relations with the advice of your attorney and corporate finance advisor. If your company utilized a public offering finance instrument (see Step 5), or your company is a public reporting company, then there will be special accounting and reporting compliance procedures. Your attorney should review with you the compliance procedures and coordinate the compliance with your corporate finance advisor.

Your corporate finance advisor should be an integral part of your shareholder relations planning. He or she can also be used to monitor the success of this program.[1] Even more importantly, if your company should ever need to inform your shareholders of some "soon-to-come" bad news, your corporate finance advisor can perform specific research projects for you prior to communicating the bad news to your shareholders. These research projects will be aimed at monitoring shareholder feedback.[2] By doing this, the leadership team has a chance to refine its messages, tactics, and tools, prior to the release of the bad news.

CAPITAL RELATIONS™ NEVER STOPS

The principles and practices underlying the development of the Financing Sequence Plan (Step 5) necessitates a long-term view of Capital Relations™. Although the initial concern of "Step 6: Creating the Capital Relations™ Plan" was with the most immediate financing round of the company, it is also concerned with the later financing needs as well. So, in effect, the Capital Relations™ program adopted by your company is a constant and continuous corporate activity.

CONCLUSION

Step 10 is the action step that allows you to pick up the investors' checks. If the previous steps have been performed well, then Step 10 will get off to a good start. Far too many companies try to execute their Offering Campaigns without adequate planning and preparation. When this happens, they face the frustrating and discouraging consequence of only getting negative feedback from investors, rather than the checks they were counting on. In effect, the

Offering Campaigns of these companies become an expensive and time consuming version of the market testing that a well-prepared company does during Step 8. The importance of solid work on each of the Investor Financing™ steps cannot be overemphasized.

Once your offering is funded, your shareholders expect your company to intensify its relationship with them. All too often companies fail to do this, since they view investors as merely a means to an end. You must keep in mind that shareholders are "Co-Business Builders" with you and they need to be treated accordingly. The success or failure of later rounds of financing can depend heavily on the word-of-mouth campaign that your existing investors will or will not provide. In reality, every one of your new shareholders is an advocate messenger for future corporate financings and strategic associations.

AFTERWORD

MY HEARTY CONGRATULATIONS TO YOU FOR MAKING IT THIS FAR. YOU now have the background you need to begin raising investor capital for your company. Most entrepreneurs looking for advice on how to raise investor capital have little patience with theoretical models or the host of other topics covered in this book. It's understandable that busy entrepreneurs want to focus immediately on specific strategies and tactics and to leave the philosophical issues alone. It's tough being the "point person" in an early-stage emerging business. There's never enough time and there's tremendous pressure to get fast results. Indeed, many of the advisors and entrepreneurs with whom I've consulted while preparing this book expressed the fear that most entrepreneurs would not feel they had the time to sit down and digest a book such as this. So I'm impressed that you paused long enough in your business building journey to study this text. You'll find that it was time well-spent.

A hallmark of the new economy is that business leaders must embark on a lifelong learning process. Those who put a low priority on the learning agenda will be left behind in the dust. It's no accident that national publications such as *Inc.* magazine began issuing warnings as early as 1997 that "Amateur Entrepreneurism Is Over—The Professionals Have Arrived."[1] Completing this book shows that you're ready to take your place among the business building professionals of the new knowledge/creation economy of the 21st Century.

I believe the Great Spirit is looking over all of us and has a special interest in those willing to create businesses for the right reasons. Business building is a special calling. If you've been chosen, nurture the responsibility and be thankful for the opportunity and challenge. Hold on tight to your dream of leading and building something important. Maintain balance. Surround yourself with only the best people, including your investors, and then respond quietly and thoughtfully to their needs. Demand a lot, and be precise about your expectations of them.

Don't worry about what you own or don't own of the company. Plan to keep your personal spending to a minimum. Your special calling is not about what you'll get at the end, instead it's about planning for high-value benefits for your customers, vendors, shareholders, and associates.

Finally, if you're ready to be a Visionary Business Builder who practices the principles advocated in this book, then Business Builders, LLC is anxious to meet you and invest in your dreams. Come spend some time in our "Money for Business Builders" clinics. You'll have fun, you'll learn, and we'll have an opportunity to connect with each other. You can contact me and my partners at: www.bbuilder.com. I look forward to hearing from you—the new economy of the 21st Century awaits us.

NOTES

NOTES

Introduction

1. Tom Richman, "Creators of the New Economy: Amateur Entrepreneurship Is Over—the Professionals Have Arrived," *Inc.* magazine (May 1997): 44.
2. Michael Ehrhardt, *The Search for Value* (Boston, Harvard Business School Press, 1994): 2.
3. Leif Evinssen and Michael Malone, *Intellectual Capital* (New York: Harper Business, 1997): 19.
4. Peter Drucker, *The New Realities* (New York: Harper & Row, 1989): 180.
5. Peter Drucker, *Post-Capitalist Society* (New York: Harper Collins Publishers, 1993): 183.
6. Ibid., pp. 183–184.
7. M. Mitchell Waldrop, *Complexity* (New York: Touchstone, Simon & Schuster, 1993): 325.
8. Ibid., p. 12.
9. Evinssen and Malone, *Intellectual Capital:* p. 19
10. Drucker, *Post-Capitalist Society:* p. 185
11. M. Mitchell Waldrop, "The Trillion-Dollar Vision of Dee Hock," *Fast Company* magazine (October/November 1998): 75.
12. Tom Richman, "Creators of the New Economy," *Inc.* magazine, vol. 19, no. 7: p. 44.
13. John Sculley, *Odyssey* (Glasgow, England: Fontana/Collins, 1987): 21.
14. James Collins and Jerry Porras, *Built to Last* (New York: Harper Business, 1994): 24.

Step 1: Designing the Phenomenal Message

1. T. Murakami and T. Nishiwaki, *Strategy for Creation* (Cambridge, England: Woodhead Publishing, Ltd., 1991): 135.
2. Stanley Davis, *Future Perfect* (New York: Addison-Wesley Publishing Co., 1987): 35.
3. Ibid., p. 36.
4. "Re-Writing the Rules of Venture Capital," *Business Week*, July 19, 1993.
5. Gene Bylinsky, "Who Will Feed the Start-Ups?" *Fortune* magazine (June 1995): 98.
6. Peter Drucker, *Innovation and Entrepreneurship* (New York: Harper & Row, 1985): 13.

7. Stephen Manes and Paul Andrews, *Gates* (New York: Touchstone, 1993): 65.

8. Bylinsky, "Who Will Feed the Start-Ups?": p. 100.

9. Ibid., 106. Also based on a report provided to the author by Venture Economics in October, 1997, showing the 25-year venture capital industry's annual rate of return from 1970 to 1996.

10. John Case, "The Wonderland Economy," *Inc.* magazine (June 1995): 14.

11. Michael Gerber, *The E Myth Revisited* (New York: Harper Business, 1995): 2.

12. Peter Senge, *The Fifth Discipline* (New York: Currency Doubleday, 1990): 175.

13. Ibid., p. 174.

14. Ibid.

15. James Collins and Jerry Porras, *Built to Last* (New York: Harper Business, 1994): xiii.

16. Ibid., p. 1.

17. Ibid., p. 1.

18. Ibid., p. 5.

19. Ibid., p. 6.

20. Ibid., p. 7.

21. Drucker, *Innovation and Entrepreneurship*, p. 34.

22. Collins and Porras, *Built to Last*, p. 7.

23. Ibid., p. xiv.

24. Ibid., p. 40.

25. Ibid., p. 28.

26. Ibid., p. 23.

27. Ibid., p. 24.

28. Ibid., p. 28.

29. Kenneth Delavigne and J. Daniel Robertson, *Profound Changes* (Englewood Cliffs, N.J.: Prentice Hall): 56.

30. Davis, *Future Perfect*, p. 5.

31. Stanley Davis and Bill Davidson, *2020 Vision* (New York: Simon & Schuster, 1991): 113.

32. James Moore, *The Death of Competition* (New York: Harper Collins, 1996): 15.

33. Thomas Moore, *Soul Mates* (New York: Harper Perennial, 1995): 42.

34. Burt Nanus, *Visionary Leadership* (San Francisco: Jossey-Bass Publishers, 1992): 99.

35. Gary Hamel and C.K. Prahalad, *Competing for the Future* (Boston: Harvard Business Press, 1994): 198.

36. Joel Barker, *Future Edge* (New York: William Morrow and Company, 1992): 89.

37. Collins and Porras, *Built to Last*, p. 95 and p. 97.

38. William Bygrave and Jeffry Timmons, *Venture Capital at the Crossroads* (Boston: Harvard Business School Press, 1992): 6.

39. Robert B. Reich, *The Work of Nations* (New York: Vintage Books, 1992): 85.

40. Ibid., p. 90.

41. James Utterback, *Mastering the Dynamics of Innovation* (Boston: Harvard Business School Press, 1994): 30.

42. Fumio Kodama, *Emerging Patterns of Innovation* (Boston: Harvard Business School Press, 1995): 7.

43. R. Buckminster Fuller, *Critical Path* (New York: St. Martins Press, 1981).

44. Drucker, Innovation and Entrepreneurship, p. 136.

45. Collins and Porras, *Built to Last*, p. 190.

46. Mike Hoffman, "Rags to Riches," *Inc.* magazine (August, 1997): 58.

47. Geoffrey Moore, *Inside the Tornado* (New York: Harper Business, 1995): 127.

48. Clayton Christiensen, *The Innovator's Dilemma* (Boston: Harvard Business School Press, 1997).

49. Moore, Inside the Tornado; p. 160.

50. Thomas F. Gilbert, *Human Competence* (New York: McGraw-Hill Book Company, 1978): 111.

Step 2: Surveying Investor Financing™ Sources and Approaches

1. William Bygrave and Jeffry Timmons, *Venture Capital at the Crossroads* (Boston: Harvard Business School Press, 1992): 1–2.

2. A. David Silver, *Strategic Partnering* (New York: McGraw-Hill, 1993): 72.

3. "1991 Annual Survey," *Venture Capital Journal*, Securities Data Publishing, New York.

4. "Price of Growth: 1993 Update," published by Coopers and Lybrand, Boston, 1993.

5. Bruce Posner, "How to Finance Anything," *Inc.* magazine (February 1993): 54.

6. Alan Deutschman, "Dealmakers for the Nineties," *Fortune* magazine, April 1992.

7. Wilson Harrell, "Keep Control," *Success* magazine, September 1992.

8. Bruce Blechman and Jay Levinson, *Guerrilla Financing* (Boston: Houghton Mifflin Company, 1992): 152.

9. "Re-writing the Rules of Venture Capital," *Business Week*, July 19, 1993.

10. Maire-Jeanne Juilland, "What Do You Want From a Venture Capitalist?" *Venture* magazine, August 1987.

11. Deutschman, "Dealmaking for the Nineties."

12 .Silver, *Strategic Partnering*, p. 1.

13. Ibid.

14. Ibid.

15. Lynch, *Business Alliance Guide*, p. 18.

16. Robert Gaston, *Finding Private Venture Capital for Your Firm*, (New York: John Wiley and Sons, 1989): 1.

17. Ibid., p. 16.

18. "Marketing to the Wealthy" seminar materials developed by Steve Moeller, president of American Business Vision, Irvine, Calif.

19. Bruce Blechman, "Step Right Up," *Entrepreneur* magazine, June 1993.

20. Arthur Lipper, III, *Investing in Private Companies*, (Homewood, Illinois: Dow Jones–Irwin, 1984): 19.

21. Ibid.

22. Thomas Stanley, *Selling to the Affluent*, (Homewood, Illinois: Business One Irwin, 1991): vii.

23. Bylinsky, "Who Will Feed the Start-Ups?" *Fortune magazine* (June 1995): 98.

24. Goldman Sachs, *Institutional Alternative Investment Report*, 1996.

25. Jonathan Morgan, "Treasure Hunt," *California Business*, November 1992.

26. John Quick, *Dog and Pony Shows* (New York: McGraw–Hill, 1992); 2.

27. Michael C. Jensen, "Eclipse of the Public Corporation," *Harvard Business Review* (September/October 1989): 61.

28. Matthew Schifrin, "Would You Buy a Mutual Fund From These Men?" *Forbes magazine*, October 12, 1992.

Step 3: Developing the Business Plan

1. Greenberg Consulting and Craig Norback, *The Entrepreneur's Guide to Raising Venture Capital* (New York: McGraw-Hill, 1991): 77.

2. Bruce Blechman and Jay Levinson, *Guerrilla Financing* (Boston: Houghton Mifflin Company, 1992): 252.

3. Paul Hawken, *Growing a Business* (New York: Simon and Schuster, 1987): 98.

4. W. Keith Schilit, *The Entrepreneur's Guide to Preparing a Winning Business Plan and Raising Venture Capital* (Englewood Cliffs, N.J.: Prentice-Hall, 1990): 20.
5. Rhonda Abrams, *The Successful Business Plan* (Grants Pass: The Oasis Press, 1993): 29.
6. Julie Brooks and Barry Stevens, *How to Write a Successful Business Plan* (New York: Amacom, 1987): 127.
7. Leech, *How to Prepare, Stage and Deliver Winning Presentations*, p. 13.
8. Harry Pickens, *Meta Marketing* (San Diego, Calif.: Pickens Group International, 1989): 66.
9. J. Morton Davis and Evelyn Geller, *Initial Public Offerings II: Public Venture Capital, Volume II of The Library of Investment Banking* (Homewood, Illinois: Dow Jones–Irwin, 1990): 87.

Step *4: Identifying Strategic Associations*

1. Mark Stevens, *Dun & Bradstreet Reports*, December 1992.
2. Robert Lynch, *Business Alliance Guide* (New York: John Wiley and Sons, 1993): 18.
3. Ibid., p. 153.
4. "The Virtual Enterprise: Your New Model for Success," *Electronic Business*, March 30, 1992.
5. Lynch, *Business Alliance Guide*, p. 7.
6. James Quinn, *Intelligent Enterprise* (New York: The Free Press, 1992): 387.
7. Robert Axelrod, The Evolution of Cooperation (New York: Basic Books, 1984): 3.
8. Dudley Lynch and Paul Kordis, *Strategy of the Dolphin* (New York: William Morrow and Company, 1988): 35.
9. Lipper, *Investing in Private Companies*, 68.

Step 5: Structuring the Financing

1. Robert Kuhn, *Capital Raising and Financial Structure* (Homewood, Illinois: Dow Jones–Irwin, 1990): 482.
2. Alvin Toffler, *The Third Wave* (New York: Bantam Books, 1980): 303.
3. "Q & A: Small Business and the SEC," published by the Office of Small Business Policy, Division of Corporation Finance, 1993.
4. Joseph Manko, Carl Schneider, and Robert Kant, *Capital Raising and Financial Structure*, p. 702.
5. Ibid.

6. *The Library of Investment Banking* (Homewood, Illinois: Dow Jones-Irwin, 1990).

7. Dorothy Dotson, *Capital Raising and Financial Structure*, (Homewood, Illinois: Dow Jones–Irwin, 1990): 167.

■ *Step 6: Creating the Capital Relations™ Plan*

1. Regis McKenna, *Relationship Marketing* (Reading, Mass.: Addison–Wesley Publishing Company, Inc., 1991): 3.

2. Theodore Levitt, *The Marketing Imagination* (New York: The Free Press, 1993): 111.

3. Regis McKenna, *The Regis Touch* (Reading, Mass.: Addison Wesley Publishing Company, 1985): 55.

4. McKenna, *Relationship Marketing*, p.85.

5. Thomas Stanley, *Marketing to the Affluent*, (Homewood, Illinois: Dow Jones–Irwin, 1988): 3.

6. Richard Wollack and Alan Parisse, *The 101 Best Financial Marketing Ideas* (Lafayette, Calif.: Sterling Communications 1989): 16.

7. Howard Shenson, *Successful Seminars and Workshops* (New York: John Wiley and Sons, 1990): 20.

8. Nick Murray, *Shared Perceptions* (Shrewsbury, New Jersey: Robert Stanger and Co., 1986): 6.

9. Rochelle Lamm Wallack, "On the Road Again," The Lamm Wallach Communications Group, Inc., Denver, Colo., 1986, 50.

10. Jane Templeton, *Focus Groups* (Chicago: Probus Publishing Company, 1987): 12.

11. Thomas Stanley, *Networking with the Affluent* (Homewood, Illinois, Dow Jones–Irwin, 1993): 221.

12. Ibid., p. 225.

13. Ibid., p. 211.

14. Ibid., p. 202.

15. McKenna, *Relationship Marketing*, p. 115.

16. Arthur Roalman, *Investor Relations Handbook* (New York: Amacom, 1974): 20.

17. Howard Hudson, *Publishing Newsletters* (New York: Charles Scribner's and Sons, 1982): 68.

■ *Step 8: Testing the Market and List Assemblage*

1. Tobin Smith and Anthony Esernia, *Small Business Capital Access Workbook* (Irvine: Dover Private Capital, 1991): Step 4.

2. William Davidow and Michael Malone, *The Virtual Corporation* (New York: Harper-Collins Publishers, 1992): 170.

3. Jane Templeton, *Focus Groups* (Chicago: Probus Publishing Company, 1987): 160.

▪ *Step 10: Executing the Offering Campaign*
1. Arthur Roalman, *Investor Relations Handbook* (New York: Amacom, 1974): 30.
2. Arthur Roalman, *Investor Relations Handbook* (New York: Amacom, 1980): 263.

▪ *Afterword*
1. Tom Richman, "Creators of the New Economy: Amateur Entrepreneurship is Over—the Professionals Have Arrived," *Inc.* magazine (May 1997): 44.

INDEX

Have You Attended America's Premier *"How To Get Money And Grow Your Business"* Program?

In locations throughout the country Mark Long and Business Builders LLC presents **The Money For Business Builders Clinic**. A one day clinic to accelerate your learning of the most important and dynamic money raising principles for success in the new economy.

A partial list of our corporate sponsors to date:

- *Arthur Andersen*
- *Silicon Valley Bank*
- *Ernst & Young*
- *Coopers & Lybrand*

- *Fulbright & Jaworski*
- *Norwest Bank*
- *Venture Law Group*

Since 1992 over 40 corporate sponsors and hundreds of boutique brokers/dealers and strategic corporate investors have participated in our programs.

For registration information call
1-800-818-3500
www.bbuilder.com

Business Builders LLC wants to invest in your company. For information on how to submit your request for funding call 1-800-818-3500 www.bbuilder.com

Find more on this topic by visiting BusinessTown.com

Developed by Adams Media, **BusinessTown.com** is a free informational site for entrepreneurs, small business owners, and operators. It provides a comprehensive guide for planning, starting, growing, and managing a small business.

Visitors may access hundreds of articles addressing dozens of business topics, participate in forums, as well as connect to additional resources around the Web. **BusinessTown.com** is easily navigated and provides assistance to small businesses and start-ups. The material covers beginning basic issues as well as the more advanced topics.

✓ **Accounting**
Basic, Credit & Collections, Projections, Purchasing/Cost Control

✓ **Advertising**
Magazine, Newspaper, Radio, Television, Yellow Pages

✓ **Business Opportunities**
Ideas for New Businesses, Business for Sale, Franchises

✓ **Business Plans**
Creating Plans & Business Strategies

✓ **Finance**
Getting Money, Money Problem Solutions

✓ **Letters & Forms**
Looking Professional, Sample Letters & Forms

✓ **Getting Started**
Incorporating, Choosing a Legal Structure

✓ **Hiring & Firing**
Finding the Right People, Legal Issues

✓ **Home Business**
Home Business Ideas, Getting Started

✓ **Internet**
Getting Online, Put Your Catalog on the Web

✓ **Legal Issues**
Contracts, Copyrights, Patents, Trademarks

✓ **Managing a Small Business**
Growth, Boosting Profits, Mistakes to Avoid, Competing with the Giants

✓ **Managing People**
Communications, Compensation, Motivation, Reviews, Problem Employees

✓ **Marketing**
Direct Mail, Marketing Plans, Strategies, Publicity, Trade Shows

✓ **Office Setup**
Leasing, Equipment, Supplies

✓ **Presentations**
Know Your Audience, Good Impression

✓ **Sales**
Face to Face, Independent Reps, Telemarketing

✓ **Selling a Business**
Finding Buyers, Setting a Price, Legal Issues

✓ **Taxes**
Employee, Income, Sales, Property, Use

✓ **Time Management**
Can You Really Manage Time?

✓ **Travel & Maps**
Making Business Travel Fun

✓ **Valuing a Business**
Simple Valuation Guidelines

http://www.businesstown.com